A Thirteen
Moon Journal

Also by the Author:

A LAUGHING PLACE: The Art and Psychology of Positive Humor in Love and Adversity

A
Thirteen
Moon Journal

A Psychiatrist's Journey
Toward Inner Peace

by Christian Hageseth III, M.D.

Berwick Publishing Company, Fort Collins, Colorado

Printed in the United States of America

Cover design by Robert Howard
Illustrations and cover drawing by Susan Maffet Peterson
Graphic images by John Schiller
Moon image on cover and title page: Lick Observatory Photograph
Rumi poem on page 302 published in *Night & Sleep,* poems of Rumi translated by Coleman Barks and Robert Bly, 1982, Yellow Moon Press, Cambridge, MA 02238

Library of Congress Catalog Card Number: 91-061903

ISBN 0-9620639-1-6

Publisher's - Cataloging in Publication
(Prepared by Quality Books Inc.)

Hageseth, Christian, 1941-
    A thirteen moon journal: A psychiatrist's journey toward inner peace / Christian Hageseth III, M.D.
p.cm.
ISBN 0-9620639-1-6

1. Psychology, Applied. 2. Peace of mind. 3. Hageseth, Christian, 1941-

BF637.P3   158.1

Berwick Publishing Company
501 Spinnaker Lane
Fort Collins, Colorado 80525

In Memory

JOHN BRUCE KERMOTT 1941 - 1966

Acknowledgements

Many thanks to friends and associates who offered kind words, careful criticism, and helpful suggestions: Mark Sloniker, Carl Spina, Karen Cushman, Jim Reid, Lowell and Barbara Jenkins, Fred and Nancy Brigham, Joachim Viens, and Carolyn Duff. Thanks to Jeanne Burns for technical assistance in manuscript preparation.

Special thanks for detailed editorial assistance from Ann Leh and Margaret Taunt.

And my deepest gratitude to my all my friends and family who are best acknowledged as they appear in my journal. Especially and forever for Carol, my gratitude is reflected every moon; thank you for your cheerful willingness to spend this life with me.

TABLE OF CONTENTS

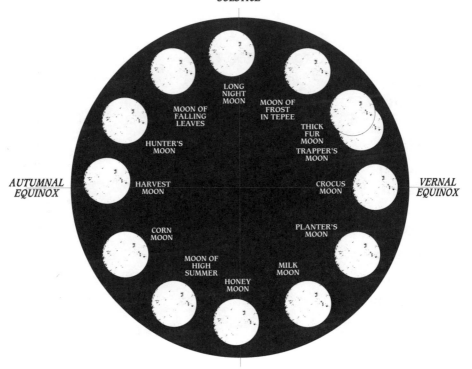

WINTER
SOLSTICE

LONG
NIGHT
MOON

MOON OF
FALLING
LEAVES

MOON OF
FROST
IN TEPEE

HUNTER'S
MOON

THICK
FUR
MOON

TRAPPER'S
MOON

AUTUMNAL
EQUINOX

HARVEST
MOON

CROCUS
MOON

VERNAL
EQUINOX

CORN
MOON

PLANTER'S
MOON

MOON OF
HIGH
SUMMER

MILK
MOON

HONEY
MOON

SUMMER
SOLSTICE

Introduction

I — THE PORTRAIT JOURNAL

Oh wad some power the giftie gie us
To see oursels as others see us!

Robert Burns

You search for a subject — everything is a subject. Your subject
is yourself, your impressions, your emotions in the presence of nature.

Eugene Delacroix

Life was meant to be lived, and curiosity must be kept alive. One
must never, for whatever reason, turn his back on life.

Eleanor Roosevelt

FEW PEOPLE know themselves. Busy living various roles, wearing different masks, they know only a thin veneer of ego, a covering they stretch over their souls, a façade they call *Myself*. They rush through their revolving addictions, constantly failing to see

9

themselves as others see them. How can you be true to yourself if you do not know who you are? If you do not see yourself? Only by seeing ourselves clearly can we hope to participate in our personal growth and come to full flower as unique human beings. Accurate self-perception requires seeing beneath our masks to our inner selves, our center, our soul; seeing clearly despite our ever-changing moods which constantly distort our perception.

From the earliest dawning of consciousness, we struggle with seeing ourselves. The first hint of conflicting views dawns on us at about age two when our parents say *"no."* We are stunned to find that ours isn't the only view of life. When they say no, they frustrate us. We begin to realize that our opinions and our perceptions are not the only ones. We don't like what we hear. We protest, but forces beyond our control compel us to submit and accept other views of life is and of who we are. Extended family and friends continue the process begun by our parents. To be accepted, we learn to stifle our rebellion, seeking instead to reconcile our perceptions with the perceptions of others. The picture we develop of ourselves is a collage of the shared perceptions of those around us; a portrait we modify by our own defenses and perceptions.

As adults, if our self-concept continually conflicts with that of others and we get roughed up too often, we may seek professional help to clarify our self-understanding. Yet, therapists are only human. Far from perfect they, like family and friends, have their distortions and agendas too. So we also have to sort through their input, looking for recurring themes that will inform us about our inner selves.

Towards mid-life, or sooner for more introspective people, we begin to settle down and attempt to look at ourselves with unflinching honesty. If we can do so without escaping to the fashionable psychological fad of the day, we are entering a fertile period of life, one of potential growth which is both the birthright and the curse of being a fully conscious human being. As we look at ourselves, we enter an inner dialogue and gradually develop a complex picture of who we are at the deepest center of our being. If we choose to participate fully in this process, we may write a journal. We commit our thoughts and speculations to paper, thus providing ourselves with a record — one we review and revise as we grow in the process of self-discovery. Our journal provides us with a way to pick up themes, stay out of ruts, sharpen our understanding of the meaning and purpose of our individual lives.

The process of journal writing is as old as writing itself. There are numerous ways to approach a journal. Most approaches stress free expression on a blank page. Write or draw whatever comes to mind. Let it flow. Adhere to no set rules. Journal without ceasing. Journal when you are in trouble. Journal in your own unique way. It helps to draw well, have good penmanship, be a Jungian analyst, and eat granola.

Such a free, unfettered approach is effective for opening yourself to your unconscious mind but it may have some drawbacks when the journal becomes a utilitarian device for self-understanding. There are two principal ways in which such an unstructured approach to journalling may fail to guide self-understanding and personal development: Crisis journalling and interminable journalling.

A few years ago one of my patients came across a journal he kept ten years earlier and was disappointed to discover that little or no movement had occurred with his internal problems. He was what I call a crisis journaller — a person who wrote only when life was so painful and confusing he had to make sense of it and, in desperation, turned to his journal. When the outer storm had passed, his journal settled to the bottom of a drawer like a toy a child discards when his attention is diverted to something newer and more shiny.

Through informal polls of individuals attending my humor workshops, I discovered crisis journalling is the most common form of journal writing. Almost like a therapist, the crisis journal serves to help when people are up to their armpits in alligators. But when everything quiets down, it is a tool they choose to do without. They don't use the journal to discover how to manage the swamp or diminish the alligator population.

11

Curious about crisis journalling, I began to talk with patients, friends and colleagues, and listened to stories of crisis-distorted journals. One woman, upon re-reading the past twelve years of her journal, was disheartened to find it contained only her pain, her mistakes, the painful betrayals of friends and lovers, but none of her triumphs, her insights, or her accumulating wisdom. Her journal of repetitive crises provided a skewed sampling of who she was, not an accurate or helpful self-portrait. Isn't that the way many introspective people see themselves? Looking only at their mistakes, their pain, their disappointments, they never see a fully balanced picture of themselves. They re-experience their failures with vivid feeling and accelerate the process of self-shaming. The individuals who choose to develop their self-understanding based upon such biased perceptions will be prone to depression. Giving up and retreating to the isolation of illness may seem a welcome relief.

As I continued to discuss journalling with patients, friends and colleagues, I discovered a distinct minority ever journalled in a consistent way. To most, the daily grind of writing seemed like too massive an undertaking. They weren't prepared to make journalling a second career. Those who did journal every day were often overburdened by the smothering bulk of their writing and rarely took the time to re-read their journals and come to conclusions about themselves. They reminded me of people who took color slides back in the fifties. The sheer mass of their slides discouraged them from ever sorting through and looking at them. Instead, plastic containers of slides accumulated in large cardboard boxes in the basement, never to be seen by the human eye. Many such boxes disappeared into the trash when the older folks moved to smaller quarters. Many daily journal-keepers store multiple volumes on multiple bookshelves where they quietly accumulate dust and serve little valuable purpose.

There are journal workshops which provide detailed plans for organizing a journal into convenient sub-journals such as a diary, a dream journal, one for creative imagination, etc. These are excellent tools, but rare is the person who actually carries through with the process for any length of time. Most undertake a flurry of journal

12

activity shortly after the workshop and then regress to crisis journalling.

In no way do I mean to criticize these methods of journal keeping nor would I ever discourage a person from taking a journal workshop. Any of these methods is better than no journal at all. It is clear that people benefit immensely from the journal process whatever the manner of their undertaking. But as I listened, it became clear that a focused method of journalling was needed if it were to provide a person with a clear self-portrait which could then serve as a guide for self-understanding and subsequent personal development.

I determined that a time-limited journal might avoid the negative bias of crisis journalling or the unmanageable bulk of life-long journalling. A time-limited journal would serve modern day individuals who explore many different avenues of personal development. It would provide an individual with a clearly defined task; one with a beginning and end; one with a clearly stated purpose and outcome. I named such a journal process *The Portrait Journal.*

The concept is simple: Develop a written picture, a word portrait, of both your outer life and your inner psychological-spiritual process. Take enough time so you can explore the major themes of your life — deep existential themes such as death, isolation, freedom and meaning. Thus you will come to see what you really believe, what is unfinished, and how you go about dealing with the most critical issues of your life. When this portrait is complete, let it season for a predetermined length of time. *Then re-read it and summarize your conclusions.* Such a document will form the basis for self-directed personal growth. Finally, you will be able to answer the question, "Who am I?"

You may choose to repeat the process several times throughout your life, especially when a clear sense of self is critical for determining the subsequent course of your life. With your Portrait Journal's help you can design your life with a more complete, grounded picture of who you are and who you seek to become.

13

Beyond the immeasurable benefit the Portrait Journal provides you, there is an additional possibility for its use. You have a personal word picture of the person you are at the center of yourself. Not a photograph or a video tape of your external self, but an honest deep look within. *What a gift to leave future generations!* How I wish I knew what was in the hearts and minds of my grandparents as they came over from Norway a hundred years ago. Nothing survives except some names, dates and a few memories stored in the minds of my aging relatives. How I would love to know the true selves of those remarkable pioneers. Your Portrait Journal may be the richest legacy you can leave the future. You may want to edit your Portrait Journal for the future. If you do, it changes and becomes *A Legacy Journal*.

Your body is one-hundred percent biodegradable. Photographs of you will dim as years go by. Your image will look like an unknown ancestor's to your great-grandchildren. Stories handed down will suffer increasing distortion and disinterest as they are passed from generation to generation. If you leave a Legacy Journal, your innermost thoughts and words portraying your deepest self will last. More than a mere historical document, the wisdom contained in your Legacy Journal may serve as a guide for the generations who follow you.

Your journal has two manifestations. First it is a tool for self-understanding and personal development — your Portrait Journal. Secondly it is a gift to the future, one that may offer understanding and personal development to your great-grandchildren and beyond — your Legacy Journal.

You should write your Portrait Journal for yourself alone. After its completion, you may decide it is too personal and not to be shared. If you start out planning to write a Legacy Journal you will create a different document altogether. You will be conscious of wanting to please or persuade some future readers. This will bias the complete candor required for writing your Portrait Journal. Write your private, personal journal first. Then edit, as needed, to refine your Legacy Journal.

II — GETTING STARTED

To everything there is a season, and a time to every purpose under heaven.
A time to be born and a time to die; a time to plant, and a time to pluck up that which is planted;
A time to kill, and a time to heal; a time to break down, and a time to build up;
A time to weep, and a time to laugh; a time to mourn, and a time to dance;
A time to cast stones, and a time to gather stones together; a time to embrace, and a time to refrain from embracing;
A time to get, and a time to lose; a time to keep, and a time to cast away;
A time to rend, and a time to sew; a time to keep silence, and a time to speak;
A time to love, and a time to hate; a time of war, and a time of peace.
Ecclesiastes

Starting your Portrait Journal is not simply a matter of choosing a date and then sitting down at a prescribed time and starting to write. Of course, starting does require a decision to undertake the project and a reasonable sense of when you will start and how long you will write. But since your unconscious mind needs to be a willing participant in this process, it is wise to be patient. Let it have a say. The underlying concept in journal writing assumes a deeper, inner self — your unconscious mind. Your ego cannot throw its weight around and expect full participation from the deeper interior of the self. So instead of starting on a fixed schedule, plan that some time in the next few months you will start your journal.

15

Then let your intuition inform you about the precise starting time. Make all the necessary preparations for writing so when the time is ripe, you can start at a moment's notice.

Such a beginning is not intended to serve the demon of procrastination, but rather demonstrates respect for your unconscious mind, a trust in the possibility of synchronicity, and a willingness to live in mythical time rather than by the clock. *To everything there is a season, and a time to every purpose under heaven.* There is a time to prepare for writing, and there is a time to wait. There is a time to write, and a time to reflect about writing. There is a time to live, and a time to forget about writing altogether. Your Portrait Journal respects the need for all such purposes under heaven.

There are several important matters to consider when you undertake writing your Portrait Journal. Commonly asked questions provide the simplest way for dealing with the details of the process.

Just what is a Portrait Journal and how does it differ from other journals?

The Portrait Journal is a time-limited journal, one you start at a given time, spend several months writing, and complete. As you go along, you edit your writing to sharpen your thinking and clarify your expression to yourself. Though handwriting is one way of writing your Portrait Journal, a word processor offers greater flexibility.

The purpose is to make a detailed statement of who you are at a given time in your life. You will include your daily life activities and explore your inner life as you experience it in the process of everyday life. What you want is a word picture of yourself, one you feel truly represents the person you are.

When it is finished, what will my Portrait Journal look like?

You will have a volume of over a hundred pages of text. You will be able to pick it up at a future time and read about your life and about your inner self. It will serve as an autobiographical statement and it will provide a rational basis for directing your personal growth. Finally, it can become a document you can leave

16

to future generations, your Legacy Journal. Depending on the sensitivity of its contents, you may never want another person to read it and you may choose to dispose of it later in your life or at the time of your impending death. On the other hand, you may edit it and duplicate several volumes of your Legacy Journal for distribution to your children, grandchildren, and on to the third and fourth generations.

Where should I write?
If at all possible, a special place for writing is best. Be it a desk, a corner of a room, a study or whatever, you will need a place where disturbances can be kept to a minimum. A place where you can think, write, revise, reflect, meditate, pray, laugh and cry. If at all possible, your writing place needs to be one where you can enjoy solitude.

What do I do when I am not at home?
You need to make plans beforehand for writing when you are away from home. What will you take along? It is unwise to take your whole journal since its loss would be a crushing blow. In his preface to *Lake Wobegone Days*, Garrison Keillor describes the loss of an entire manuscript when his briefcase was stolen from a men's room. " . . . the best work I had ever done in my life. . . . I couldn't recreate even a faint outline." Take along what is necessary for your writing while you are away and little more. Leave the main part of your journal in your writing place.

Writing while away from home is particularly enlightening since the change of scene provides a different lens for looking at your life, one you don't often use unless you are away from your familiar surroundings. Writing on airplanes, trains or in the car is stimulating and offers a fresh new perspective compared to writing when sitting still. Writing in the company of strangers can provide for your solitude. We all know how lonely one can be in a crowd.

When should I write?
You will need to be flexible when it comes to time of day to write. As a rule, the early part of the day is when you are fresh and most creative; plan to write during the earliest hour when you can find a period of solitude. This is a general guideline, not a rule etched in stone. Different hours of the day offer different perspectives and different emotional tones. Each should be represented in your Portrait Journal. Sometimes a day will have been filled with trials and you will need time to reflect on them. Such writing may wait for morning but then again, the pain might be particularly acute at night and your clearest insights may occur then. Be prepared for an idea to shake you from sleep and demand you write it down. Get up. Don't ignore the urging. Such ideas may be the clearest expressions of your unconscious mind.

Be flexible about the time of day you write and be prepared to drop everything when the spirit moves you. Let your unconscious mind guide you. Without it, your journal will degenerate into a simple litany of the woes of your ego. When a thought seizes you, write it down while the passion is fresh.

Do I need to write every day?
No. But plan to write about five days in seven. You need that level of intensity to develop continuity in your writing. You need to write regularly enough that your journal is in the back of your mind nearly all the time. Each event of the day needs to be considered for inclusion. Certainly every daydream or period of silent reflection is ripe fruit for your project. The dedication to writing is somewhat akin to athletic training. Your Portrait Journal has to be of utmost importance and your schedule adjusted to fit your writing, not vice versa.

How long should I plan to write each day?
This will depend on the day, the availability of time, the urgency of the idea and your own freshness or fatigue. In general, fifteen minutes should be a minimum. Thirty to forty minutes may be an

18

average. Plan one to three hours when you have the time and you are coming to terms with a particularly fruitful or troubling part of your life.

How many months should I plan for completion of my Portrait Journal?

Similar to the other answers, there are guidelines but no absolutes. You need to take *enough* time, however long that may be. Plan for three months to a year. Three months is truly a short time when you begin to consider the meaning of your life, your career, your honest feelings about death, your reminiscences of childhood, and your hopes for the future. If you take much longer than a year, you will run into problems of length and redundancy. In many respects, a year is an ideal length of time since you will write through the cycle of the seasons. You will see what memories or hopes are evoked by every point on the calendar.

This sounds like too big a job. Should I plan to undertake it? After all I am not a writer.

Most people spend at least this much time in idle, inconclusive worry. The Portrait Journal simply provides a structure for recording the mental activity that is always going on inside your mind. Personal growth is not cheap. There is no Royal Road to being a complete, fully-realized individual. Anything of value takes time and work. The project is time-limited. You will not make a career of it.

How private should I keep my journal?

Very private; only your mate, your most trusted friends or counsellors should see your writing. Potentially, there is a benefit in letting those closest to you comment on your writing. Their observations may stimulate new ideas or help you past a block you have been blind to. Share, yes; but share selectively. Use others' input as food for thought. And then again, there will be sections you choose to share with no person. So be it.

This brings up the whole concept of confidentiality, the privacy of your writing. Your journal needs to be secure. Those with whom you share living space need to respect your journal and your privacy. Tell them what you are doing and ask for their cooperation. Consider a note at the beginning of your Portrait Journal such as, "Thank you for respecting my privacy," or perhaps, "If you read this journal, may you spend eternity watching daytime television." If you cannot be assured of privacy, you are in a tough spot. Every person deserves privacy. If you don't have it now, get it! You need to find ways of securing your journal from the curious eyes of those unwilling to respect your privacy.

It is wise to instruct the person closest to you about what to do with your journal in the event of your death. Throw it away? Keep it and read it? Pass it on to specific family or friends? It is your journal. It is your decision. Just like any other part of a will, make your needs clear to those who survive you. I know a woman who has been keeping a journal and has requested her husband destroy it in the event of her death — *Destroy it and not read it.* This is a matter of deepest trust. I know her spouse. He can be trusted to carry out her wishes. His love is stronger than his curiosity.

Should I keep a back-up copy of my journal?

Anybody who has had Garrison Keillor's experience or has lost data stored in a computer can attest to the importance of back-up copy. Since a Portrait Journal differs from other journal techniques by the use of editing, a back-up copy is a good idea. The only issue is that of confidentiality of the back-up. If you choose to use a word processor, back-up copies on diskettes are simple and a sure-fire way to preserve your work. Otherwise, duplicate your written material at a copy shop and keep the back-up in a separate place.

While writing my *Thirteen Moon Journal*, I kept one hard copy in my study and a second at my office. I backed up my work on two sets of diskettes. One I kept at home and the other at my office. Even if my house or my office burned down, I was not going to lose my most precious work.

It sounds like the Portrait Journal is very precious. Is it?
Yes, it is as precious as the finest gold. It is the distillation of
the activity of your innermost self, your soul. It is precious indeed,
because you are precious indeed. This journal is of greater value
than all the photos ever taken of you in your life. We don't know
what Plato or Jesus looked like. What we care about is what their
lives manifested and the words they left behind. *In the beginning was
the Word.* After you are gone, what will be left of you are *your words.*

**Word Processing? This is a journal; aren't all journals
supposed to be hand written?**
Why not let technology be an ally instead of an adversary?
Usually a journal conjures up an image of a hard bound book with
virgin, white pages awaiting the pen. Completed, it is a well-worn,
dog-eared volume with numerous scratch outs and one's own
distinctive handwriting. In fact, many people who keep a journal are
just the sort of individuals who hate modern gadgets. Putting
contrary emotion aside, word processing is an absolute joy once it is
mastered — and that only takes a week or two. Word processing
comes in various packages from sophisticated software programs on
a personal computer to inexpensive, dedicated word processors sold
at mass outlet stores.
Consider word processing first, typing second, and handwriting
last. The art of fine penmanship is fast disappearing from our
culture. It is slower than word processing and the editing process is
much more difficult. Though it is true that history's greatest novels
were written by hand, word processing, now merely fifteen years old,
is the way of the future. The great novels of the twenty-first century
will be written on word processors. Why not the great journals as
well?

Do I include my dreams in my Portrait Journal?
Of course. All experiences from your inner life and outer life
are fair game for your Portrait Journal. Dreams are particularly

important messages from your unconscious mind. The problem is, most individuals are not Jungian Analysts or even trained therapists. (We can all take some comfort in that observation.) So deciphering the meaning of a dream may take some work. Write your dreams down, particularly those that awaken you. Look for themes. Consult books about dream interpretation, but beware of books with titles like *1001 Common Dreams Interpreted.* Dreams are very personal matters. Though all human beings share common elements in their unconscious minds, and there are common themes in our dreams, your individual history may use specific dream symbols in ways contrary to the popular interpretation.

Don't let your dreams overwhelm you. Write them down. Look for themes. Look for repetitive dreams. Pay attention to nightmares or disturbing dreams, they have the most to tell you. Even if you don't understand a dream, if it was particularly vivid, save it. It may become clearer in the future. You will be glad you saved it when your understanding deepens.

Should I prepare myself mentally before I write?
If your schedule allows, yes. Take some time for silent reflection. Don't plan your writing during the silence, simply let your unconscious mind have greater access to the present moment. Then again, there will be times when something is burning within you and you will sit down and write in a frenzy.

How much attention should I devote to my interpersonal problems?
Though we may learn much about ourselves from the way we bump up against one another in life, too often we use such psychological collisions to buttress our defensive armor and not as opportunities for self-understanding. Do not neglect interpersonal conflicts, but don't dwell on them either. Your Portrait Journal is *about you, not about your companions in life.* Distill your interpersonal conflicts to understand what they say about you. If you edit to create a Legacy Journal, you might even consider speaking of

certain individuals in your life anonymously. Be considerate of your companions in life, let them tell their own story if they want. Just as a photographic portrait is of one individual alone, so your Portrait Journal is about you alone. Fill in interpersonal details as they inform you about yourself and then let them go. As they say in AA, take your own inventory, not somebody else's.

Should I include my special relationships in my journal?
People who are important to you will manifest their importance by their inclusion in your activities and conversations. If you wish, say more about them. But, in general, the Portrait Journal process shies away from focusing on relationships when such focus may divert attention from dealing with your most special relationship with your deepest inner self.

Should I include past experiences in my journal?
When past experiences are stimulated by some present event, include them by all means. Your Portrait Journal provides a way of achieving closure. Past events don't emerge easily unless there is an unfinished quality about them.

What if I get writer's block?
Sit down at your regular writing time and wait. Put in the time you planned for writing and be patient. Don't walk away. Don't declare you have nothing of value to say. Don't chuck the whole process. Sit back and wait it out. But wait it out in your writing place with all instruments at hand. Consider writing about the block or having an imaginary conversation with it. "What are you hiding from me?" Or if that seems too direct, "Would you like a cup of tea?" All writer's blocks clear and there is almost always gold waiting for you behind the block.

III — EDITING

If you would not be forgotten,
As soon as you are dead and rotten,
Either write things worthy reading,
Or do things worth the writing.
                        Benjamin Franklin

Reading maketh a full man, conference a ready man, and writing
an exact man.
                        Francis Bacon

      Anybody who has ever written seriously, whether it be an essay, a book, or a poem, has confronted the reality that the first words on the paper are not the best. Certainly, whatever the writing, the first draft needs to be uninhibited, free-wheeling and bold; always ready for surprise, ready for the unconscious to break through and splash across the page. A problem with most journals is they stop with the first draft. So convinced are the authors that their first draft is their truest representation of themselves, they look upon their rough draft as sacred. The thought of changing a single dot smacks of desecrating holy scripture.

      As I developed my writing skills, I learned that the task of writing is not simply writing, but re-writing, re-writing, re-writing. Famous novelists have gone through twenty or thirty drafts before being satisfied they had adequately conveyed their meaning. And even then they weren't quite satisfied. When I sent my first (never-published) novel to an agent, he quietly admitted that "some of it worked," and then firmly suggested I "get professional help" with the editing. Thereafter, he never returned my phone calls. His rude treatment bothered me, but it forced me to face the truth. So I found a professional and sought her counsel.

When she was finished with my manuscripts, they were richly decorated with pencilled comments and corrections. Everywhere unnecessary words were deleted, and comments like "what are you trying to say here?" filled the margins. As I edited my writing, *what I was thinking became clearer to me.* That is the point. *When we edit our writing, we come to a more precise understanding of what we believe.* Forcing ourselves to be precise in our writing forces us to be precise in our thinking.

To edit your journal is to take a magnifying glass to your thinking and scrutinize it. What are you trying to say? Is this really what you mean? How could you express this more clearly?

You will find grammar and punctuation serve an important function. They provide structure and clarity. The rules of English usage exist to help us say what we mean and avoid ambiguity. The rules are there to serve us, not restrict us. If a grammatical rule hinders your writing, feel free to break it. Then re-read the passage later and see whether you were successful in conveying what you intended to say. In my *Thirteen Moon Journal* you will see how incomplete sentences succeed in communicating an idea.

The concept of editing is one of the principle ways a Portrait Journal most differs from other journal methods. Edit your writing to sharpen your expression and to add precision to your self-understanding. The editing process will actually open you to new levels of insight about yourself and will confront you with your vague generalizations, unconscious assumptions and muddy logic.

This editing process is where sharing your journal with others may be helpful. Not only will you be sharing yourself with a person close to you, someone whose opinion you value, but you will also benefit from their looking at your writing with new eyes and offering you a different perspective. Their evaluation of your writing may make you go back, think it over, and then express yourself more precisely.

25

Editing is one of the reasons I suggest you consider word processing. Editing on a word processor is a piece of cake. The ease it offers is a whole order of magnitude greater than typing or handwriting. The word processor also saves you the problem of misspelled words and typographical errors. Some software programs offer a thesaurus to check whether a different word might fit your ideas just a little more clearly. But word processor or not, editing is central to the Portrait Journal method.

Editing is done most efficiently if you do it as you go along. Don't put off your editing until later. *Procrastination is lethal.* If you let several days of material accumulate, the job will become tedious and your love of the product will wane as you re-experience composition assignments written to please some long-forgotten English teacher. Edit as you go along to stay sharp. Challenge yourself. Do your words accurately portray what you think, what you feel? You will find the English language a wonderful and complex tool. It evolved for just such a purpose — to provide precision in personal expression. Whenever a word did not exist to clarify some distinction, a new one was created to fill that purpose.

There is a potential problem with the editing process you must be aware of: Rationalization. If you become preoccupied over how your journal will sound to others, you will modify your writing to make yourself look good. You will erect excuses to account for your mistakes and transgressions. You will deny your shadow. As soon as you do this, the whole purpose of journalling has been scuttled and you might as well drop the project. Your Portrait Journal depends on your willingness to conduct an unflinching moral inventory. If you rationalize, you are lying and your journal will be of scant benefit. Your Portrait Journal exists precisely because you want to get beneath your everyday psychological defenses and discover your deeper self.

If you catch yourself rationalizing or otherwise avoiding your inner self, good. Stop. Look deeper. Don't punish yourself. Simply adjust and go on. If you continue to rationalize or use other defenses, you will have failed yourself. Avoiding rationalization is

26

another reason to share your journal with your most trusted friends or perhaps a therapist or clergy-person. Such individuals can help you see your defenses. *Caveat:* Don't offer them a portion of your journal to read unless you are willing to listen to their most honest comments.

As I wrote my *Thirteen Moon Journal*, my wife read every word. She often caught me on rationalizations and other unconscious defenses that I had conveniently overlooked. Certain portions I shared with friends and colleagues (though most often, such sharing was not of my deepest struggles). I know a woman who shared too much of her journal with too many people. It was a great mistake to share the intimate details of her inner struggle with acquaintances too peripheral to care. They were embarrassed at her disclosure and her teenage daughters were beside themselves with frustration. Ultimately she concluded she had betrayed herself and regretted her naïve sharing.

When you share your journal with others, be thoughtful. Provide them with edited copy. Don't make them wade through misspellings, scratch outs and cumbersome grammar. Give them something clean enough so they won't be distracted by the writing and can focus on your message.

The goal of writing and editing is to state what you are thinking in clear, simple-to-read terms. Here are some guidelines:

1. Use simple sentences rather than complex ones.
2. Be as brief as possible. Avoid clutter.
3. Punctuate sparingly. Use more periods, fewer commas.
4. Use exclamation points liberally in your rough draft; rarely in the final copy.
5. Use fewer adverbs, fewer "*-ly*" endings.
6. Adjectives color your writing. Tasteful color never draws attention to itself.
7. Metaphors and similes arc rich. They turn your technical journalism into poetry. Make love with them, but never commit adultery with them.
8. Use active voice whenever possible.

9. Write in the present tense, the better to show rather than tell.

10. Avoid cliches like the plague.

11. When you start writing, remember points 1 through 10 are guidelines, not commandments.

IV — The Legacy Journal

The absence of romance in my history will, I fear, detract somewhat from its interest; but I shall be content if it is judged useful by those inquirers who desire an exact knowledge of the past as an aid to the interpretation of the future, which in the course of human things must resemble if it does not reflect it.

Thucydides: 431 B.C.

The mind of man is capable of anything — because everything is in it, all the past as well as all the future.

Joseph Conrad

A hundred years from now your biological body will have been completely recycled. All the molecules which now comprise you will have been re-constituted into plants, soil, the ocean or other animal life. Memories of you will have faded to a few anecdotes. Photographs of you will be quaint reminders of some person's heritage. But the essence of who you are will be gone. Nothing about you is permanent except the ideas you leave behind. Your identity is not dependent on the persistence of your physical body, it depends on the persistence of your words. Whether a part of you is immortal remains to be discovered after death. But your ideas can enjoy a sort of immortality if you record them and preserve them. Journals have been the primary way the identity of a historical figure has been preserved. Monuments don't do justice to the inner person; words do — words are the vehicles for ideas and human beings are the bearers of ideas. Our stewardship of ideas is really what we are talking about, not some sort of immortality for our egos. How we carry, interpret and modify ideas is our principle role in human evolution.

Famous people are shrouded in myth — not informative myths, but falsehoods conceived to further political aims. The records of the lives of famous people may in fact seriously distort history. For history to be accurately portrayed, it must be conveyed in the lives of ordinary people.

Besides the history of nations and peoples, there is the micro-history of particular families. The history of the Hageseth family is of scant interest to anyone except we few souls who bear that surname. I would love to know our family history. Never before has the means been so readily available to record and preserve a family history. Never has it been simpler to preserve your life as a legacy for the future — your very common, very real and very special life.

The Legacy Journal is a spinoff of your Portrait Journal. When you write your Portrait Journal, you write it for yourself alone. When you prepare your Legacy Journal, you do it for the future. Its integrity depends on the candor and honesty inherent in writing deeply and personally to yourself alone. Don't undertake the Portrait Journal for an audience, that would compromise its purpose. But once you have completed your Portrait Journal, you are in a position to decide whether you want to save any of it for the future. If you do, the process of editing is simple. You eliminate the parts which are too intimate or might be harmful to yourself or others. Add some orienting comments and then copy it on acid-free paper and bind it. A copy shop can to the job for you; it need cost no more than ten dollars. More fancy and sturdy library bindings are nice. Use them if you like, but they are not necessary. You may also want to include an abbreviated family tree and some photographs.

The first step is to *decide*. Do you want to leave a Legacy Journal? If the answer is yes, then go over your Portrait Journal and decide what to leave out. Save what you want to keep and discard what you don't. It is entirely appropriate to make these choices. It is much like asking yourself what clothes you want to have on in a picture of you that will be passed on to your great grandchildren. What typifies you? You would not leave them a photo of yourself in the nude, nor should you plan on leaving them your Portrait Journal with your soul similarly bare. It is proper to keep some thoughts and memories entirely to yourself. That is one of the reasons we have thoughts and don't have to speak them out loud. That is one of the primary differences between a Portrait Journal and a Legacy Journal. Nothing is held back in the Portrait Journal. In contrast, you need to be careful about what you expose in your Legacy Journal. That is as it should be. Every writer does it. Every journal does it. Every person has the right to secrets.

You may add information to describe relationships in more detail since future readers will not know who is who. Explain enough to orient your readers, but then let the journal portray your thoughts and feelings. Show, don't tell. You may want to add some more comments about the larger historical events of the day. Thus you will orient your readers to your particular time in history.

How much should you preach? There will be a temptation to tell future readers what you want them to think or believe. I would say, go for it. Speak as boldly as you want. Such statements represent your most heart-felt dreams for your progeny. Go ahead; say whatever you like. Perhaps such statements are best expressed in a letter at the end of the journal — your letter to the future.

If you include a family tree, it does not have to be anything genealogically profound. Just include your parents, grandparents and first degree relatives; who is living; who is dead; what they have done. Be as detailed as you like. The principle of the Legacy Journal is your ideas are the most important part of your legacy, everything else merely orients your reader to understanding those ideas.

You may choose to include some photographs. Talk to a professional photo finisher and see what types of dyes will last a couple hundred years. Find out what you should do to a photograph to preserve it. Avoid posed professional portraits. Instead, use common, everyday snapshots of yourself. They will round out your presentation more adequately than a formal portrait would.

Finally, make several copies, as many as you think you will have grandchildren. If you don't have children or grandchildren, provide copies for younger people who are important to you — individuals who will appreciate your journal and keep it for the future. Let your children read your Legacy Journal, but make sure it gets into the hands of your grandchildren. The tension between parent and child may distort your children's reading of your Legacy Journal. It is a different matter with grandchildren. Consider stipulating the distribution of your Legacy Journal in your will. Store copies for safe keeping.

That is how easy it is. No life is so uneventful that it shouldn't be remembered. The job is not that big. Once you have completed your Portrait Journal, you can complete and package your Legacy Journal in just a few hours. Wouldn't you love to know the deepest thoughts and feelings of your grandparents or great-grandparents? Consider your great-grandchildren. They would too. Your Legacy Journal may be one of the primary ways of projecting your values and beliefs into the future. Think about it.

V — SEE ONE, DO ONE, TEACH ONE

The great poet, in writing himself, writes his time.
T. S. Eliot

Being entirely honest with oneself is a good exercise.
Sigmund Freud

As an inexperienced medical student, I needed to learn a wide variety of techniques and procedures. I had learned the basics. I knew what made the body tick. I knew more detail about obscure diseases than would ever be of any value in my practice of medicine. But I could not *practice* medicine, I only *knew* it. I had to learn how to put my "book learning" into action. There is a well-known process for doing this, one that might frighten the average patient in a university teaching hospital. If, for example, I wanted to learn the practice of venipuncture (inserting a needle into a vein and withdrawing blood) I would first observe as another student or intern performed the procedure, describing exactly what he was doing. Next, we would go down the hall to another patient and I would perform the procedure with my teacher watching. Finally, I would repeat the process on yet another patient and would teach the process as I was doing it. We called the process *See one. Do one. Teach one.* It was an efficient teaching device, one that provided maximum learning.

Books on journal writing usually provide small excerpts from various individual's efforts, but rarely do they present a complete journal. Such a teaching technique is similar to instructing a student to perform a symphony by only playing an isolated three or four bars at a time. The gestalt never emerges. In order to understand the Portrait Journal process, you need to read one. The closest examples I know from current writers are Thomas Merton's *Sign of Jonas* and his *Asian Journal*, Etty Hillisum's *An Interrupted Life*, and May Sarton's *Journal of a Solitude*. Though none of these writers had heard the term "Portrait Journal" when they wrote these journals, each did an inspiring job of writing one. Each writer was, of course, uniquely talented and lived through moving experiences which rivet the reader's attention. But your Portrait Journal is no less unique. Every life is special. There can be no boredom when the singularity and subtlety of an individual life is gently analyzed. No life is so routine that it is not a candidate for a Portrait Journal.

With a certain amount of fear and trembling, as well as some brash confidence, I now share my Portrait/Legacy Journal — all the time bearing in mind the admonishment: Self-disclosure is merely self-serving if it does not have a higher purpose. At least that is what we instruct young persons learning the art of psychotherapy. My *Thirteen Moon Journal* is my Portrait Journal with some editing in the direction of a Legacy Journal. I wrote it near the end of the fifth decade of my life. I offer it as an example of what a completed Portrait/Legacy Journal might look like. A secondary purpose is to share the inner mind of a contemporary psychiatrist. After all, we psychiatrists look inside the minds of so many persons, turn-about is fair play. I grant that I am not in the mainstream of psychiatry, what with my spiritual orientation and my love of nature. Yet I believe my thinking is representative of middle-aged men of our time who ask the deeper questions of themselves . . . . . and then attempt to answer them. Asking is important, answering is too.

The layout of the chapters presents *A Thirteen Moon Journal* in a standard typeface. Running throughout are notes inserted in the text in italics which are my comments to the reader. They are intended to provide instructions as you read along. This is the *See one* part. Just as the intern would describe what he was doing as he went along, I offer comments as you follow *A Thirteen Moon Journal* along, relating how you might adapt sections in your own way.

Because of the nature of my profession one obvious disclaimer must be stated: The confidentiality of my patients is paramount. To quote *The Principles of Medical Ethics With Annotations Especially Applicable to Psychiatry*: "Clinical and other materials used in teaching and writing must be adequately disguised in order to preserve the anonymity of the individuals involved." I have adhered to this ethical standard and have disguised all patients mentioned in my journal. This is a record of my inner process and my outer life — an outer life which is intimately bound to the triumphs and tragedies parading through my office every day. But it is *my life, not theirs,* so all facts have been altered to guarantee my patients' anonymity.

Let me offer some orienting information at the beginning. I am married for the second time. My wife's name is Carol Nees. (I elected not to take her last name when we married.) I have two

33

biological children, John and Chris. And, I have two step-children, (I hate that prefix, step-) Allison and Steve. I have a sister, Beverly and a brother, Gaylord. My parents are deceased. I practice with two partners, both social workers, Carl Spina and Lowell Jenkins. Carl is married to Karen and Lowell is married to Barbara. Other friends, colleagues and relatives will be obvious by the context when they appear. I live in a lovely middle-class community tucked on the edge of the Rocky Mountains, Fort Collins, Colorado. I spend my professional life practicing psychiatry and travelling around the country teaching the art and psychology of positive humor.

Now sit back and follow along as you *see one,* a Portrait/Legacy Journal in thirteen moons.

A THIRTEEN MOON JOURNAL

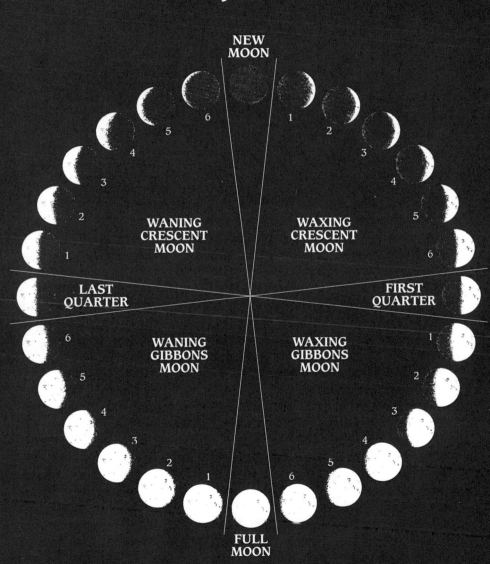

NEW
MOON

WANING
CRESCENT
MOON

WAXING
CRESCENT
MOON

LAST
QUARTER

FIRST
QUARTER

WANING
GIBBONS
MOON

WAXING
GIBBONS
MOON

FULL
MOON

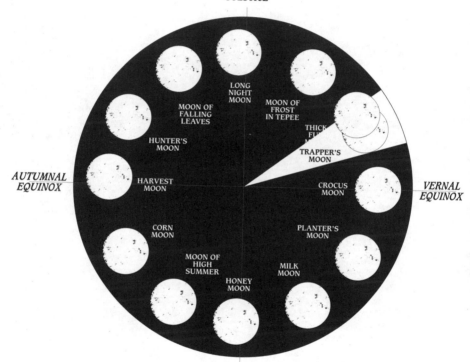

WINTER
SOLSTICE

LONG
NIGHT
MOON

MOON OF
FALLING
LEAVES

MOON OF
FROST
IN TEPEE

THICK
FU...
...

HUNTER'S
MOON

TRAPPER'S
MOON

AUTUMNAL
EQUINOX

HARVEST
MOON

CROCUS
MOON

VERNAL
EQUINOX

CORN
MOON

PLANTER'S
MOON

MOON OF
HIGH
SUMMER

MILK
MOON

HONEY
MOON

SUMMER
SOLSTICE

Chapter One

TRAPPER'S MOON

I AM AN ANALOG man living in a digital world. My work is meaningful and important, but it alone fails to express my passion for life. I live by schedules, chided by impersonal technical devices that torment rather than assuage my harried soul. Unfulfilled, I chase myself through years of adult life longing for something different; a life of awe and mystery, one of inner peace, as if seeking a monastery within myself.

I have learned to behave very digitally in this technical, over-scheduled world. I diagnose patients by the numbers, work a forty-five minute hour, and show up for appointments on the minute, even the second, but never late. My watch is digital. My finances, plastic. My days are shrink-wrapped. I cook with microwaves, write on a computer, and faithfully monitor my cholesterol.

37

Within me, I sense a rebellion brewing. I yearn to live in harmony with Nature as my ancestors lived for millions of years: The moon marking the passage of months and the sun counting the years. Seasons, tides, the flooding of rivers, the mating of God's wild creatures and even the moods of human beings undulate with the ever-changing patterns of sun and moon. After all, it is only recently that we started living indoors; even more recently that we agreed to measure time in a linear, mechanical fashion. Little wonder I feel cut off from something basic, something very important. Our cities are filled with savage human beings, devoid of roots, devoid of altruism, devoid of myth; filled instead with violence, drugs and despair.

I want to live out my natural analog-ness. I want to throw away my watch, tear up my calendar, and destroy my phone in a blazing ritual sacrifice. I want to sing in the moonlight with wolves. I want to run through the summer rain, feeling wind-driven needles pricking my bare skin. I want to burn autumn leaves for the wonderful aroma of it all. I want to build bonfires at the winter solstice to call the sun back so it won't abandon us forever.

Ah, but what I long for and what I feel I must do are vastly different. I have three, soon to be four, kids in college. I have income taxes, social security taxes, property taxes, malpractice insurance, disability insurance, health insurance, a couple of mortgages, and my retirement to worry about. I contribute my money and my labor to those causes which work for justice, peace and preservation of our natural world. And I have patients who depend on me; many of them are more like friends than patients. There are valid and loving reasons why I should not drop out. There are people and causes I should not abandon. Maybe I will stay put. But, if that be the case, deep within me something must change. My frantic life pace cannot persist without grave consequences for me, for my physical health, for my very survival.

There are risks in such inner revolutions. I have seen self-centered, asocial dropouts who, pretending to be free spirits, became possessed and bound by the demon of their own narcissism. They pretend to live in harmony with nature, while longing for some ill-defined past epoch when they should have lived. Using the excuse of avoiding the rat race, they live a parasitic life. Ridiculing people who plan for a future as spiritual midgets, the dropouts have little awareness of the logs in their own eyes.

I must discover and practice more analog-ness. I am not sure that running away will do any good. Perhaps I need to wrap Nature and Spirit around my digital life. For now, I will continue to go to work, be on time, and provide care for the beleaguered souls who seek my counsel. But I will start to watch the movement of the moon more closely. I will meditate upon bees, birds and blades of grass. With reverence and awe, I will withdraw into an inner space for silence, seeking there to meet God, The Origin of The All. I will seize precious time to savor God's gifts in the natural world around me, even when that world consists of my own very ordinary back yard. I am looking for inner peace. When I discover it, I will not just practice peace, I shall *become* peace.

Comment:

I waited three months for the right moment to start. One morning I awoke and knew this was the day. My conscious mind had been playing with the analog-digital polarity as a metaphor for the tension I was experiencing in my life. What poured out surprised me. And I liked it.

If you can wait for inspiration before starting your Portrait Journal, good. If you want to start without delay or are afraid of procrastinating, get going. You don't have to start with a bang. Since it is your journal, any way you start is fine, just start.

Any author knows the book he starts to write and the book he finishes are two completely different things. That is the nature of creativity, of unconscious material breaking through. You may have some idea where you are going when you start, and if you are open to your inner self, prepare to be surprised.

It was very cold yesterday. It snowed enough for snow to fall into your shoes as you walked. And the wind blew. They said the wind chill was 29 below. I don't know about that. How cold was it? I had to turn my head from the wind because my forehead, pierced by needles, stung too much. This morning the recently-arrived red-winged blackbirds sit in a subdued silence on skeletal cottonwood branches. I wonder what they think after having spent the last week basking in warmth and singing their cantatas as if life were a summer marsh. Perhaps if you are a red-winged blackbird, you are accustomed to such stormy reversals. Save your songs for warmer days when more of God's creatures have their ears open; not only their ears, their hearts.

The sun comes out at midday and quickly transforms the road surface into steaming asphalt as if some giant burner were turned on beneath the streets. In no time the promise of spring reasserts itself. The thermometer announces it is twelve above. I don't care about such numbers, it feels warmer. I shovel the walk wearing only cotton gloves and my hands stay warm. I pause to talk with neighbors taking care to turn my face towards the sun for added warmth.

Tonight the sun is setting nearly two fist-breadths south of Horsetooth Rock. If I want to see the moon, I will have to wait for morning. It is rising in the middle of deepest sleep now. Not being a morning person, I will not check on it. I trust it hasn't played any tricks on me.

I talk to B* on the phone this afternoon. She is still too close to suicide. For her, life is so black, so empty. Despite my psychiatric training and years of experience, I still don't know how to transfuse another soul with the joy that can come from simply being alive. It is hard for her to respond to words. Her brain chemistry is so disturbed, but she is hanging on and her spouse is supportive. But will she cash it in? I honestly don't know. She said she will see me in a couple of days. She is future oriented, so maybe we're OK for the moment. I would love to talk to her about the coming equinox and the beautiful, orderly movement of the sun. Incessant talk about her feelings and relationships only seems to drag her down more. The next full moon falls on the vernal equinox. Will she live to see it?

We need to live our lives in small pieces, savoring what is here for us now, whether comforting or disturbing, whether of our choosing or not. I didn't choose the snow and the cold. I don't particularly like it. But I am choosing to savor it and in the process I am more alive.

waning crescent₅

At silent meeting this morning I can't settle down and find unity with the Light within. I try words. They don't seem to work. I visualize the awesome scope of Hawking's universe, seeking to appreciate the span of God in time and space, but that doesn't help either. So, remembering my biofeedback training, I warm my hands and relax my shoulders. What does my mind settle on? The tracks I saw in the back yard this morning, rabbit tracks. Tracks of a little creature of no strength, dominance, or cunning. Just a soft, furry creature capable of incredible feats of propagation.

The children at the Montessori school named him Sherbet, but that name never stuck; we just called him Bunny. Much as in my childhood, my parents disagreed on calling me Ellis or Christian, and finally settled on calling me *Baby*. That continued until the age of seven when I realized such a name was a substantial handicap. It was during the harvest moon two years ago that Carol was given the small, red satin rabbit for the classroom. He paper-trained easily and became an accepted playmate in the kindergarten class. The following summer, spent alone in a hutch, seemed to alienate him from the kids. So he passed much of the next school year in the hutch taking daily outings in the giant tractor-tire sand box. Then last summer, hormones rising, he longed for companionship other than human beings. A horny fellow of poor discretion, he settled for

41

masturbating on any warm object near him such as feet, ankles, or arms. He became a social misfit. So we brought him home, housing him in our abandoned dog kennel. At the vet's advice, we neutered him. (We don't call it getting fixed, since nothing was broken in the first place.)

Bunny, no longer tormented by hormones and no longer interested in human contact, began living in direct contact with the earth. For the first time in his life he became one with his rabbit ancestors. He experienced the ground (real dirt) rather than wood or wire beneath his feet. He set aside the far corner of the kennel as his latrine and then went about carving out a room beneath the abandoned dog house. Throughout the fall we saw more dirt mounding up in the kennel; he was getting into his bunny-ness. At the first snow fall, he made his break. As skillful as any prisoner, he had tunnelled under the back walk and had come up beneath our back porch. He was free. I discovered the kennel-break the following morning as I looked into the backyard and saw Bunny eating the remaining green leaves of last summer's strawberry plants. No longer did he let us touch him. Approach yes, touch no.

We worried about the predators of the neighborhood. Fortunately most of the dogs are well controlled. The two shelties who live next door don't have a mean-spirited bone in their bodies. All they want to do is herd other creatures. When ducks land in the greenbelt, the little sheep dogs go out and do their thing with no urging, no training. "Head 'em up, move 'em out." It seems to satisfy some deeply ingrained instinct. No danger to Bunny, those two dogs.

Cats are another matter. A smallish black cat from nearby started visiting us more frequently. Finally one day, I saw the confrontation. In his crouched-down, tail-twitching feline-hunter way, Cat stalked Bunny. But then Cat stopped, seeming to reason through a problem that had not occurred to him while stalking: Bunny outweighed him three to one. So, not to lose face, Cat sat upright, washed a paw in a nonchalant way and walked off, announcing to all the world that he was not interested in Bunny for now, but one day he might be.

Then came the very cold weather during the Moon of Frost in Tepee. The thermometer stayed below zero for four days. Bunny was nowhere to be found. When it finally warmed up, we discovered his tracks and eventually saw him surveying the various flower beds of our neighbors, apparently deciding where he might choose to live. Seeing his coat more luxurious than ever, I understand why the early settlers called this time of year the Trapper's Moon.

We were just getting used to his daily appearance on the greenbelt when suddenly, one day, he was gone. No trace, no good-bye note, just gone. For nearly a moon, there was no Bunny, not even any tracks. We worried about him. Perhaps better to have a short life of true bunny-ness than a long boring life in a hutch.

Then this morning, as I looked out through the back window, I saw tracks — giant rabbit tracks — Bunny's tracks. He had sauntered over from the neighbor's juniper bushes to check out his old homestead.

I spend my silent meeting time reflecting on living with my feet on the earth rather than on wood or wire floors, of digging my way to freedom, of facing the predators of life, and of experiencing life as it was intended for me.

Comment:

Early in your Portrait Journal you will need to decide how you want to measure time. For my purposes I didn't want to go by the calendar, too digital. I elected to use the lunar cycle. Use any method you want. Certainly the conventional calendar is the most convenient. If you are feeling creative, you might come up with some novel concept to engage your creativity and playfulness. Your Portrait Journal should not be serious all of the time. Feel free to appropriate my lunar time idea. It certainly didn't originate with me.

Write your journal in the present tense as much as possible. It is more alive and keeps you a participant rather than a bystander of life.

It also provides future readers with a sense of seeing rather than being told.

waning crescent$_6$

What do you say to yourself when the police dispatcher says his family wanted you to know he just committed suicide? You say it can't be true, he was just here an hour ago. When the dispatcher goes on (not knowing you were talking to yourself) and says he shot himself, you deny it happened; you press the thought, "No, not K* He was just here with his family, they were going off to alcohol treatment. Everything was going to be all right."

The dispatcher provides dry, emotion-free information only, "The family just wanted you to know."

You hang up the phone, look at the stack of waiting phone messages, and note you're twenty minutes behind. Trying to pull it together, you are interrupted in mid-swallow as Carl comes in and asks you to come next door. One of his patients is suicidal, *right on the brink.* She is deeply depressed again and feels hopeless.

Not up to sharing about K* just yet, you say you'll be with him in a minute, you just have to look at your messages. Where is the one from B*? There. Give her a call.

"Hello . . . . Dr. Hageseth? . . . . OK . . . . A little better than yesterday. When will this ever stop? . . . . Yes, I'll be in tomorrow . . . . Thanks for calling."

Somehow the day finishes with no more tragedies. I am home communing with the protective darkness of this moonless night. Alone with myself, I am not sure what I think. I feel a strange muted stillness inside like the quiet on a battlefield as the dead are counted, tagged and placed in body bags — a stunned sort of silence. I didn't see it coming. Nobody did. I hadn't seen K* in over a year. He had just dropped out of sight. Last Fall Carl had gone to his condo, no answer. Then suddenly last week, his family came from Missouri.

They called me and we arranged for K*'s in-patient treatment to start this afternoon. His family was well-intentioned, right behind him, supporting him, pushing him, encouraging him, all at the same time. They did their part as well as they could. I think I did too, but then again . . . .

It is chilly tonight, but not cold; warmer than it has been for awhile. I go out into the back yard walking on hard, crunchy snow and count some stars. I look for Bunny. This morning I discovered he has a playmate, a little cottontail about a quarter his size. I saw the little one hopping along Bunny's tracks and sniffing. I'll name this new character, Flasher. I wonder if Flasher will have any idea what to do with this handsome, "big lug" of a neutered male rabbit. I guess that depends on whether Flasher is a he or a she.

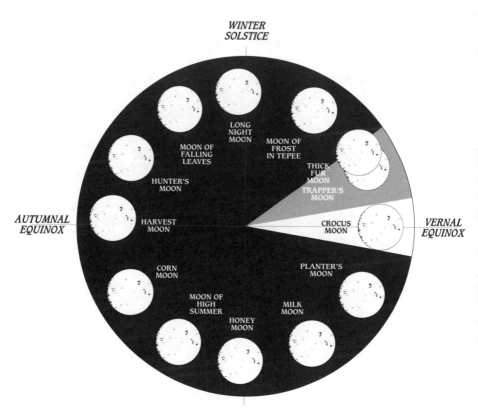

WINTER
SOLSTICE

LONG
NIGHT
MOON

MOON OF
FALLING
LEAVES

MOON OF
FROST
IN TEPEE

HUNTER'S
MOON

THICK
FUR
MOON

TRAPPER'S
MOON

AUTUMNAL
EQUINOX

HARVEST
MOON

CROCUS
MOON

VERNAL
EQUINOX

CORN
MOON

PLANTER'S
MOON

MOON OF
HIGH
SUMMER

MILK
MOON

HONEY
MOON

SUMMER
SOLSTICE

Chapter Two

CROCUS MOON

NEW MOONS ARE shy, introverted. They hide in the daytime sky where nobody can see them. But today, this new moon creeps up on the sun and takes a healthy bite. The morning starts with too many clouds. Just before midday I steal out to the parking lot. I have poked a pinhole in a piece of cardboard to project the solar eclipse. And then, as if just for me, the clouds tease apart just long enough for me to project the image of the eclipse on the back of my hand. Alone, I crouch in the parking lot and play with the image. And then I return to my office and call the coroner.

Somewhere in my brain I file the details of K*'s suicide with other mutilating destruction of bodies I have seen, starting with my cadaver in gross anatomy. As I talk with the investigator, I come to realize I didn't blow it. No matter how conscientious you try to be, when your patient commits suicide, you wonder if you may have failed in some way. K* was schizophrenic and abusing alcohol to boot. Schizophrenia, another name for hell on earth.

47

This evening Carol takes me out to our muddy flower bed. There is a small family of yellow crocuses proudly proclaiming arrival of spring. They are coming out, ready or not. Damn the blizzards, full speed ahead.

The Nez Perce call this the Flower Time Moon. I like that better than the old colonial descriptions, lenten moon, fish moon or worm moon. I proclaim this third moon of the new year to be the Crocus Moon.

waxing crescent₁

Thermometers vie for attention today. Five days ago they were recording all-time low temperatures, today they are proclaiming all-time highs. This welcome warmth has converted playgrounds into ponds. It's tough on the high school rugby team, but they don't care. Getting cold, wet, and otherwise banged up is just part of the process.

At lunchtime I go out to sample the air. Appreciating the warmth, I savor the spring bouquet. The sense of smell imprints memories more indelibly than any other sense. I remember the distinctive smells of my father, his cigar, his aftershave, the fresh rubber smell where the tires were stored in the warehouse. Another favorite smell of mine: The sharp, freshly-waxed smell of the first day of school. Standing in the sun, I smell a bold scent but I can't place it; loamy, ripe, rich, not unpleasant. I pick up the dried pine needles at my feet but it's definitely not them. I check the direction of the breeze. Out of the east. That's it! Feedlots. At a distance, a scent that's pleasant, refreshing, almost sweet.

waxing crescent₂

I arrive for my appointment at 10:00:04. (Digital watch.) The visit goes well and then I drive back to Fort Collins. Taking country roads, I pass a wheat field, now a temporary lake. A flock of pintail ducks wheels around in sheer delight. Pintail drakes, clad in formal dinner jackets. How splendid.

Carl asks me how my fast is going. Pretty good, but after seven days I'm tired of the watery nutritional supplements and waking up hungry. For him, fasting is a spiritual experience. Not for me. It is a holistic health experiment.

Tonight Carol fixes our first meal, vegetable soup with a couple tablespoons of brown rice. Head bowed, holding Carol's hand, I meet several little pot-bellied African children and two emaciated Jews from Nazi concentration camps. Standing at the far end of our table, their wordless stares tell me they never had a choice about breaking their fasts. Their hunger wasn't for their health or some lofty spiritual exercise. Standing in silence, they look at me. They don't accuse me of any sin, nor do I feel guilty. Their presence is not wasted; clearly, I must do more than just talk about those who starve. One small bowl of soup fills me nicely.

_waxing crescent_3

Hospital committee meetings, too many phone calls, charts to complete; the day opens at its usual frenzied pace. I am careful to seclude myself in my office for a long deep silence. I need all the serenity I can muster before meeting with K*'s family.

K*'s Mom, dad, sister, brother, Carl and I meet. A hot liquid pain fills the room. His sister blames herself. Carl's words touch her gently. She relaxes, cuddles my teddy bear, and cries from some deep hollow cavity in her soul. The abscess drains. K*'s father seeks relief another way, humor. Recalling K* was always strange as a child, difficult to understand, his father talks about the afternoon after the suicide. The family wanted to have the room where K* ended his life with a single round from his shotgun cleaned. No cleaning service responded to their calls, so rather than risking an odor the next day, they cleaned the carpet and the walls by themselves. They placed pieces of K*'s brain and cranium in a cereal

49

bowl. Jaw twisted, laughing and squezing tears through clinched fists, K*'s father blurts, "I always said I wanted to get inside K*'s head." We laugh — a needed break in the tension. I don't think he knows I wrote a book about humor.

Tonight the moon floats higher in a fully black sky. The dark side is so voluptuously spherical. Why have I taken so long to notice?

waxing crescent₄

I jog around Warren Lake this morning. A comfortable, though muddy, three miles. Despite the recent warming, winter continues to cover the lake with a solid sheet of moaning ice. Snow crouches along the north side of houses but has disappeared everywhere else. Birds are everywhere. And so many of them; common birds: Finches, sparrows, blackbirds, robins, mallards, geese, even a flicker playing castanets on a dead log. I nearly run into a pair of mallards flying eyeball high right down the middle of the street.

I stop and check out our crocuses. Yellow, white and purple, the race is on to see who is fully flowered first. To supervise the process, a bee is out like a building inspector forcing her way into each open blossom. She seems to prefer the yellow ones. Never in my forty-eight springs have I lingered to watch a bee probe the first flowers of spring. Little wonder I have felt something lacking.

Comment:

Your Portrait Journal will influence you to look more closely at the details of life: The everyday commonplace details that you may overlook when you are not actively reflecting on life.

waxing crescent₅

As a boy I saw them colored yellow in comic books. The enemy, combining the worst of the Japanese and the Russians. In college I debated whether we should grant them diplomatic recognition. It seemed foolish to ignore one fourth of Earth's population. But they said I didn't understand. They were communist and "they hate us so."

Tonight we celebrate the thirty-first birthday of Wu Deng. He brings three other Chinese students with him. We feed them spaghetti with venison sauce, garlic bread, salad, and chocolate cake, complete with candles. We hold hands, heads bowed in the name of peace among all peoples. They have no problem with our silent grace. We have no problem with their atheism.

Foreign exchange students will insure peace far more than a million MX missiles ever could. What a short distance it is from enemy to friend.

waxing crescent$_6$

In my morning silence, a recurring phrase repeats in my head, "I pray for the peace of the world." I will dwell on that phrase whenever my mind needs a place to rest. It sure beats the hell out of worrying.

Four years ago I bought a computer for my bicycle. It tells my speed, distance, average speed, maximum speed, pedal cadence, time elapsed, and total miles ridden since the battery was changed. It measures my distances and provides times to shoot for as I train. But over the years, I became a slave to it. I often spend my ride watching the computer and pushing myself. And what for? I'll always be a last-third-of-the-pack racer, whatever I do. I was born a golden retriever, not a greyhound.

Today I get my bike out, pump up the tires, and re-attach the computer, but it is blank, the battery dead. I go for my first ride of the season. It is splendid. I don't know the distance, average speed, or how long I was gone. But, I do notice how the air cools as I ride next to the lake, how the sand on the streets makes steering tricky, and how my mind wanders about. And I remember the phrase, "I pray for the peace of the world." I won't replace the battery for now.

At home, Carol is cleaning the winter debris from the flower beds. She shows me what tulips look like when they first push up through the surface of the ground. Our local geese mill around the lake as usual, while high above, a long strand of geese work their way directly north, migrants on their way to the arctic. It is extraordinary how spring barges in. As I lay on the ground watching the geese, I realize the ground is not chilling me. It is almost warm. Mother Earth.

FIRST QUARTER

The local geese, who mixed randomly all winter, have suddenly paired up. Just yesterday the flock grazed the greenbelt in general disarray. Today they are all couples; courting, and claiming nesting boxes with loud honking proclamations.

waxing gibbous₁

The wind blew hard last night. The numbers were interesting: Gusts exceeding eighty miles per hour. Our barbecue grill was blown about the back yard as if made of aluminum foil. Our lawn chairs were all plastered up against the kennel. It is gray and raw today. I like immersing myself in the weather whatever its quality. Thank God I'm not at its mercy as my ancestors were. I'm sure weather was a demanding and cruel teacher.

B* calls me at home. She just wants to hear another voice on the phone. She feels lonely and frightened. I tell her I am frightened for her too. There are no guarantees.

waxing gibbous₂

A day like any other day — a non-descript morning, a few high clouds, a cool breeze. The ice has finally receded from the edge of the lake leaving the center a large white plate. My jog is average. Then it's off to work.

My first appointment is a no show. It was a _freebie_ for a local peace activist who called in distress a couple days ago. It is strange how frequently those who don't pay are the most likely not to show or even call to cancel. I pass the hour weeding out old charts from the archives. A thick folder demands my attention for just one more time.

She was a most delightful woman, but tormented by schizophrenia. On meds she was unassuming, plain, a bit odd, but devoted to her nephews; she never had children of her own. Off meds she was tortured by a pack of demons who dragged her into Dante's Inferno. Once in the hospital, she refused to eat the hamburgers served at dinner, "I won't eat them. That is meat from my nephews. I murdered them this morning. I ground them into hamburger." More medication and she came back her odd, likeable self. Last winter, she went off her medications. God knows why. Her landlord discovered her . . . . dead. She had slashed her body all over with a carving knife and had run around the house breaking everything in sight, even swallowing some silverware. The mortal wound was the carving knife thrust into her vagina. What demons pursued her that day?

I had to assist the police and I then worked with her family, helping them to understand she was murdered by a terrible disease. She did not commit suicide. The investigation complete, I can put her chart in the archives. I will try to put her memory in a similar place in my mind. If I were to remain conscious of every tragedy, I would go mad. The hardest part is that she just wasn't an old lady, she was a _person_. I liked her.

Second session, I see half of a couple who came to me for marriage counselling. She couldn't get off work, so he comes in alone. In his late forties, he (like so many men) knows little about what a woman really wants and needs in a relationship and what his wife wants in a sexual experience. It is good his wife isn't here. I take off my analyst's cap and give him an Old Uncle Chris talk.

Your presence, your little acts of caring, your casual caresses are more important than any orgasm. When you make love, take time, talk with her. Pause in the middle, eat an apple or drink a glass of wine. Surprise her by coming home in the middle of the day for no reason at all. While making love, let your hands speak love to her, don't leave them dangling like inert lumps of bread dough.

He is attentive, but will he translate my advice into action? He has read *PLAYBOY*, but magazines like that teach men to seduce, not to love. They fail to teach how to love one woman forever. Adding to his problems, like so many middle-aged men, his passion is business, not his wife.

Then I see an old friend — a woman nearly disabled by obsessive-compulsive disorder (OCD). When I first met her, she lived in a world of bizarre magic, terrified that if she didn't undo a thought with some ritualistic behavior, a tragic accident would befall a family member. We have worked with medication and therapy in a long, laborious way — slow, steady, successful. Now she is finally in love for the first time in her life. She has come to terms with her disease and is ready to get on with life. She is thirty-seven and her biological clock is running. Will she succeed with love? I don't know.

Next I see a young manic-depressive woman who is finally controlled on medicine. For years a variety of therapists thought she was a product of a dysfunctional family, co-dependent — a hyper-adolescent creature with an eating disorder. As a last resort, she came to see me, a psychiatrist. All the evidence for manic depressive disease was there. I started her on lithium and she got better. "Normal for the first time I can remember." As part of her treatment she has been abstaining from all addictive behaviors: Sex, overeating, alcohol. Today she tells me she is founding a club, *The*

54

Born Again Virgin Club. So much of sex in her past was a manic escapade. She says she wants to re-experience virginity. The next time, sex will be for love. And she will be sober too. Hooray. For now, she is returning to college; a little bored, but accepting that life has its boring times.

Next I see a tall, blond bisexual man whose father died when he was young. His mother was seductive, controlling and confusing. He has seen three therapists before — lots of analysis. His problem: "I get too mad. I hurt people." A gymnast, he cultivates every muscle of his near-perfect body. He has never emerged from his narcissism. I am taking an intuitive approach and have challenged him to sit in silence for fifteen minutes every day. "You mean meditate?" His competitive juices would like to see him as an advanced practitioner of zen. No, I say, just sit in silence, count your breaths and if you must do anything, pray for the peace of the world.

He is experiencing a transference with me. I have become the good father he never had. He wonders if we could go jogging or work out at the club together. I tell him no, but I'll be here for him every week. He needs a therapist, not another companion. Treatment is going to be a long process. The outcome is in doubt. A lot will depend on how we negotiate the time when his anger turns on me.

Finally, I have my afternoon break, telephone time. I catch up on eleven phone calls and pick up the mail. I also sneak a drink of water and visit the patio to breathe some fresh air. I close my eyes, tilt my head back. No feedlot today.

I have three more patients before I can finish up and go home to Carol's welcoming embrace. How nice it is to look forward to going home. Our embraces are the high point of my day.

First I see a young stout dark-haired woman. A victim of a recent armed assault, she hasn't been able to sleep in three months. She keeps hearing her assailant in the house at night. She refuses medication, fearing it would impair her if she has to confront him. Her past history is a disaster. At nine she was held at gunpoint by a sadistic adult cousin. He played russian roulette with her, but she was always the target. She never dared tell her family, "Tell them, and I will kill them one by one. But I'll let you live so you know it was you who really killed them by opening your big mouth." He still calls her every year, just to let her know he is still thinking of her. No wonder she finds it so hard to talk. Sometimes we pass the whole hour in silence.

My next-to-last patient is a deeply depressed grade school principal who is being sued for the wrongful death of a mentally retarded student at her school. Since she is the administrator, she has to go to trial and listen as attorneys describe her as a negligent, insensitive bureaucrat. All of her good intentions and victories with countless other students go unheeded; not admissible. Philosophical and bitter, she offers her summation of the whole process, "Shit flows up hill." The trial is scheduled at the next full moon.

I finish the day off with one of my Viet Nam vets. He has killed too many people. Once, somewhere along the Ho Chi Minh Trail, his squad was directed to stir things up, live off the land, and come back in a few months. One day they decided they wanted roast beef. To do so required they killed every person in a small village in order to get their cow and go unrecognized. They did. They killed seventeen people, women, old men, and children . . . . and one cow. As the war went by, his buddies were killed so often he stopped learning the replacements' names. Isolated, depressed and alcoholic, he spends his days poring over Viet Nam documentaries. This year he has managed to stop drinking. But the guilt; is it within my power to help him experience forgiveness?

Comment:

This was a full routine day. Select one of yours and tell its story. This is the outer part of life. You may include several such days in your Portrait Journal. It will be clear what day you want to include when the day is over.

Crocus Moon

Patients gone, I fill out the daily ledger, return three calls, and finish off the mail. A few checks, too many advertisements, a couple of throw-away-journals, and one big thick envelope from a law firm. What?! They are suing one of the non-medical therapists for whom I provide consultations. I have never seen the patient in question. Of course, they are suing me too. They see me as the responsible supervisor, not a consultant. *Respondeat Superior*, complete vicarious liability. And I have deep pockets, or at least my insurance company does. The alleged malpractice took place several years ago. I really don't like this part of my profession. Then I remember the teacher's comment. I smile, duplicate the letter, lock my file cabinet, and head home to Carol's embrace.

waxing gibbous₃

Finally the lake is open. The ice is gone. On the banks patches of grass are greening, while everywhere else it remains so much shabby straw. The waxing gibbous moon lolls above in the evening sky. What a planet! *A good planet is hard to find.*

We dine at Carl and Karen's tonight. Lowell and Barbara are there too. The theme is fish. As usual, we eat too much. What is not spoken of is the most important issue for our group this year. Barbara's cancer is more active again. She has *maxed-out* on radiation therapy and her chemo options are getting slim. She's not so sure she wants any more treatment. I don't blame her. She has beaten the odds already, working both conventional therapy and the holistic side as well. She limps now, experiencing constant pain. What does Barbara talk about? Feeding the homeless at the shelter. She volunteers every week for the evening meal. And now her church is opening at lunchtime for the homeless too. We don't talk about cancer because we don't want to dwell on it, as if giving it attention will somehow encourage it.

Stomach full, I pick up Badger, Carl's *zen dog*, and lean back in a reclining chair. Over a hundred moons of age, Badger is unaccustomed to being indoors. He adores warmth and human attention and expresses his pleasure lying on his back in my arms and groaning occasionally. I love it too. I miss having pets. But I know my travel schedule won't allow me to give a pet the attention it needs. I'll just have to stick with borrow-a-dog for now.

waxing gibbous₄

The issue isn't analog instead of digital. The issue is restoring an analog balance to an over-digitalized life. Analog isn't somehow better than digital, but it is being supplanted by digital's arrogance and influence. Digital gets jobs done; jobs in the material world anyway. But our world suffers because of the increasing lack of analog-ness in life. What is needed is a restoration of balance.

ANALOG	**DIGITAL**
curved, waving, undulating	straight, choppy
intuitive	analytic, logical
musical	mechanical
feminine	masculine
mystical spirituality	organized religion
awe	respect
flexible	legalistic
quantum mechanics	Newtonian physics
language is fluid	language is fixed
truth is biographical	truth is absolute
poetic	technical
Native American	European
mystery	certainty
unconscious	conscious
right brained	left brained

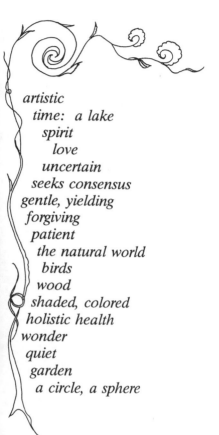

artistic	graphic
time: a lake	time: a river
spirit	matter
love	needs-gratification
uncertain	deterministic
seeks consensus	power dominates
gentle, yielding	demanding, rigid
forgiving	an eye-for-an-eye
patient	hurried
the natural world	the city
birds	airplanes
wood	plastic
shaded, colored	black or white
holistic health	allopathic medicine
wonder	curiosity
quiet	show-off
garden	supermarket
a circle, a sphere	a square, a cube

Comment:

Your Portrait Journal will insist you clarify your thinking. An idea will germinate, grow, and develop an identity. Were you not writing a Portrait Journal, the ideas would gradually regress as more pressing matters occupy your mind.

59

_____*waxing gibbous*₅_____

The Vernal Equinox

Not much of a show, today is a cold snowy day, hardly one for celebrating re-birth. Of course, inside my heart I have been celebrating spring for the last half moon. Clouds block any view of sunrise or sunset. My mood is consonant with cloudiness and cold. I spend the first half of the day talking to insurance adjustors and attorneys. I am getting started on that great American exercise in futility. I am preparing to defend myself in a lawsuit. And what gets me: I never even saw the person.

_____*waxing gibbous*₆_____

Bright sunshine and my mood responds. Today is a fasting day. First, I descend into a deep, rich silence. Then I take a run. The geese, now in twosomes, greet my passing with sonorous honks. Actually only one member of a pair sounds off, the other keeps its head in a lower, deferential position. As I admire the couples, I take note of something I have never seen in all my life: Goose Breath. With each honk, the exhaled air hangs golden in the morning sunlight. It is just like my breath as I pant along. Shouldn't be too remarkable an observation, but how rarely do we see, *really see*, the little touches of life, golden goose breath lingering in the morning air?

Today a tragedy is discovered next to the Montessori School playground. Mr. Herbst, who keeps a small flock of Banti chickens in his yard next to the playground, discovered that every last hen had been killed by a dog who broke into the chicken house. When Carol tells me, I feel a mixture of sadness and anger; sadness for the very gentle Mr. Herbst, anger over useless death. Carol brightens, saying that he's just going to get some more and keep raising chickens for the kids to enjoy. Resurrection doesn't have to be mysterious;

60

sometimes simple day-to-day human kindness promises new life after tragedy.

Later in the sunny afternoon, all the children are congregating along the fence where the old gentleman is spading the dirt of his garden. Carol notices he is handing something to each of them. Many are engrossed with the little gifts, examining them closely, while others pocket them and scamper off. What were these fascinating objects? Earthworms. Thus the name, Worm Moon.

FULL MOON

As we watch Steve's rugby game at sunset, I scan the eastern horizon for the full moon's appearance. It seems delayed and, for a foolish moment, I wonder if it will show. Isn't that the way we worry ourselves unnecessarily? Pester ourselves about things over which we have no control and that will turn out just as they should.

Later now, as I write, I marvel at the beautiful, white full moon beaming in at me over my computer monitor. She is a lovely companion. How slowly time has passed since I started savoring her appearance every night. I may not live longer this way, but it feels longer. After all, time is relative, biographical; more a lake than a river.

Comment:

Time will slow when you start observing your life in detail. Time is relative to the freshness and novelty of life. When life is repetitive and mundane, time flies. When life is new and fresh, it slows to a crawl. Your Portrait Journal calls you to rediscover the newness of life.

waning gibbous₁

A sunny morning. After my silent time I take my daily jog around the lake. Once out the door, I am greeted by the local redwing community in the cottonwoods across the street. Rounding the south side, I meet the Canada Geese. They are experiencing a housing problem. Several couples are checking out the peaked roofs of homes along the lake shore since all the nesting boxes have been claimed. One goose stands alone on a lawn. The only solitary goose I see. Is he too young or too maybe undesirable to win a mate? Or perhaps he had a mate who fell to a hunter's gun last fall and he chooses to be alone.

Further around the east side, I am dazed by the iridescent green of a drake mallard's head; perhaps the most splendid green in all of nature. When the sunlight catches it just right, it reveals a hint of purple.

Finally on the north side I am surrounded by a robins' chorus punctuated by a loud echoing tap-tap-tap of one small downy woodpecker. I reflect on the design of a woodpecker's head; how utterly shock resistant the system must be for protecting his brain from trauma. If not, woodpeckers would have become extinct long ago from being punch drunk.

I didn't intend to bird-watch this trip, but how could I avoid it? The only digital intrusion on my run is the sound of the jet planes high overhead, coming from the south out of Denver.

This morning I see only one patient and then go to the airport and board a metal bird. I read three short stories and then arrive in Arizona to see the boys. Interesting how I still call my sons *the boys*. They are both fine young men over twenty. I guess parents are like that, their children remain children well into adult life.

----------------------------------*waning gibbous₂*----------------------

Tempe, Arizona

Too blonde. Too sun-tanned. So many young men drinking too much beer. John takes me to Schooner's, his favorite hang-out. It overflows with beautiful, muscular young people engaged in an archetypal ritual which, in the current vernacular, is called *scamming*.

John looks around the room: "Dad, this is a target-rich environment."
Following John, I tour the site. I feel like an anthropologist observing an unfamiliar culture. Then I take a seat off to the side, nurse my schooner of beer, and feel just slightly the spiritual superior. After a while, I begin to recall my college years. Professor Jaffe, who I haven't thought about in twenty-five years, pops into mind. He had studied in Paris after the First Great War. What was it like in Paris in 1920? No young Frenchmen. They had all been killed in the War-To-End-All-War. There were boys, old men, and foreigners. Young women, yes. Young men, no. Professor Jaffe didn't use the words, target-rich environment, but he implied as much. As I continue to gaze about the crowded room, I become thankful for seeing so many young men. Too blonde. Too sun-tanned. Drinking too much beer.

Comment:
   Present day experiences will call up old forgotten memories only to synthesize a new perspective on an otherwise seemingly common event.

_____*waning gibbous₃*_____

This morning the boys and I take time to talk more. Our absence of this past year and their growing maturity have opened pathways of communication previously strewn with rocky rebellion, thorny misunderstandings, and parental speed-bumps. I speak my heart. They do, too. Our comradeship is growing. They are so alive, vital, and happy.
   Later, we jog around the park across the street weaving our way among several man-made ponds. In the desert, such scarce open water abounds with a special richness of life. Birds everywhere. Some I never see in Colorado, like small nervous flocks of Inca Doves. We happen upon a flock of widgeon, American Baldpates, trim little ducks who whistle rather than quack. Not as bold as the

mallards, these late migrants swim off a safer distance from shore. Soon to head north, they are fair-weather cousins of the pintails who, by now, are challenging spring in Canada.

Along the way we come to a fenced-in area strewn with little plastic easter eggs, containing jelly beans and chocolate. We see beautiful children, dressed in their Easter finery, wait with empty easter baskets in hand, for the go-ahead. To them, is this another opportunity for getting something material for free? Are we teaching our children to love or are we mistakenly trying to love them so hard that we prevent them from learning to give and to love, giving and rarely requiring? Are we providing plastic sugar-filled eggs to our children instead of real flesh-and-blood, life-sustaining psychological and spiritual nourishment?

After the run, the boys, tired from too many late nights, need a nap before attempting one more restaurant meal with dad. While they sleep, I exercise some more by walking the entire four-mile length of the park across the street.

More a walking meditation than an aerobic workout, I relish the hot afternoon sunshine. Skateboards. Rollerblades. Bicycles of all designs. Big dogs, little dogs, old dogs, and puppies leading people of all ages. The park parallels a golf course where adult *homo sapiens* swing at little white dimpled spheres. When I caddied as a boy, all the golf balls were white. Now they come in a wide array of brilliant colors. When I caddied as a boy, all the golfers were white. Now, they too, come in a wide array of brilliant colors.

On the path, I discover a blue egg shell. It is streaked with dried albumen and a little bit of blood. A boat-tailed grackle, has discarded the shell from her nest atop a palm tree. Blue eggs are not just for robins. Big shiny black birds have soft blue eggshells too. I like that. I carry the shell for most of my walk and begin to reflect on Easter.

As a boy I had been taught that this was the day Jesus was comforting the souls in hell. "He descended into hell and on the third day . . . ." As a young man, I regurgitated The Apostles Creed as I had been taught. As an older man, I am not sure what I know

64

about Jesus. I do know I'm not much into creeds anymore. And I do know I am open and ready to experience passion, awe, and mystery.

I was told to worship Jesus. Blind, unquestioning faith. I was told to ask for anything in Jesus's name and it would happen. I tried several times and it almost never worked. How much do we really know about Jesus? What should we know about him that we don't? Can we ever know? Well, if time is a lake and death merely a transition, Jesus may be mystically closer than I know.

And he called his followers *friends*. A nice word. He didn't call them slaves, but friends. I think of my friends and I smile. I walk with that feeling for a while and think of Jesus. I smile again. I make up a mantra: *Friendly Jesus*. Mercy! That sounds dangerously close to being some sort of a fanatic. I walk with the blue egg shell of a large black bird, watching black and white men hit white and neon golf balls. It is evening of the day before Easter.

---

waning gibbous$_4$

The first Sunday after the full moon following the Vernal Equinox. Easter. Here in central Arizona, it is raining torrents; the first significant rain in over a year. The park across the street has become a lake. At silent meeting, I speak of Friendly Jesus.

---

waning gibbous$_6$

Home

She greets me at the door and then ushers me directly to her room. I pause to pet the dog and exchange greetings with her house-mates. She walks briskly, shoulders square and back straight. Arranging the cushion on the rocking chair for me, she sits in a straight-backed chair, fixing me with a clear, gentle smile. I have waited over a moon for our meeting; I have so much to say.

I always longed for a mother who would be wise, gentle, and encouraging. I briefly experienced such a relationship in therapy with an older Jewish woman psychologist. Now I meet with this eighty year old Catholic nun. A friend of Thomas Merton during his later years, Mary Luke Tobin directs the Thomas Merton Center for Creative Exchange. For the past year she has listened and offered advice as I have undertaken the exploration of my inner self. Not one for solemnity, she counsels as much with her earthen laughter as she does by sharing her encyclopedic knowledge of saintliness and total commitment to social justice.

I tell her about the *Thirteen Moon Journal*; she is encouraging. We talk of my silent time, K*'s suicide, the lawsuit, and many other events of the past moon. Though superficially similar to psychotherapy, spiritual direction is a much different process. We don't dwell on my family of origin, my defensive style, or discordant relationships. We look more deeply at the underlying purpose of my life and consider the combined wisdom of many cultures not just our Judeo-Christian background. We explore the spiritual domain beneath the psychological veneer. Things aren't always as they appear to be. When I withdraw from the hustle of life, I see things in a different light. I tell Luke I want to quit psychiatry and maybe even run away for a couple years. But I don't know how to do so and remain a responsible person.

Follow your inner leading. If you do, changes will seem natural, not miraculous. Leaving psychiatry for a life of writing may follow as a part of your growth. And, then, maybe not. There are plenty of therapists in the world, enough to go around. Maybe it is time for you to touch people in a different way. It will become clearer as you spend more time in prayer. You want to become a writer? Do it! You want to run away? Do it! . . . If you can. And she twinkles.

Luke offers some words of a colleague: To live a spiritual life requires you become humble. A humble person has a good-humored detachment from his own self-importance. He is willing to give up materialism and he is willing to give up the need to control others.

Humility is something I need. I think I practice it in my own odd sort of way, though many who know me must consider my outgoing extroversion to be the antithesis of humility. Could be. But to me, humility is the right-knowing of my relative size and importance in the universe. Next to God, who birthed the big bang by merely uttering a word, I am a temporary particle of dust come together for a purpose beyond my knowing. My first response, as I come to appreciate my size and relative insignificance, is fear. But when I do not run from the fear, when I sit in silence and be with the fear, what follows is acceptance. Acceptance of my utter smallness and willingness to follow my purpose whatever that may be. Acceptance and willingness, the underpinnings of humility. I don't become humble to gain favor, that would be a manipulation. How incredibly narcissistic to think I could manipulate God.

I drive home through ever-changing weather. The wind spurs tumbleweeds across the highway with terrible ferocity; big ones often bounce up over my car as we collide. The word, tumbleweed, may be the most appropriate descriptive noun in the whole botanical lexicon. I encounter three varieties of snow, a bit of sleet, a light rain shower, and then bright sunshine and calm air.

waning crescent₁

A pussy willow sky comforts the awakening spring landscape. As I enjoy my morning jog, I consider how clouds may comfort rather than depress. These soft, low clouds seem to nurture, to invite a pause in the seemingly hectic onset of spring. Ms. Nature, good mother that she is, allows her children time to fully awaken before getting on with the business of growth. The aspens dangle their wooly-worm buds anticipating the first spring showers that will wash them away, making way for leaves that will dance in summer breezes. The weeping willow branches have blushed a muted chartreuse, forecasting the emergence of their long graceful leaves. The ash and the cottonwood buds fatten and smile as they emerge like little birds from tight brown eggshells. Only the linden trees in the backyard show no signs of life; they are always the last to get the word.

The land is beginning to stir with a great expectancy of spring. Though the crocuses have displayed their best, the tulips and daffodils aren't quite ready. More color, lusty breezes, and spring fever will celebrate the season soon, but not now, not yet.

waning crescent₂

I speak at a local church this morning. I ask how many people have had experiences they would classify as extraordinary, as mystical. The responses come in, secret-ballot style. Sixty percent of this audience of middle aged, mostly college educated, predominantly white, men and women answer *yes*. What I actually asked was, "Have you ever had an extraordinary, a mystical experience — one which you rarely share with others because you fear they would think you to be *crazy*?"

Even though a majority have had such an experience, the tyranny of the digital mind-set holds the individual hostage, threatening him with being thought to be *crazy* if he shares his mystical experience.

waning crescent₃

My first love was not psychiatry, it was veterinary medicine. As a child, I found more solace in my relationships with animals than I did with human beings. The softness of my cat offered comfort as I avoided the turbulance of my family. More than anything, my mother loved doctors, real doctors; her internist, her psychiatrist, and her gynecologist — *especially her gynecologist*. After Jimmy poked me in the penis with a stick (I was five and involved in a normal sexual behavior of childhood, displaying myself) Mom tried to shoot his father. So the sheriff took her away to the mental hospital where they gave her *shock treatments*. She came home a sweeter and more easy-going person. Unfortunately, the treatments (or her own repression) wiped out all memory of me so I had to live with neighbors for awhile. She thought I was "that little bastard, Jimmy." So to gain her good graces, I told her when I grew up I would become a psychiatrist.

I forgot that promise shortly after she accepted me as her child, and I returned to the comfort of animal relationships. All through junior high, I read everything I could about being a vet. But with the stirring of spiritual restlessness, and realizing I loved the stage, I felt called to be a minister. (A fate worse than death!) I compromised with God by becoming a doctor, a *real one*, one who takes care of humans.

With single-minded purpose I ripped through pre-med in four years, med school in four years, endured an internship, served a stint in the military and then found myself out in the world unsure what I really wanted to do when I grew up. It was then I entered therapy and remembered my promise to Mom; I was to become a psychiatrist. I spent six months in therapy considering the idea and concluded if I were to be a psychiatrist, I wouldn't be like those arrogant, insensitive, white-coated analysts I met in med school. And I wouldn't be like those distant God-like giants who erased my mother's memory of me.

Now I have practiced psychiatry for fifteen years. I stay current with the scientific side and I continue to feel great compassion for those I treat. But inside, I am yearning for something different. Medicine and psychiatry were right for me when I started out, but lately a new self is emerging, wanting a different life. But a man of forty-eight summers isn't in the best position to shift careers.

I have remained true to my promise by remaining different from those analysts I abhorred, but there have been a few twists. For several years I stubbornly refused to perform shock treatments; the more proper term now is Electro-Convulsive Therapy or ECT. Reluctantly, I came to realize ECT was life-saving in many situations; sometimes nothing else works. So now I perform ECT, whether

Mom blotted me out of her mind or not. This week I am in the midst of providing ECT to two elderly women; one who attempted suicide and another who only sits and weeps. Therapy and medications have failed to help them. Three mornings a week, I hold their hands as they are put to sleep and then I pass a brief pulse of direct current electricity through their cerebrums. I seek for them another opportunity to find purpose and even joy in being alive.

Comment:

> *Your Portrait Journal will recall past decisions which shaped your life. Many of the behaviors and attitudes you practice in the present were determined by a decision you made earlier in life, often in childhood.*

waning crescent₅

I wouldn't call it a shortcoming, it's more of an inconvenience. I am not a morning person. I enjoy mornings, I only wish they didn't come so early. This day starts before sunrise as Carol and I savor the dim morning light, awakening and positioning ourselves in one-another's arms, waiting for the clock radio to click us awake.

NPR's news is the usual — a huge oil spill in Alaska; an inebriated ship's captain; dead sea otters, birds, and soon-to-die salmon fry. The corporation offers an inadequate effort at amends. That news is followed by more assault rifle murders and news of another airplane crash. Inflation is going up, the trade deficit is going up. The educational achievement of school children is going down, and there are more hostages and artillery duels in Lebanon. Chinese students are rioting in a place called Tianenman Square. It is time to shower.

I clean up and leave for the hospital as the sun just breaks the horizon. I skip breakfast in order to get my cholesterol checked today. Meeting my ladies in the treatment room, I can see that each seems to be improving already. I spend the necessary time electrically evaporating their depressions. Then it's off to the lab, become a patient, get my blood drawn (I still don't like needles) and go home for a quick bite of breakfast.

Then I begin another typical day in the life of a generic psychiatrist:

#1. A young female college teacher has fallen in love with, and had an affair with, one of her students. She is not sure she wants to stay with her husband and children. I am helping her sort through her feelings, understand how she came to this place in her life, and look realistically at her options. She feels as though I am pressuring her towards staying in her marriage. In a way, she is right. I'm not neutral about marriages, I like to see them succeed. Divorce is pretty devastating business, even if it is simple and, in many cases, absolutely necessary.

#2. A middle aged stock broker came in two months ago and challenged me on why he should stay alive. A tall, dark, imposing man, he once was an All-American linebacker. There have been seven suicides in his extended family during the past decade, his second marriage is failing, and he is addicted to alcohol. He tried sobriety and AA for several months; but he felt more depressed. Unable to sleep, he returned to the relative tranquility of alcohol. We are making a little headway, he is down to four drinks a day and beginning to believe I can help him find a reason to live. But he is crystal clear on one matter. If I ever try to hospitalize him, he will play the game, leave the hospital and kill himself by driving into a bridge abutment. *Make it look like an accident.* Today his desire to commit suicide is as strong as it ever was. And with a sinister laugh he tells me he has good life insurance, all his family would need. I eye-ball him and reply his family needs a husband and father, not his money. You're lying to yourself if you think your family will be happy with your money. He agrees to postpone his suicide for now, to see me next week, and to cut down to three drinks a day.

#3. A wonderful lonely elderly woman who simply needs some guidance on how to find and maintain friendships. She is not depressed, so no meds for her, just some brief therapy.

#4. A most difficult couple. Previously in marital therapy with a female colleague for four years, they have a decomposing marriage. She is incredibly cruel to him and he takes it. Like so many men, he settled for outward physical beauty only to be cursed with a narcissistic woman who likes other men and belittles him every step of the way. I don't let on that I see her as the primary fault. The therapy would go nowhere then. But the fact is, though it takes two to tango, *one person can destroy a marriage*.

#5. A new referral from another therapist for a medication evaluation. A young woman, clearly depressed, a victim of incest, and she is unwilling to take any medication; she just wants my opinion. She will go home and talk to her husband first. She says he doesn't believe in therapy, much less medication. He believes there is nothing wrong that they can't straighten out between the two of them. Why tell your problems to strangers? She should just straighten up and stop dwelling on her past. Still dominated by males, she has yet to discover the power within herself. When she does, he will be in for some interesting lessons.

#6. Finally, a repeat visit for a mildly schizophrenic woman who shares my birthday. The voices aren't bothering her at the moment, but she is sure she is condemned for some unknown sin and is going to hell. She can't sleep lately and has shooting pains in her neck. I'm worried. The lack of sleep is an ominous sign; hallucinations will come soon if I don't do something. I adjust her meds and instruct her to call me if anything changes and she agrees to see me in a week.

Then I handle my phone calls, all eight of them. B* is worse. She stopped her lithium a week ago because we thought it might be contributing to a recent catastrophic weight gain (sixteen pounds in the last eight weeks). But now her mind won't turn off. All she can think about is suicide. She promises she won't do anything impulsive and agrees to a medication change.

Therapy day complete, I drop my paperwork so Carol and I can meet Nancy and Fred for oysters and beer. Nancy has a wonderful story about Forrest, her grandson. "Nanna, when I grow up I will have to work very, very hard, because I will be in kindergarten and I'll even have to buy a pencil."

Carol offers the Montessori observation of the day. One of her kindergartners was watching Missou, her uncoordinated iguana. The poor guy (if he is a guy, who knows an iguana's gender for sure) never learned to climb very well. In his new, taller cage he stumbled and fell clumsily on his side. A little boy covered his face with his hands and in a very adult voice exclaimed, "I can't watch, I'm so embarrassed."

What a nice break, listening to stories about children. Simple, happy children. As Carol and I leave, I look for the sun over Horsetooth Rock, but once again, clouds block the view. We have had clouds almost every evening for the past two weeks just as if to thwart my observing the gunsight juxtaposition of the sun atop the rock. Maybe tomorrow I'll see it.

The night is rounded out by my returning to the office and catching up on insurance forms, sorting the mail, and reading my colleague's account of the therapy she is being sued for. I can't see any negligence. Her insurance company may offer a *nuisance settlement*. It will be cheaper for them in the long run. What a mess. Pay people off because it is cheaper than fighting. Now that's what I mean by a too-digital world.

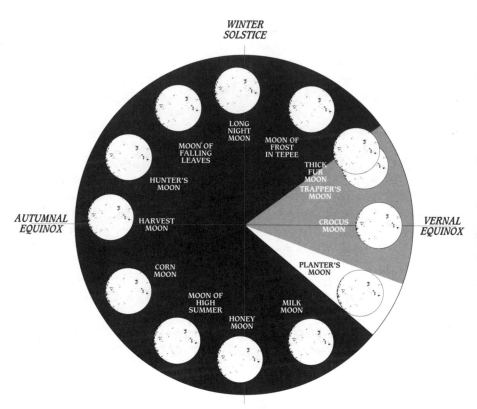

WINTER
SOLSTICE

LONG
NIGHT
MOON

MOON OF
FALLING
LEAVES

MOON OF
FROST
IN TEPEE

THICK
FUR
MOON

HUNTER'S
MOON

TRAPPER'S
MOON

AUTUMNAL
EQUINOX

HARVEST
MOON

CROCUS
MOON

VERNAL
EQUINOX

CORN
MOON

PLANTER'S
MOON

MOON OF
HIGH
SUMMER

MILK
MOON

HONEY
MOON

SUMMER
SOLSTICE

Chapter Three

PLANTER'S MOON

      I GO TO THE encyclopedia this morning hoping to learn about wind. The entry is detailed, scientific and disappointing. I want to learn the mythology of wind, how primitive man related to the wind, the names of winds. But, alas, no such. Why do I want this information? The last weeks' winds have been howling, belligerent, confronting, intruding, unsettling. They have put me on edge, interrupting my sleep, discouraging my running. They have silenced the birds. This morning as I get the paper, I hear no songs. A pair of sea gulls float silently overhead, hanging motionless in the wind. Spring in Colorado isn't sunshine and flower blossoms; it is windy, irritable, and repressive. These winds should have names.

      Carol shows me the most beautiful eggs this morning. A parent at her school has hens which lay different-colored eggs. We have pink, green, blue, brown and white eggs. Since my cholesterol is only 195, I eat bacon and eggs for breakfast.

      Speaking of colors, I am starting to use a variety of different colored pens in my office charts. I select the color of ink depending on my mood or to contrast the previous entry color. One more occasion to play in the midst of my often too-serious consultation hours.

waxing crescent₁

Today is a workday, but I stay home. I'm sick. The weather makes this a good day for being sick: Gray skies, blustery winds, rain and snow. I pushed too hard last week, skipping my exercise and only taking time for silence twice. Not good. Yesterday I was struck by some bug, a cross between Montezuma's revenge and a brain tumor. I dragged home early and settled into my ill health, letting Carol nurture me. It is easy to see why people stay ill; for some it is their only opportunity to receive nurturing.

Why am I sick? One of my patients came to see me two days ago, he had been up all night with a similar illness. We shook hands and I caught the virus from him. Of course.

But, now *really*, why did I get sick? The truth? I need time out. I need to retreat from life for a while. My immune system knows my needs and it knows how I drive myself. It knows my inner restlessness and worry. It welcomed the virus with open arms: Come on in, make yourself at home. Today, I take a two hour nap. The first time in years I have accomplished such a feat. Normally, I can't nap. My body tries to relax, but my mind roars along. But not today. My mind is quiet while my body goes about the chores of restoring health.

I once heard that illness is Western Man's response to needing a retreat, time for meditation. Usually we drive ourselves so hard, even in our leisure time. Today is a good day to be ill. It is so miserable outside that no part of me wants to be there.

The dysentery has stopped, thanks to a miraculous medication named Lomotil. I know it is a product of a very digital world, and for that I am grateful. But in my analog mind, Lomotil is a Mayan god.

76

Snow. Deep, wet, slushy, subduing snow. Par for the course lately. We know better than to expect spring to come in smoothly. The farmers call this kind of spring storm a million-dollar snow. The winter wheat has been parched by the recent drying winds. The fields have yet to achieve the billiard-table green appearance of a healthy young crop. This snow will change that. As it melts, it will soak into the soil and launch the wheat on its way. For us city-folks the snow is an inconvenience, a disappointment. But deep inside, we know we are one community with the farmers. Better to be covered with the white stuff now than see dry, bare, lifeless fields in mid-summer.

As I reflect on my bug and the readiness of my body to embrace the illness, I wonder what I need to do differently. The answer is obvious: *Go back to the basics.* If you are drawn to the life of a contemplative man, don't operate on the schedule of an organization man. My consciousness still busies itself with the more superficial level of day-to-day existence. *My first priority must be my silent time.* My commitment and my primary goal must be to deepening my spiritual life.

Silent time is that very special period of seeking to experience the presence of God. It has elements of biofeedback, meditation, visualization, and prayer. In an unpressured life, I would like to spend an hour or more in silence each day. In fact, I would like two such periods in a day.

I start by centering, using biofeedback techniques to calm my body and thus quiet my mind as well. I deepen the process and open myself to the presence of God like a flower opening to the morning sun. I then begin to experience a special, quiet, comforting presence. I enter a time of mindlessness, feeling like an infant cradled in the arms of a loving parent. The infant gazes into the eyes of the parent, the parent smiles in return. Words have no place. The infant does not understand verbal language. It does understand comfort, security, and loving presence. I am the infant. I don't understand the

77

language of God, but I do experience the comfort, the security, and the loving presence. I linger in that vision as long as possible. Usually, however, my digital mind interrupts with some inane exclamation like, "Hey, it's happening!" So then I move into mental prayer, a time when I use words to talk to God about what seems important. But it is interesting how, after the silence, I find little need to say much. It is as if everything has already been said for me. And I conclude by praying for the peace of the world. Then I read something contemplative, just a few paragraphs at a time, and lapse back into wordless reflection and simply experience the silence, letting the thoughts germinate within me.

Perhaps this period of silence bears some similarity to planting time. Seeds are planted, they germinate out of sight, and later grow a hundredfold. I am responsible for the seeds planted in the soil of my mind. I must keep my mind fertile, well-nourished, well-watered, free of pests. And then I must harvest at the appropriate time. I suspect these metaphors occurred to our forefathers as they planted crops during this, the planter's moon.

I wonder if it is easier for a farmer to be closer to God. In the past, I'm sure it was, but nowadays, with government interference, mechanization, competitive markets, fluctuating interest rates, and fuel shortages, the poor farmer probably has little time to reflect. He is caught in the same digital trap as his urban cousins.

Comment:
This is an example of what writing about the inner life looks like. This is my inner life. Yours will look different. The process of reflection and writing about that reflection is what you need to see here.

_____ *waxing crescent₄* _____

When I embarked on this journal, I did so uncertain where it might lead. Writing can lead to seeing yourself more clearly than you might like. After all, we usually keep our dark side hidden, fearing to look at it, much less make friends with it. I am finding my shadow everywhere now as I see the feebleness of my attempts to change, as I question my career, and as I indulge my fantasies to retreat not only from psychiatry, but from life.

Medicine has been a very special career for me. I loved it wholeheartedly. As a med student, I spent extra time in the emergency room, I assisted on every Code Blue within earshot, I truly wanted to touch the souls of the patients I cared for.

Psychiatry was right for me. I was a clear communicator, spontaneous with my feelings, and sincerely empathic. My own history of psychological pain prepared me to resonate with my patient's lives.

Yet now I find myself feeling as if I have spent my whole life in the company of people struggling with illness. I'm tired of illness, of depression, of suicidal intentions, of lives encumbered with violence and abuse. I want to spend some years with optimistic, altruistic people committed to growth, to the life of the spirit; people who dare to conceive of a world dominated by love. Perhaps, if I were an engineer, I would throw away my computer and bake bread. If I were a soldier, I would bury my medals and grow flowers. Adult life is not supposed to be a stagnant end-point, it should be a creative, developmental process. Few adults seize the opportunity to follow their unique development. Some who do, go off half-cocked and, in the process, pursue a superficial goal at the expense of their loved ones. On the other hand, some never risk a change, feeling corralled by life circumstances and all the demands of security. These next ten moons will reveal whether I take the chance, whether I make a leap. Will the leap mean a change in career, a retreat to a desert island, or a radical change deep within me?

Comment:

As your Portrait Journal takes on a life of its own, don't be surprised if you find yourself questioning some of your deepest assumptions or confronting the very course of your life.

FIRST QUARTER

Our back porch faces west. Tonight is warm, quiet, and clear. Carol and I seize the moment and sit outside. The half moon hovers twelve-o'clock high, bathing the landscape in soft white moonglow. The final traces of snow have evaporated in the afternoon sun. Our Albert Einsteins, the yellow-on-white daffodils, remain cowed by their recent burden of wet snow, bearing witness to their untimely appearance in the midst of our last blizzard.

Earlier this evening, I had a clear, unobstructed view of sunset. It is now nearly a fist's breadth north of Horsetooth Rock. The next chance I will have to see the juxtaposition of the sun atop Horsetooth Rock will be the autumnal equinox. I'm in no hurry.

waxing gibbous₁

Claire calls,needing to speak to me ASAP. I hate those letters, ASAP, an impersonal order barking at me from the telephone note. Then again, she never has used them before. Generally, when another therapist calls with such urgency, someone is about to commit suicide. The morning paper says that suicides have accounted for half of the coroner-investigated deaths in our county this year. And this moon is the leader for suicide in the northern hemisphere. A similar phenomena occurs in the southern hemisphere, highest number of suicides just as they emerge from their winter.

But Claire doesn't have a suicidal person for me to see, she has a woman with a demon. Is she psychotic? Will she need medication? Hospitalization? Can I see her ASAP? Yes, I will be glad to.

I am familiar with demons. My openness to see evil as discrete personalities dates back to the ripe old age of six, when I would (with brazen naivete) ask God to "tune the devil in" and then give him a piece of my mind. I wanted to make him feel bad and let him know

I was his enemy. I don't think I made much of an impact one way or the other, except on myself. My older brother tried to scare me with threats of boogy-men and devils. More often than not, he succeeded. One night I actually hallucinated a fiendish *glowey-man* running in the alley behind our house.

In college I undertook an independent study on the topic of evil. It was just an academic exercise until I had a significant dream experience. As a member of the university's pistol team, I had returned early one spring break for a match and was sleeping alone in the empty dorm where I was a resident counsellor. While asleep, I heard my gun rattling around in the dresser drawer, tumbling over and over, calling me to come and shoot my brains out. I experienced a cold, black, empty and totally evil presence next to my bed. I was utterly alone. In extreme terror, I finally gathered all of my strength into one final protest and spoke "NO!" out loud. I awakened suddenly, standing next to the drawer that contained the gun. Sobbing, I felt I had come within a millimeter of my own suicide. I then locked the gun in another room and put the key in a bathroom two floors away. I was going to assure myself plenty of time if the dream recurred.

I went to a psychologist after that. After several sessions, he told me I wasn't crazy. I was relieved. We acknowledged, however, that suicide was high in my mind since my father always threatened it. Our family had both friends and relatives who had committed suicide.

My next foray into the dark world came in a most unexpected way nine years ago after reading *A Road Less Travelled*. Impressed with its message and wanting to get on with my spiritual development, I visited Scotty Peck. For reasons beyond my comprehension, I spoke to him of my experience in college. He gave me part of his manuscript of *People of the Lie*. Later he solicited my help with patients who felt themselves to be demon possessed. I was suddenly in the demon-busting business. A couple of my patients who had failed with every sort of conventional psychotherapy, drugs and hospitalizations sought out clergy for exorcism. I accompanied them

81

through the process. Then I assessed how they did. At first they did great: New, transformed, delighted. Then almost all of them gradually returned to their previous patterns — some in a few days, others in a year or two.

Then I reviewed cases from all over the country — probably a dozen or so. The information was very revealing: All but one were female. All but three were incest victims. Most came from religious families.

These tortured women were victims of their fathers' sexual appetites and distorted religious fervor. But since "daddy was Jesus's friend," it left the little girl certain she must have been evil. She would go out of her body to escape the abuse and her personality learned to split into different parts in the face of the unspeakable. One part, an evil one, became a demon, often Satan himself. Interestingly, the demons were always male. All this was then stuffed into her unconscious (repressed) before she entered adult life. And the stage was set for her believing she was possessed.

By and large, exorcism doesn't work. In conjunction with competent, experienced, compassionate, and professional therapy, what does work is a supportive system of loving family, steady friends, and then, if the individual is so inclined, a religious community providing prayerful support and nurture. Perhaps, one day, secular minded scientists and unscientific minded religious practitioners will give this difficult area a solid, cooperative, scientific examination.

I believe evil is too slippery to be so easily contained in the human construct, demon. Evil is mystical goo, oozing like Faustian silly putty everywhere the psyche has a crack. Whenever a person thinks he has evil externalized, he better look again . . . inside. I think this is why contemplative spirituality is so important. I think this is why tele-evangelism, with its lack of (and even disdain for) contemplation, scholarship, and psychiatry, manifests evil so flagrantly.

I see Claire's patient. For two years her nearly-sexless marriage has been failing. Feeling dirty and evil, given to unexplained rages, she vented her fury on her husband. Fortunately he is a man who knows how to love and has stayed with her. Especially he didn't push sex or religion. Two months ago, she entered therapy as nightmares began to dominate her few sleeping hours. Claire saw the evidence of incest long before her patient recovered any memories. Then suddenly, the memories, a raging torrent of poisonous recollections engulfed her. Father and brothers raping her. Satanic rituals. Animal sacrifices. The repressive barrier was shattered, and with it, a red pointy-faced devil took up residence in her solar plexus. She could feel it, see it, and even smell it rotting within her.

Her husband, never left her. Gently attempting to understand the grotesque, he comforted her. Knowing of no other way out, she asked him to pray for her. As he did, the demon threatened her life. Terrified, she defied it and after more than an hour of struggle, she vomited it out. She saw it on the floor in front of her; it shrivelled and died. Then she felt inner peace for the first time she could remember. That night, last night, she slept the night through and then came to my office this morning.

In no way does she appear psychotic at this time. Her thought processes and her patterns of associations are normal. She and her husband are open, simple people, sincerely wanting my opinion. I tell them she is not crazy. The evil visited upon her in childhood became so real she hallucinated it as a demon. Love and therapy will free her. I offer no medicines for now, none are indicated. But I will be glad to see them again, any time.

Demons are like PAC-MAN figures. They are representations on the screen of our consciousness. But dealing with them in the midst of psychological combat demands pressing the right buttons at the right time, dealing with them as if they were *real*. Later, when the game is over, we can discuss how the little computer is made and how the images are projected on the screen and how the program was prepared by some distorted computer programmer in the past. They are images from our unconscious mind, constructs we derive, attempting to comprehend the evil besetting us.

The concept of demon is too-analog. The digital approach I made in evaluating contemporary exorcism provided essential insight.

Analog is not inherently good. Like overly-digital approaches, it can be misused. It was misused for centuries. Consider the Inquisition and the Salem Witch Trials as occasions when fine digital information could have prevented wholesale atrocities. The retreat from analog tyranny by the use of honest scientific (digital) inquiry has saved many incest victims from being burned at the stake as witches.

_____ *waxing gibbous₂* _____

The winds have stopped. Warmer and more sunny, the wintry hiatus of the past few weeks appears to be over. Hopefully we can pick up on spring and get going again. I haven't had much time to exercise. And I have taken precious little time for silence. This is not good. If I am not careful, I will have to relearn last week's lesson.

_____ *waxing gibbous₃* _____

Carol and I seize the warm, sunshiny afternoon for a long bike ride along the Spring Creek Trail. The ride is glorious; particularly the birds. Flocks of red-wing blackbirds storm through the barren branches with jolly ferocity. Pied-billed grebes demonstrate their best submarine performances, settling low in the water on our approach and then disappearing in a ring of water, only to pop-up twenty yards away. Meadowlarks, yellow breasted minstrels in black V-necks, get the award for best stereophonic performance. Often they sing on cue, serenading us as we pass.

_____ *waxing gibbous₅* _____

Today, I buy a new watch. The old one just won't do anymore. It is still working well, but it is simply too digital. Watches don't just tell time, they make statements. In my anti-materialistic stance, I have worn a black rubber, digital watch; no fancy Rolex to waste money on in an effort to impress others with my success. I couldn't afford one anyway.

In my pursuit of the analog life, I am now the proud owner of a watch with hands that sweep along. Its only digits are the 12 and the 6, all the other hours are simple small marks on the circular face.

waxing gibbous$_6$

This morning, long before even the faintest glow materialized in the east, a songbird calls to me to awaken. For a while I resist, knowing it is too early to get up. But the bird persists till I go to the window and look out. The moon is breathtaking. Hovering high in the western sky, nearly full, she feels alive as she drenches the landscape in bridal whiteness. The bird, like jolly old St. Francis, is singing a canticle to Sister Moon. I join with him, my heart singing with wordless delight. Brother Bird, Sister Moon, and me . . . . the three of us, created elements of some great plan, pausing to reflect on being.

FULL MOON

Finally. Summer weather. How abrupt. The thermometer says it is eighty-eight. How warm is it? Cardboard screens appear behind car windshields and air conditioners awaken from their winter hibernation. Our down comforter is put away, making way for lightweight cotton blankets. Short sleeve shirts and cotton trousers move into the closet. Sprinkler systems chug-a-chug through the early morning hours.

Carl and Karen join us for dinner; we eat on the back porch. Lingering till midnight, we remain warm and mosquito free. Our friends have just returned from Honduras where they scuba dived off the Caribbean coast. But what most excited them was not the diving, it was the unspoiled tranquility, the slow pace of life, and the simple, friendly people. Carl muses about quitting the therapy business and going down there to make a living while helping a people emerge from poverty. Tempting idea. Anything but the same old routine is tempting.

waning gibbous₁

She called him Mishu, a name that was a play on words. Carol's Montessori iguana: Iguana Mishu. Sounds like "I'm gonna miss you." Carol has known Mishu for six years. This reptile grew to the size of a small Komodo Dragon. I would quip, "Eat any children today?" Carol was very attached to him and tolerated my jibes gracefully. I never have been able to muster up much feeling for reptiles. Mammals? Yes. Birds? Yes. Reptiles or amphibians? No. Must be something about the inferiority of their central nervous systems.

Mishu died today. Our only warning was a dream I had a week ago with the simple statement: Mishu died. Carol is sad. I comfort her tears, feeling compassion for her sadness, but it is hard to feel any loss myself.

Then I ruefully reflect that my absence of feeling is just the excuse that provides for racial prejudice, justifies genocide, and extinguishes whole species from the face of the earth. When humans have no feelings for other creatures because of their differences, their death is of no consequence. For example, war is more efficient when the combatants are of different races, it makes it simpler to _off_ them. In Viet Nam, we didn't kill _people_, we killed _gooks_. We extinguish species from the earth by treating them as mere objects; so much clutter to be cleared away or exploited until they are no longer needed. Passenger pigeons, buffalo, whales: Use them and then discard them. Rather than saving the earth, our superior brain may prove to be its executioner.

Carol's feelings form the fabric which the survival of the planet depends on: Compassion for the loss of any creature regardless of the make-up of its central nervous system, its softness to touch, or how it responds to humankind. Unconditional compassion is the key. Practiced globally we would achieve peace among all people and plot a course for saving our mother earth. Carol chose a most correct name for her coarse, dry-skinned reptile. Yes, Iguana Mishu.

waning gibbous₂

A hot, dry steady wind blows out of the southeast. Not the punishing winds of the new moon, this wind coaxes flags to stand partially unfurled. It bounces small tumbleweeds across the road. I take a bike ride out to Severance.

First passing the partially-completed psychiatric hospital, then Hewlett Packard with its new construction, I cross I-25 and come to Swet's place where a welder with a keen eye and a sense of humor has fashioned all sorts of prehistoric beasts from old farm machinery. I continue due east into the quartering wind. I pass the trap-shooting club. The parking lot is filled with pick-ups, mostly Fords and Chevys. Bumper stickers proclaim the need to ask before hunting or fishing on private land and a few say negative things about Jane Fonda's mother.

Once in Severance, I stop outside of Bruce's Bar, a local color spot that specializes in Rocky Mountain Oysters. Not seafood, these delicacies are deep fried beef testicles removed from calves in the process of making them into steers, gentler animals who gain weight more efficiently. Thirsty, I drain my water bottle in one long gulp. It was ice cold with six ice cubes when I left home, now it is warm, nearly body temperature. That is how hot it is. Hot enough to warm a liter of ice water during a thirteen mile bike ride.

Returning to town with the wind at my back, I get a boost. I hear the hum of the tires as if I were riding in still air. Along the way I come upon a prairie fire. Ignoring the wind, some fool decided

87

to burn his trash and succeeded in setting fire to a quarter section of wheat stubble. The fire engulfed a few wooden out-buildings and then made short work of a wind-break. Eighty years ago a home-steading family hauled water by hand to start those trees. Trees don't grow on these arid plains unless helped along. And nowadays digital farming techniques are slaughtering the trees to squeeze out a little more arable acreage. Not good. Trees are analog. Planting trees may be one human activity that has nothing bad to say for it. If our planet isn't going to turn into one hot greenhouse, we must plant more trees and burn fewer of them.

Finally home, I drink three mugs of water. Then I replace the batteries in my bike computer. I guess I'll give in on this digital point. I do enjoy knowing how far I have ridden. But if I start torturing myself over my average or maximum speed, I will disconnect it.

waning gibbous$_2$

We were across town last night when the lightning started. At first, so far away it was just flashes of light, no sound. Then gradually, it rumbled upon us. We went out to smell the air; that special fresh rain smell, absent here for many moons. Delightful. We listened and admired as the rain came, the thunder crashed, and the lightening shimmered. Then we heard a harsh, unmistakable sound . . . hail. At first scattered, then dense; pea-sized and a little larger, it beat down the tulips who were just beginning to strut their colors. About fifteen minutes and it was all over.

On the way home, we passed cars covered with more than an inch of hail. Approaching our neighborhood, the streets were drier and, at home, our tulips stood tall and bright, not knowing that their cousins across town had just succumbed to the first summer storm. Humans are like tulips. Even with the advantage of TV news, we usually go our way despite adversity striking elsewhere in the world.

I just read about AIDS in Uganda. Perhaps a third, or more, of that East African country has AIDS, more getting it all the time.

_____ _waning gibbous_6_

36,000 feet above Tennessee

If I talk to St. Peter when I die, I expect to be asked one important question: Did you *make a difference*, a real significant difference? I doubt I will be asked to recount my sins. Though they are numerous, I have it on good report they have been forgotten. No, the test of the value of my life will be whether my life moved in the direction of peace, love, beauty.

Last night I listened as a compact Honduran woman belted out her message in well-articulated Spanish. Fortunately, she had an impeccable translator. My Spanish is just so-so. She spoke of atrocities against the peasants, against women, against anyone who resists the militarizing of her country. She spoke of how poor children lack food and basic medical care while the dogs of rich families eat beef and have the finest veterinary care. In the end she decried even the Peace Corps and the Mennonites. Well-meaning though these volunteers are, they form part of the whole fabric that is stifling her poor country. Couldn't we just leave them alone and let them work out their own life and their own peace.

As a youth, my patron saint was Tom Dooley, the young navy doctor who returned to Laos in the late fifties to serve the poor and the suffering. His life and his writings encouraged me to follow and bring modern medicine to the third world. Tom also saw communist atrocities and prophesied the holocaust. Perhaps that vision triggered his terminal cancer at too-young an age. Tom Dooley made a difference. But his work and his writing also served militant anti-communist sentiment and in some twisted way may have paved the way for our armed intervention in Viet Nam. Rather than pursuing a peace-waging campaign on a scale the world has never witnessed before, we tried to bomb Viet Nam into the stone age. We nearly succeeded. It is clear that war just doesn't work. But who wages peace with equal resolve and adequate economic backing?

I wanted to be like Tom Dooley, but I started a family before I completed medical school and so gave up that dream. Lately with my family nearly grown, I have wondered about going to Central America . . . to make a difference. But she said, "Don't come. Leave us alone. Create peace in your own country." How often are good intentions subverted by some mysterious evil?

LAST QUARTER

Orlando, Florida

Gardenias, jasmine, eucalyptus, orange blossoms, magnolias, hanging moss. My parched sinuses delight in the humidity. I am here in the sub-tropics to teach positive humor to a group of interested psychotherapists. But while I am here, I am going to enjoy what this place has to offer. Here in Florida, there is much to savor, especially the gardenias.

I think the average length of time people linger over a flower's bouquet is three seconds. The digital mind snaps in with "That's a gardenia all right" or "Yep, that's a rose." And having attached a word to the experience, our left brain hurries us along to some *important* endeavor, such as worrying about how to call the whole trip a business expense and get the tax deduction.

Our hosts have a splendid gardenia bush. Shoulder height, with a positively wasteful surplus of gardenia blossoms. It beckons every minute to come, smell, delight, intoxicate, but *never name and then walk away*. We spend our evening hours sitting in the screened-in back patio, experiencing what moist air feels like and appreciating gardenias.

My best friend and I spend the whole day with Walt Disney. We take every ride, eat all the wrong foods, wait in footsore lines, and buy small souvenirs that will one day find their way to the bottom of a drawer or sell for ten cents at a garage sale. I buy a little Brer Rabbit to ride atop my computer monitor, the better to remind me of my laughing place.

We both bring our inner children along. And do they play! We close the park down, staying through till closing despite a tropical cloudburst. What a treat! This is a very digital place, serving a very analog purpose. People of all sizes, ages, languages and colors hurry about laughing and succeeding in being delighted. I nominate Mickey Mouse for analog man of the century.

As I think about my work, encountering broken lives, confronting addictions, and aborting suicides, I sometimes feel like a Disney character in a Franz Kafka play. The painful and often meaningless tragedy that confronts me daily tries to make me relinquish dreams of love and play as though they are mere fanciful whims in the *real world* of sexual abuse, suicide and depression. Perhaps my challenge is to legitimize our Disney-ness. We don't seek play to deny the adversity of the world, we seek play to cope, to grow through, and to overcome the pain and adversity. And we seek play, *simply because it is fun.*

Drying your body after a shower in Florida is a relative sort of process. In Colorado, drying is prompt, complete, and excessive, so much so that my skin itches and my hair is like straw. But not here. I run long and slow, enjoying the moist air, intoxicatingly rich with oxygen. On my return I cool down, exhausting myself on the gardenia bush before my shower.

While I was out running, Carol received a phone call from Allison. An acquaintance of hers committed suicide last night; a surprise to all who knew him. We talk long, listen well, help her come to grips with the tragedy and promise we will talk more when we get home.

Undeterred by Allison's tragedy, we go air-boating in a swamp; they say gators live there. Our guide is no stranger to beer, his opulent girth and red face bear witness to his passion for the malted beverage. The lettering on his olive drab tee-shirt sums up the flavor of this place, *If you're dumb, you gotta be tough.* Despite intermittent rain from heavy multi-layered clouds, we skim out over the swamp. Our guide says we are going over forty miles an hour. In analog terms, we are going so fast that a surprised gallinule fails to get out of our way. Unlike a Roadrunner cartoon, the gallinule will not get up for another adventure.

We see egrets, herons, coots, gallinules, sora rails, frogs, fishermen and gators. The little ones measure a foot long, "But he can bite your finger off." We admire the big ones (about four feet long) from a comfortable distance.

waning crescent₃

Home

The flight home is flawless. In fact, the day is about as smooth as any in recent memory. I get in a splendid morning run, beautiful silent time, wonderful conversation, and have adequate time to read.

As we unpack and look over the half bushel of mail, Allison calls with more disturbing news: Her acquaintance's death may have been a homicide rather than a suicide. The police are investigating.

And then, even more disturbing news: Looking through the newspapers, I check the obituaries. Something I reluctantly, but routinely do. I discover my alcoholic stockbroker patient has died in a motor vehicle accident. Authorities believe he fell asleep at the wheel and his car collided with a bridge abutment.

A sour lump extends from the pit of my stomach to the base of my tongue. They say things come in threes. Hopefully this will end it. If the digital world doesn't subdue my spirit, the evil in the world will.

Kafka   3

Disney   1

---

waning crescent₄

I have this dream, actually more of a memory fragment, almost every time suicide visits me:

"Dad, Mom says for you to come in for supper."

He doesn't answer me. He just sits silently in the front seat of his '46 Ford, staring into the distance. As I approach the car window, I swallow my message in mid-sentence when I see his .32 caliber automatic in his lap.

"Dad, don't do that. Please. Come in to eat."

Looking at me, he sighs. "You go back into the house. I'm going to get it over with."

"No you won't. Come in . . . . come in now . . . .please."

He seems to ignore me. I turn and walk slowly back to the house. Wincing. Waiting for the sound of the pistol. No sound. No gunshot . . . ever. Dad threatened suicide all the time, but finally died of cancer in his seventies. I think he did hear me. I'm convinced he did love me; that's why he stopped and came in to eat. Thank you, Dad. I know it wasn't easy. Thank you very much.

Suicide has haunted me all of my life, sort of my special adversary. During the first few years I practiced psychiatry, I had no suicides. Lately, that has changed. I haven't changed what I do, but more people I see are committing suicide.

Cancer can be cut out, TB can be chemically sterilized, a clogged artery can be reamed out. But the mysterious evil of suicide is not so easily dealt with. The leading cause of death in psychiatric patients is a spirit as destructive as any cancer, but it cannot be

93

located and simply removed. In many cases, it is a biological depression. Too often, it is associated with alcohol. Regardless, each suicide involving people I have cared for drives me one step closer to quitting. If I didn't care about them as individual human beings, as real people, perhaps it wouldn't bother me as much. Teaching love and compassion and positive humor is my heart's desire. Fighting in the psychiatric trenches is simply becoming too painful.

waning crescent

At the office I catch up on five days of accumulated calls and mail. A hectic and intense time. The high point of my day is news of Bunny. I have been reluctant to admit the obvious. Bunny has been notably absent again. Cottontails are scattered about, but no big fat satin rabbits.

Most unexpectedly, while presenting a workshop this afternoon, a participant introduces himself as a neighbor, the one with all the bushes around his back deck. Had he seen Bunny? Seen him! Bunny has been living at his house. His daughter named him Cinnamon. They rescued him from another neighbor who had seen her crocuses disappear in a single evening banquet for the big guy. She was about to call the humane society and have Bunny locked away in the pound. Another neighbor, a rabbit person, brought a black and white, lop-eared male rabbit over to mate with Bunny. She had checked Bunny out and assured his new family that he was a she. No testicles, right? (Things aren't always what they appear to be.) Imagine the indignity of it all.

So it looks like we will get Bunny back. His new family wants a litter of young rabbits. Unfortunately, Carol has given away the hutch and we cannot let him out to experience his bunny-ness in our neighborhood anymore unless we are prepared to bail him out of the humane society, a mere twenty-five bucks for the first offense. I'll be out of town. Bunny's domicile will be Carol's problem.

waning crescent[6]

Kansas City, Missouri

The trees in Kansas City are full and green while back in Eastern Colorado the fields are a drab winter brown and the trees bare and gray. Spring is a very uneven affair.

As I was leaving this morning we learn that Allison's acquaintance's death was ruled a suicide. With that information she can start to put it behind her. Suicide is tragic, but it is a bit easier to swallow than homicide where your anger boils over and you want revenge. There is no revenge to be sought when the dead person is his own executioner.

I am in Kansas City to teach more positive humor to a group of businessmen and their wives. I shift gears and prepare for the show.

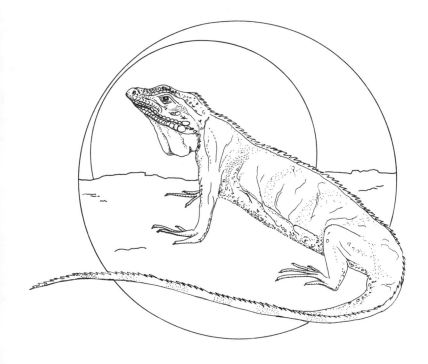

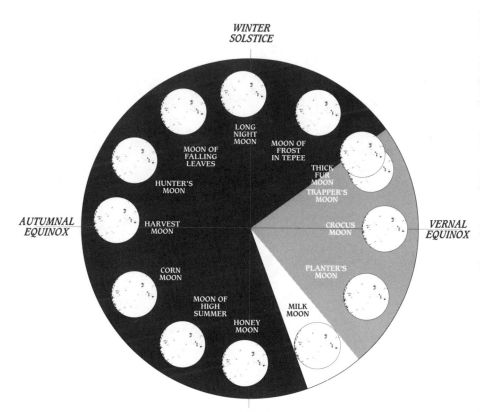

WINTER
SOLSTICE

LONG
NIGHT
MOON

MOON OF
FALLING
LEAVES

MOON OF
FROST
IN TEPEE

HUNTER'S
MOON

THICK
FUR
MOON

TRAPPER'S
MOON

AUTUMNAL
EQUINOX

HARVEST
MOON

CROCUS
MOON

VERNAL
EQUINOX

CORN
MOON

PLANTER'S
MOON

MOON OF
HIGH
SUMMER

MILK
MOON

HONEY
MOON

SUMMER
SOLSTICE

Chapter Four

MILK MOON

Home

A DAY OF CONTRASTS weaves a bewildering web around me. During my morning run I encounter two fresh mallard hatches. The first, a mated pair, has ten ducklings and the second, a single-parent hen, has eleven. My dark side reflects how nature provides abundant young in those species which serve as prey to their carnivorous neighbors. Of course, that doesn't exactly apply to human beings, we are prey to no species but ourselves and presently are breeding ourselves out of room on this precious planet.

During work, another grotesque narrative bludgeons my neutral psychiatric ear. A bald, black-bearded Viet Nam vet recounts his special training in survival. If he allows himself to really *feel*, it would draw from his heart a wail so deep the echo would penetrate the core of hell itself.

"They said we had to live off the land. Our sergeant made his point so we wouldn't forget it. While telling us about different plants

97

and such, he held a small rabbit and petted it. Then, to make his point, he bashed the rabbit's head and with his own mouth tore its throat out with one bite. In the next instant his other hand disemboweled the rabbit and he threw the guts at us. With blood running down his chin he hollered that *this is how you survive. You eat what's at hand.* The rabbit's body was still moving."

How do I de-program something imbedded so graphically? I listen, reflect, re-frame his experience. I let him curse, wish he would cry, and then allow him to change the subject. All the while I don't let myself feel.

waxing crescent₃

San Francisco, California

It's a long way from Colorado to San Francisco. I jog this morning over a series of hills that only go up. Glimpses of the Bay Bridge greet me as I amble past streets leading down to the water. In a small park, old Chinese men share in Tai Chi, while on a nearby bench a bum, his brown bagged wine bottle lying empty by his side, sleeps a dazed alcoholic slumber. The moist air blesses my troubled sinuses.

I am here for the latest scientific information in psychiatry. There is little art taught here, but there is a whole lot of science. Analog vagaries are so prone to being personalized and distorted. In the past (e.g. Freud and his disciples) ideas, mere theories, were canonized as *truth.* I have no quarrel with the straight science of psychiatry. But how are we ever to develop our spirits and those of our patients? Or do we just ignore the whole concept? Perhaps life of the spirit depends largely on time spent in solitude and contemplation.

My recent reading reminds me the issue of life is not what happens to us . . . . rather it is *how we adapt to what happens to us.* Recently I have been grumpy, almost on the edge of depression. Carol has been able to tell; I have seemed more distant. In my mind,

98

I feel my mood is an inevitable response to the recent stresses of my life. While it is true that I have had my share of adversity, my task is not to justify my grumpiness. My task, like the alchemist of old, is to create gold from the base elements of my existence. No matter what, I commit myself to finding positive paths out of whatever adversity I encounter. I don't descend into the inferno with the intent of staying there. I will not resign myself to being a grump.

Tonight, after the meetings, we go to a cabaret. It is bawdy, to say the least; not the kind of thing we get in Fort Collins. After all, Colorado is very far away from here.

First Quarter

Positron emission tomography. Quantitative encephalography. Serotonin depletion. Trichotillomania. AIDS-related dementia. And the list could go on and on. For these several days I have been immersed in the science of the human mind and its pathology. I can scarcely hold any more information. The drug companies and hospital corporations are generous with lavish buffets and fine California wine. I doubt I can hold any more rich food.

But other images whirl about, taunting my comfort, crying out for attention, crowding into my consciousness, demanding reflection.

Civilization? Tumult! Too much stimulation. Too much noise. Too many cars, buses, and sirens. Too many street people. Dirty and foul smelling, they talk to themselves and beg for money. All genders, races and ages. Mothers with children — even with new-born babies — sit outside our fancy hotel holding cardboard signs asking for money for food, while we, on the inside, pay twelve dollars for a continental breakfast. A woman with a harmonica cradled to her lips mournfully plays her private requiem in Union Square, while at her feet huddles a large german shepherd dog and too many puppies all wrapped in a filthy wool blanket.

Homelessness is complex. As a psychiatrist, I know one particular facet of this complex social plague. I know that many street people are schizophrenic or alcoholic; others victims of abusive childhoods. Many have had their poverty passed on to them by their parents.

Jesus said we would always have the poor with us. Does that mean we must accept the present state of affairs and let capitalism go its way? If they won't work, won't pull their share of the load, do we just leave them to their sorry state of life? No! That is not right! Jesus didn't have the word, schizophrenia, at his disposal. The street people during his days in Galilee must have included a large share of schizophrenics and alcoholics too. Schizophrenics have always made up a significant portion of the poor, the homeless. Though they have always been with us, we must find better ways to care for them.

But I don't give capitalism the whole rap. Many homeless are on the street because the ACLU and a host of other ill-informed, though well-meaning liberals, have succeeded in preventing them from taking the very medication which would make their brains more chemically normal. Back in the fifties, some mental patients worked at a state hospital's dairy or vegetable farm. It was simple work, slow-paced, and free of time demands and other employment pressures. But the ACLU came in, demanding they be paid minimum wage or not be forced to work. Since schizophrenics were of such low productivity, migrant laborers were hired instead (at minimum wage, or less) while the patients were then locked into their hospital units with single television sets for company or were released to fend for themselves on the streets.

Outside our hotel, demonstrators carry signs claiming *Psychs Kill*. They decry every tool of our trade and imply we are an inhumane, unsympathetic collection of cruel demagogues; first cousins of Nazi physician conspirators. All the while, across the street a filthy, emaciated schizophrenic man passes the entire afternoon in his autistic world, examining the configuration of his knotted shoelaces.

If we took the money from the B-2 bomber project and put it into caring for the chronically mentally ill, the problem would be solved. Of course we would have to muzzle the ACLU and other ill-informed liberals who seek to protect those with dysfunctional brain chemistry from us *psychs* and our science. As I think of the insensitive, paranoid, militaristic conservatives on one hand and the naive, paranoid, fault-finding liberals on the other, I respond: A curse on both your houses.

waxing gibbous₁

Home

It's a sensitive gray day; one with low, sober clouds, laden with misting, soft, female rain. One that nurtures the earth and greens the land. Even the linden trees are beginning to show signs of life. No leaves yet, but their buds are pregnant, swelling and promising shade by the solstice. This is a good day for sleeping, reading, and catching up on the jobs I put off while in California. And it's a good day for robins too; the moist earth extrudes its earthworms, feeding another mother with life growing within her.

I love to travel, but there is a cost. I don't mind airports, delays, different beds, and variable schedules. What I find difficult is falling behind in my reading, eating too much rich food, exercising too little, gaining weight, not spending enough time with nature, and (most importantly) failing to achieve sufficient quality time in silence.

Today I catch up on my writing. I run long and easy in the cool rain and I luxuriate in two long periods of silence. The more I experience the timeless peace of it, the more taking time for silence is like drinking from a deep, cool mountain stream when you are very, very thirsty.

waxing gibbous₂

Hamlet was troubled by it. King Saul, Abraham Lincoln and Winston Churchill too. (Unfortunately, Ronald Reagan wasn't.) Insomnia comes in many shapes and colors: Difficulty falling asleep, middle of the night awakenings, early morning arousals, shallow-fitful

101

sleep. These symptoms are daily subjects of my inquiries with patients. Depression, anxiety, stress, age and physical illness all disturb sleep. Facing a day unrefreshed by sleep burns the eyes, squeezes the chest, and makes every nerve tingle. But it seems the human mind just doesn't want to turn off at times. The little squirrel just keeps running, running, running. The treadmill spins, creaking and going nowhere. The vast majority of the time I succeed in helping my sleep-impaired patients. I feel a genuine empathy for them. Insomnia is my problem too.

Off and on for years my sleep has come and gone. Clearly it is a psychological issue. When I am away from all my cares, I can sleep like a baby. I have tried to help myself, sought help from other professionals, practiced biofeedback, prayed, taken a variety of pills from time to time. All to no avail. My poor sleep is a red alarm light on my brain's console.

The past months have been touch-and-go as far as my sleep is concerned. The last few nights my sleep has been filled with long, boring, tedious dreams. They stretch out like a fool telling endless tales of no consequence. I awaken with a tight neck and a sense that I still need a good night's sleep. I value informative dreams, they are guides even though at times they are troubled with frightening images. But these last few nights have been B movies portrayed on black and white TV, only I can't seem to turn the TV off. I know something must change, but what? Or how? I won't simply drop out, run away, leave my kids high and dry in the middle of college. I can't become financially irresponsible letting my house and plans for retirement go. I am deepening my life, but my insomnia tells me what I am doing is not enough.

waxing gibbous₁

The Ditch Company is filling Warren Lake. As I jog this morning, I see the water flowing beneath the bridge for the first time this year. Lakes in Colorado are digital affairs. Man-made, they are actually reservoirs for The Ditch Company, the outfit that created the whole system of irrigation in the first place and now oversees its distribution. The eastern, flat half of Colorado is nearly a desert; only by harnessing the spring runoff have we ever managed to farm this land. A good use for the digital mind.

I notice that the winter toll of dead trees can now be counted. Our intense, dry cold kills many of those trees which are better suited to Ohio than Colorado. Those that succumb are usually the very young or the very old. I count seven wooden corpses on my run.

I check on the ducklings I discovered a quarter moon ago. I see the hatch of eleven is intact with both parents looking on. Unfortunately, the other hatch has only the solo hen and three of her ten ducklings left. As I watch, I become aware of icy-blue hunter's eyes near the water's edge surveying the same hatch. A siamese cat studies the scene but then, disturbed by my intrusion, silently vanishes in the tall grass.

All around the lake, the geese are keeping a low profile. No flying, honking or displaying. Couples lower their heads and quietly go about the job of incubating their families. We should be seeing their young ones pretty soon.

Closer to home, a pair of red-wing blackbirds make life miserable for a magpie. Chasing him, driven by some deep primal courage, they dive-bomb, even snatching a feather from the bigger bird's behind. The magpie is a nest robber. Parents must protect their eggs. Smaller and more vulnerable, the redwings can't sit in stately, dignified quiet like the geese.

There is life and there is death to be seen on a simple morning jog in my very ordinary neighborhood. And, I am not deceived, I am as mortal as any of these.

Comment:

Your Portrait Journal will demonstrate that in the most common and everyday experiences, the profound exists. No life is without constant access to the very depths of life. Your Portrait Journal will force you to look and to see.

103

---
waxing gibbous₅

What a perfect day: Buoyant blue sky, trees and grass that shout green out loud, a light caressing breeze, and warmth as soothing as a lover's lingering kiss. Through my morning silence I sit on the back porch in the company of the neighborhood birds. They seem to feel the same as I; some out enjoying the day, flying about, singing, while others meditatively preen their feathers.

I visit Mary Luke today. Between the two of us, we have much to say. She has been at a Buddhist peace retreat. She brings me two pearls of great price. First, a simple meditation exercise to accompany breathing:

In....................Out
Deep.................Slow
Calm.................Ease
Smile................Release
Present Moment........Wonderful Moment

I especially like the part about smiling and releasing.

Her second pearl is a rebuttal to the old gestalt self-centered number: "I'm not in this world to meet your needs and you are not here to meet mine. If we meet and it works out, fine. Otherwise it cannot be helped." (I paraphrased.) Rather she offers: "I am here to alleviate your suffering; you are here to give me joy." How rich we would be if we all lived these every day. More food for silence.

---
waxing gibbous₆

How do you make a grown lawyer cringe? You throw your head back and laugh at him when he is trying to be deadly serious and hoping to clinch his argument. You don't really laugh *at* him, you laugh at his attempt to be intimidating. Easy to do when you are merely an expert witness. Harder to do if you are the defendant. I spend my morning enduring a corruption of our society; I am deposed for too long about a case which everybody knows will settle out of court the day before the trial. But we go through the expensive process, maximizing the expenditure of money.

I don't criticize lawyers alone, since experts (including physicians) often extort abusive fees for their testimony while insurance companies play the numbers game as shrewdly as any Las Vegas gambler. The pity of the whole process is it doesn't contribute to any psychological or spiritual growth. Quite the contrary. Those who lose, pay out their money, feeling defiant and betrayed. Those who collect feel smug and self-righteous. Neither state of mind is particularly helpful for spiritual development. It is a self-absorbed, self-perpetuating, deceitful system.

Perhaps, though, it is like politics. Perhaps I am the fool; I don't see the complex correctness of it all. To be sure, suing someone is better than shooting him over a disagreement. But the psychological violence of this ponderous, snail-paced process is plenty damaging in itself. It is too digital. It has no sense of humor. It expresses no love. Feigned altruism deceives even the chief deceivers.

My laughter feels good this morning. I don't think I offend him, I merely surprise him. Whether or not he thinks I am particularly professional is his problem. I have a full moon to talk with tonight and my son has just come home.

FULL MOON

This vision has lingered on the periphery of my mind, sort of a quixotic notion. Drive to a Minuteman missile silo, get there in time for the rise of the full moon. Meditate on peace for the world. Pray that wisdom will be reborn in the hearts of earth's children. Contemplate the incredible destructive power lurking nearby. No greater dragon ever slept in all the myths of humankind, and no dragon was ever imagined that could awaken so quickly. Already targeted on some distant Soviet city, a single missile holds hostage a million Russian souls. There is a Russian counterpart targeted right here, this spot, one more Ground Zero.

Then when the contemplative period is finished, open a bottle of wine, offer some to our Mother Earth, and toast the dream of a future free of war. After that, return home feeling warm and complete. A nice fantasy for this warm weather full moon. But it is uncommon for our expectations to turn out the way we plan; there are simply too many variables.

Comment:
In every life there are things dreamed of but never done. As your Portrait Journal becomes more alive, you may find yourself acting upon what you only dreamed of. When you act upon your dreams, your life enriches and you come to realize yourself more deeply. Count on being surprised in the process.

The day is once again sensational, warm with a light breeze and blue crystal skies. We finish more jobs around the house than we planned. Chris and I refinish the picnic table. For dinner, Carol and I take Chris and Allison out for Mexican food. Afterwards it is nearing sunset and I ask Carol if she wants to join me for the-full-moon-by-a-Minuteman-missile-silo project. Always agreeable, she says sure. We gather a couple of lawn chairs, a blanket, but pass on the wine. I look at my map marking all the missile silos in Colorado, Nebraska, and Wyoming. The nearest appears to be about fifty miles east, out Highway 14.

As we leave town, I am surprised how far to the south the full moon is rising, almost due southeast. Most people think the moon simply rises in the east, not so. It rises and sets all over the horizon.

Heading due east Highway 14 is a straight asphalt line stretching into eastern darkness. It demarcates a remarkable scene. To the north of the line is a massive thunderhead with its lightning shimmering, dancing and galloping from east to west. To the south,

106

the serene flat prairie lies quiet as if a sleeping virgin, simply illumined by a soft ice cream moon. Our map is small and not too descriptive, so we miss a couple of turns ending up in a small village named New Raymer. The map marks a missile site one mile due north of town. By now the wind is blowing hard out of the southeast, threatening us to go no further. Unnamed gods are displeased with our boldness. Overhead, the thunderhead spreads its gigantic black silhouette, towering to the apogee of the sky. Tchaikovsky's Fifth Symphony adds drama to the scene as we follow the gravel road north to the missile silo. North, away from the quiet, virginal prairie.

What we find is not just a simple missile silo, but a command post for several missile silos. A large compound, it proclaims its presence with gigantic mercury vapor lamps, dominating squatty, low frame buildings. And everything is secured by a tall chain link fence. We park on the approach a couple of hundred yards from the gate. As we get out of the car, the driving south wind hums loudly through the power lines and rattles the rope on the compound's flagpole causing a loud, irregular metallic clanging sound. Positioning our lawn chairs on the leeward side of the car, we settle down and observe the dazzling lightning display. The thunder is muted by the wind; the only sounds we hear are the humming power lines and the clanging flagpole.

Meditation is impossible. So at first, I study the enclosure. There, in the surreal yellow brightness, some men come out of a building speak loudly, mill around briefly, and then vanish. Do they know we are here? Do they wonder what we are doing? Will they come out to investigate? Will I tell them I am a Quaker or will I tell them I used to be a Lieutenant Commander in the Navy? Are any of them too young to be trusted, inexperienced, or even trigger happy?

Then we continue watching the lightning show. I comment on how awesome this must have for the Arapaho, the Pawnee, and the Cheyenne; Native Americans who, living upon this very land, once saw the divine in every blade of grass, every turn of the weather. The word, *awesome*, does scant justice to the feeling surging within me as I witness this spectacle. And to think the nearby warheads would pale the power and the damage inflicted by this giant storm as if it were a child merely blowing the fuzz from dandelions. I feel the spirits of war all about. I feel small and puny and scared.

After several minutes of watching the evolving thunderhead, I suddenly discover figures moving in the field. Men, two of them, running and crouching down, about a hundred yards out to our left. Guards. Why didn't they just drive out in a pick-up to check us out? Mouth dry, heart beating more loudly, I experience the fear of one about to be preyed upon by the workers of war. I look back to the compound but see no activity. I look back at the crouched figures. Carol breaks the silence, "Tumbleweeds."

Feeling an odd mixture of fear and relief, we continue sitting a little longer and finally agree meditation is out of the question. Sensing our mission complete, we gather our chairs and blankets and drive back to Fort Collins. Mark's *Paths of Heart* is playing on the radio station. What a nice contrast to the angst of Tchaikovsky.

I don't sleep well this night. I awaken with Mexican heartburn. . . . And dreams. . . . Fearful, Kafka-like dreams with bloodied creatures, devoid of all hope . . . only some sort of empty, meaningless survival. I had visited a nuclear dragon's lair and encountered the spirits of war. Now they mock me, spinning about in my unconscious. I am very small; no match for them, no match at all.

waning gibbous₁

I spent yesterday recovering from my missile silo encounter. A passionate imagination may be a blessing for creativity, but it can be a curse too. It is easy to see how writers are often victims of depression. Their mood disorder inflames their creative passions; driving them to write, to paint, to sculpt, to create, to express some oceanic depth of human experience. And the shadow side: More than one has succumbed to suicide when the passions grew larger than life and turned on them like Frankenstein's monster.

This morning is gorgeous once again. My bare-chested run around Warren Lake is rewarded by all sorts of discoveries. The carp are spawning. Twisting and turning over one another beneath the flotsam along the bank, they nearly beach themselves in their passionate ritual of propagation. Further along, I come across the first goslings of the year; four of them out with their parents grazing along the greenbelt. As I pause to admire them, the parents (with their long necks stretching full length) scrutinize me carefully before returning to graze. Nearer home, I am nearly knocked down by the positively wasteful aroma of some newly blooming lilacs. Their humble servant, I caress them, savor their aroma and never once name the experience.

Comment:
Your Portrait Journal will provide another storage place for the details of your life so you won't have to depend on simple recall. Memories fade and change through time. Your journal might fade slightly but the recorded events will not change at all. The details will be there for you forever.

---

waning gibbous₂

Bicycle riding in a breeze is . . . well . . . a breeze. Bicycle riding in a wind is work. My morning ride starts out pleasantly and then becomes work. Not that I mind really, I need the workout. I indulge a variety of aromas on the ride: Silage, a faint touch of skunk (not unpleasant in small doses), lilacs, and the most wonderful first sweet clover of the spring. All sorts of common birds are out. A crow gracefully suspends himself in the wind while I, in my playfulness picture him to be a sea gull in black-face on his way to a minstrel show. All in all it is a beautiful ride and a thoroughly delectable morning . . . a good morning to sum up my recent thinking about death. Better to consider this most existential of all subjects when well rested, happy, and clear-thinking.

Several years ago, I was so down that I welcomed the idea of a permanent break with life. Through many sleepless nights my heart sputtered and coughed its way from dream to fitful dream. I had PVC's, irregular contractions of the heart related to anxiety. Probably not serious, but then again PVC's have been known (rarely) to lead to an instant fibrillation. The thought of "passing away" was welcome. Probably that is what is in the mind of most suicidal people. Life isn't that great and passing away would be welcome. Probably such a feeling explains the cheapness of life in inner city ghettos as well. Then after marrying Carol and tasting the sweetness of love once again, death loomed as an icy cold emptiness threatening to rob me of not only joy, but my very existence. I then began to fear death so much I shuddered when thinking of it.

Lately I have been coming to terms with it. By coming to terms I mean I am coming to *accept* death with all its uncertainty and utter finality, knowing that it is part of a master plan which I have no ability to influence or revise. Whatever existence there is, if any, beyond death will greet me when the time comes. By living a moral or godly life, I am not so sure I will tilt the tables of the next existence in my favor. I live a moral life because it is the right thing to do; something I feel intuitively; something I do whether there is another life or not. I seek a godly life because something within me yearns deeply for unity with the Source of all life. That yearning is a gift to me, not something I have achieved by some sort of spiritual scholarship or talent.

Thus it is now that I think about death every day. I am glad it is far off. (I hope it is far off.) Thinking of death causes me to savor all aspects of living — most especially love, contemplation, and the marvels of our Mother Earth. I accept I will die and that may be all there is to it. Whatever lies beyond death is beyond my comprehension. All ideas of the afterlife are approximations — projections of the human mind and all must fall woefully short of what that transcendent reality is like. I hope to savor my death in advanced years, feeling a sense of completion as I look back over my life. But should I die soon, I at least have come to some sort of terms with it and I no longer feel the empty, icy terror as before. A side benefit of facing death is that other problems pale in comparison. I was awake worrying about money for the kids' college last night. When I found it hard to let go of the worry, I recalled coming to terms with death. The money seemed pretty trivial after that and I drifted back to sleep.

Comment:
Your Portrait Journal will require you contemplate the deepest issues of your life. Your answers are for you alone so they need not conform to any other person's expectations or beliefs. Here you answer what you really believe.

_____ *waning gibbous₃* _____

Last night the wind tested the durability of the trees' new growth. It whipped and gusted, tearing small twigs off the cottonwoods. Our maple's weak points showed up as two larger branches half-ripped from the trunk and draped to the ground. It wasn't a particularly intense wind, just one to test the new growth and provide a stimulus for reinforcing the growth already begun.

Unfortunately a pair of nesting birds did not fare so well. Their whole nest lay on the greenbelt, empty, lonely and useless. It is this year's nest. I can tell. The twigs and grass don't look weathered by the winter. But there are no tell-tale feathers and no evidence of eggs. I muse about the dilemma of the nest builders. Isn't the female about to lay her eggs? Can she delay their maturing within her body while building another nest? Will she deposit her eggs in an unsuitable place? Will she even try to care for them if she doesn't have a properly prepared nest? These questions remain mysteries to me. In any case, I take the nest home for Carol. It will make an interesting addition to the school.

waning gibbous₅

Just slightly larger than a half circle, the waning gibbous moon hovers in the soft blue, late morning sky just above the southwestern horizon. These beautiful days simply cry out for humankind to stay out-of-doors and enjoy. We drive up the Poudre and walk along the river in the forest. A soft pine fragrance suffuses the air and the tumbling river rhythmically suggests we relax and forget the concept of linear time. In the distance a single hermit thrush sings a blessing upon our visit. We promise ourselves to take more time in the forest this summer. Carol will be out of school. But my schedule, poking its digital nose into our analog life, insists that our breaks be short and not interfere with my work. And we have teenagers at home who still require supervision. Our absences better not become too frequent, too long, or too predictable.

waning crescent₃

Lowell comes to borrow our hanging bags. He and Barbara are off to England for a couple weeks; their first such vacation in over twenty-five years of marriage. How absolutely splendid. At the moment, Barbara's cancer is not causing much of a problem. Lowell will carry the two hanging bags so Barbara need only carry a lightweight backpack. For years, they have deprived themselves of so much in order to give to others, I am glad they are going to give to themselves. They are masters at the art of loving.

I am just a bit ill today; probably the result of some questionable chinese food last night. But as the day progresses, I feel better by the hour. Such an illness serves as a reminder to be thankful for health and life. I know Barbara has many, many days of feeling much worse than this and, despite her long-term prognosis, she lives each day with such richness.

112

Vandals cut down forty-six trees at Roland Moore Park this morning. Why? Behavior has its reasons, no matter how warped the logic. Often I have been called on to describe the workings of some criminal's mind. Too often, they have failed to attach to a parent during early childhood and hence live their lives without empathy, without compassion, without love. Was it some unattached young person who vented his passion for destruction on the trees? Or was it just a teenage prank? I don't know, but it's sad. Trees are so hard to grow here. But this event goes to show: There are those in our world who, for complex and often unconscious reasons, pursue the destruction of life, beauty and order.

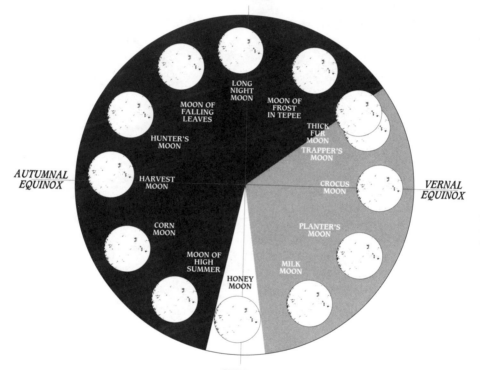

WINTER
SOLSTICE

LONG
NIGHT
MOON

MOON OF
FALLING
LEAVES

MOON OF
FROST
IN TEPEE

HUNTER'S
MOON

THICK
FUR
MOON

TRAPPER'S
MOON

AUTUMNAL
EQUINOX

HARVEST
MOON

CROCUS
MOON

VERNAL
EQUINOX

CORN
MOON

PLANTER'S
MOON

MOON OF
HIGH
SUMMER

MILK
MOON

HONEY
MOON

SUMMER
SOLSTICE

Chapter Five

HONEY MOON

THE FULL MOON nearest the summer solstice has a variety of names: The strawberry moon, the rose moon, the moon when-buffalo-bulls-are-rutting, and most familiar of all, the honey moon. With this new moon, I am on my way to retreat at the Trappist monastery near Snowmass. I relish the six hour drive through snow-capped mountains singing their anthems to a cloudless sky.

As Carol drives, I play with my new toy, a lap-top computer. It has all the capability of my computer at home, but weighs a mere twelve pounds. As a young man, I always wanted to write, but revisions on a typewriter were so painfully slow, my retarded fingers so clumsy, that I usually lost interest in my project part way through the rough draft. But no more. Now I create and edit as I go along. I could write forever. Had this digital wonder been available to me in college, I may have become an English professor or maybe a journalist.

My mind keeps returning to the digital-analog polarity. Balance is the key — not dominance of the analog world nor dominance of the digital — just balance.

waxing crescent₁

Tall and bearded; his searching gray eyes look two ways at once; slender to the point of being gaunt; right out of the middle ages or fresh from a Union Square park bench: Theophane, our retreat master is more than I imagined a monk to be. He drives up in a dusty old Oldsmobile and proceeds to instruct us in the art of _walking meditation_. I have a difficult time concentrating on his message, a house finch on the tree branch above his head sings so joyously, I can't decide to whom I should listen. Is jolly old St. Francis playing a trick? Theophane picks up on the distraction and weaves the bird's singing into his message. When you meditate, work, or live with adversity, don't struggle to ignore your experience, whatever it is. _Incorporate all of life into your meditation or your work._ Never fight it. _Dance with it!_ Theophane goes on talking, St. Francis sings, the mountaintops pulsate with ancient geological rhythms. I open myself to the concert and _I dance._

I respond to one of Theophane's rhetorical questions replying that God is everywhere. Theophane is disturbed when I answer so quickly. Never answer in less than twelve hours, otherwise it looks like you didn't thoughtfully consider the question fully. He suggests we all need a quiet place, one free of distractions where we can _experience_ God and the fullness of that meeting. Then, when we seek the peace of God in the midst of the stress of daily life, we will have practiced well enough to find Her, despite the din.

Vespers flood over us like precious oil. They massage our souls with emollient Gregorian chant. The white-robed monks, the cool brick walls, the echoing medieval acoustics . . . . captivating. Yet I am comforted that as beautiful as this place is, I have found more of

116

God within my deepest self or in Nature with all her diversity, than I have in all the buildings built by humankind.

Afterwards, my best friend and I linger outside in the cool evening air. Evidently the monks have decided that dandelions are God's most perfect flower for their lawn; never have I seen such a thick carpet of this special flower. They are in all stages from yellow blossoms to gray puffs to green pitchfork leaves splaying all over the ground. And in the midst of this special blanket hops the most perfect snowshoe hare the world has ever seen; right there just for us. We laugh out loud but we do not speak. Then we walk the mile and a half back to the guest house in silence. As the sun sets, I search the western horizon for the sliver of the new crescent moon. There it is, just above a solitary gray cotton cloud. Greetings, Sister Moon, everything is right with the world.

waxing crescent$_2$

A deep sleep with sweet dreams; somehow being away from the phone is conducive to letting go. On the way to mass, Friar Tuck, in the personage of a large brown marmot, inspects us from atop a small boulder. Whether he approves of us, I don't know. He doesn't say.

The haunting beauty of the mass bonds me with countless forbearers who have sojourned with hospitable monks. Having been accepted and rejected and accepted again at the Catholic Eucharist, I long ago concluded that rules ordained by whatever ecclesiastical authority will never stand between me and The Origin of All Life. Hence I observe, rather than participate in, the sharing of the sacrament. A couple priests ago, I was told I was welcome at mass but was not, under any circumstances, to partake in the sacrament. You're not Catholic with a big C. It was similar to being invited for dinner provided I didn't eat any food. At first I was mad, confused, rejected. Then the dawning came: No person or rule or organization or religion can prevent me from communing with our Sacred

Mother/Father, the Origin of our whole universe, The Breather of Life, The Origin of all wisdom, all laughter, all silence, all love. *Nothing can!* That is when I descended within my deepest self and found the Light shining, a bottomless Source available whenever I simply take the time for silence. Study and dialogue are crucial to my growth, but silence is where it starts, where it continues. *Silence is the answer.*

After lunch, I go off by myself to climb an unnamed mountain nearby. It has a sharp peak overlooking a vast rock-slide shoveled out by some cosmic giant a million years ago. I choose the steep, trail-less approach off to the right side of the slide. Pulling and clawing my way up a couple of thousand feet through the dense brush and scrub oak, about two and a half hours of steady work, I arrive at the summit. All alone, I sit at the edge of the precipice and retreat into silence. As a child I may have feared a fall from such a height. Later, there were times I feared I might impulsively jump. But now, I fall only into the welcoming, nurturing silence and watch as green and white swallows demonstrate their aerobatic best, soaring and diving around the peak in the process of lunching on the plentiful fly population

My meditation centers on my feelings of guilt. Cheap forgiveness, offered by some religious counsellors and numerous therapists, provides a shoddy solution to the problem of guilt. I have my share of serious sins. I have confessed my transgressions and I have done my best to mend my ways, but my sins still haunt me. I would love to be free of guilt, so that remembering past events or hearing songs associated with painful periods in my life would not cause my stomach to roll.

I continue to sit in silence; sun baking my back, flies buzzing about, swallows twisting and plummeting, and an occasional ant crawling into my navel. Looking down at the monastery, I feel peaceful, rightly placed in the world, and generally lacking in holiness. Gradually, a solution comes to me. *Accept* guilt as a teacher. Journey with it. Learn from it. Dance with it. The purpose of guilt is not to make me feel depressed or inadequate. Guilt is not human experience to be exterminated, expunged, displaced or otherwise avoided. Guilt is my teacher. It reminds me of my capacity for failure. And guilt reminds me to be compassionate towards other people's shortcomings, their failures. I will not judge others too readily while I am reminded of my own capacity for wrongdoing.

As I turn to descend the other side, a gentler slope with a trail, I wonder about my angel. Walking along, admiring the profusion of Indian paintbrush blooming everywhere, I look about but don't see him. (I refer to my angel as him, though angels have no gender.) Finally, I look back up to the summit and I experience an impression of a presence: Quietly joyful, watchful, seemingly thoughtful, as if he approved of my conclusion. He offers little communication save a fleeting sense of his presence. That is enough. My conscious mind perceiving the projection of its deepest desires? Of course.

The trip down is long but not steep. The weather suddenly changes as clouds come in and a cold wind challenges my peacefulness. Descending a cattle trail behind the monastery barns, I find a gift on the middle of the path. Thirty feet from the nearest tree, there is a sky-blue robin's eggshell. Recalling my Easter walk in Arizona, feeling twice blest, I laugh. Snow billows in over the Capital Peaks. The air grows colder. I jog the rest of the way back to stay warm. Just as I arrive at the guest house, a harsh, intense, male rain starts pelting the valley.

waxing crescent₃

The crescent moon hovers respectfully above the early nighttime horizon. Theophane passes the evening reflecting on the walking meditation. He liberally sprinkles his discourse with anecdotes from Hindus, Buddhists, and Zen Masters. He concludes by suggesting we take the heart of Jesus very seriously. Don't just content yourself with the pleasure of feeling holy, set apart. He somberly explains that the most optimistic experts only give our world fifty years (at the present rate of destruction) until the environmental cataclysm. Pessimists give it sixteen years.

Then the gaunt old monk suggests we sing a song in closing. A diverse group with no guitar, we uncomfortably stumble around the idea. Favoring his back, he stands up stiffly, his gray eyes looking at both sides of the group at once; then he leads us in song:

Cigareettes, and whiskey, and wild, wild women,
They'll drive you crazy, they'll drive you insane.
Cigareettes, and whiskey, and wild, wild women,
they'll drive you crazy, they'll drive you insane.

waxing crescent$_4$

Snowmass snapshots:

The monks wear white medieval cloaks, all right. And they wear Rockports, Nikes, Reebocks, hiking boots, or suede desert shoes; most of which are liberally coated with *barn-carpeting*.

Commuting in Levis and baseball caps, carrying shovels or hoes, the monks ride Suzuki motorcycles between the Monastery and the outlying farm buildings. They don't speak to us. This is their home, we offer our courtesy and respect by not seeking to be familiar. They sing for us, pray with us, and bless our presence.

Three a.m prayers are too early for most retreatants. Not for the monks. They awaken then to pray and meditate till daybreak.

"Retreatants, please do not let the yellow cat in the guest house, it is not housebroken. Signed, Brother Mouse." The well-fed cat stays outside. The mice usually show up after dinner as we chat around the kitchen table.

Honey Moon

A monk, with a lariat in hand, chases a hobbling sheep around the corral. Finally, with help from another monk, the lassoed sheep is gently rolled on her back so the two men can gently minister to the injured hoof.

The resident llama oversees monks, guests, and sheep with lofty disdain. I suppose I would feel superior too if my eyelashes were that long.

Three crosses on the side hill above the monastery mark depressions in the earth, graves of departed monks. They are simple wooden affairs with no inscriptions. There are clusters of silk flowers in the dry, brown grass at the base of each cross.

Hermit thrushes sing from every aspen grove. They seem to sing for the sheer glory of it. They can't be mating or marking their territory all the time. Oh, Great Spirit, when I die, may I sing with the voice of a hermit thrush.

The old guest house has stairs so steep you need a grappling hook to climb them and a rope to rappel your way back down. No building code in the country would allow them nowadays. Bedrooms are upstairs, bathrooms on the main floor. The fire escape is a knotted rope at the foot of our bed.

I wash dishes whenever I can. It dries my skin, but moistens my spirit as I perform menial work that has a clear endpoint.

The phone rings in the guest house and in the barn at the same time. I never answer it. It isn't for me.

The yellow cat doesn't try to get in the house, but regularly and deceitfully it persuades more than one guest that it hasn't been fed today.

My best friend and I pause on a mountain trail commenting that this is as happy as we have ever been. All is right with the world.

Theophane teaches us how to bless in the process of blessing meditation. Each of us has our own unique way of doing it. I picture the person to be blessed, smiling brightly, surrounded by a mystical white light. She is held in the palms of God's gigantic hands. I dwell with that image and then, at Theophane's suggestion, I experience the reverse and accept the blessings of others.

_____ *waxing crescent*₅ _____

Clouds subdue this, our final morning. We walk in silence to lauds. In the darkened chapel, I stop listening to the words of the chant. Closing my eyes the chant becomes a grand large owl. I climb on her broad shoulders and she bears me into a great darkness. She flies on, weaving in and out through unseen obstacles and menacing shadows. Her giant wings undulate with the cadence of the chant. She soars and dives through the octaves. I lay my head against her giant feathers and dig my hands into the soft down beneath. Gripping her shoulders, I thrill to her strength and silent wisdom. I feel an odd mixture of childlike trust and almost erotic anticipation. The darkness: My shadow . . . . and more . . . . much more. The voyage frightens me, but as long as I remain with my guide I am safe. Then the darkness engulfs the whole world and I sit alone in the now-empty chapel. I sit in silence. There is no such thing as time.

Outside, we say farewell to Theophane. I promise him a copy of *A Laughing Place* for the "Hall of Laughter" in his *Magic Monastery*. We return and clean the retreat house. A sharp contrast to San Francisco's finest of a couple weeks ago, these accommodations are far more luxurious.

Our retreat group attempts to close our time together with one more season of silence, this time out-of-doors. But the birds, the monks, the Suzukis, and the loudly purring yellow cat all crowd our senses. Finally, reluctantly, with quiet efficiency, we load the cars to leave the real world and return once again to the false one.

Somewhere within me, a place known to no person, not even to myself, windows open. A clean fresh breeze breathes through. Something has changed. What? I don't know. Only whatever it is, it is very lovely and peaceful.

waxing crescent₆

Home

Mail by the bushel, telephone calls to return everywhere; life goes on at the office even though I retreat. I catch up by handling each piece of paper once only. My lawyer calls to say that if I approve the deal, my insurance company will pay ten thousand dollars to the woman I never saw five years ago, the one who never kept her one appointment with me, the one who feels the therapist I supervised failed to provide her with proper psychotherapy.

"No, Paul, I won't do it. Why should I?"

He explains it would be cheaper than the cost of defending the case. Besides, word of it could get leaked to the newspapers and damage my reputation.

"No, Paul, I won't do it."

He explains that the plaintiff's lawyer is on a crusade against therapists. Besides her noble vendetta, she is making a substantial profit. Just one four hundred thousand dollar case pays her handsomely for a year. She has succeeded with three such cases in the last six months.

"No, Paul, I won't approve."

Inside my head I hear, "Dance with it." And for a moment I am transported to another dimension, flying through the darkness, swerving to avoid a towering, dark, cold form in the darkness. I smile and then I take the lawsuit in my arms and I dance with it.

Tonight Carol has the first three strawberries from our garden waiting for me on the kitchen counter. I eat them straight, no sugar, no nothing; just the naked berry. This is called the strawberry moon for very good reason.

FIRST QUARTER

Living an analog life to its fullest requires a special sort of consciousness, an awareness of the richness of life and its ever-changing appearance. Analog living embraces birth, maturity, and death; not just one's own, but that of all creatures. And in the process, it passionately experiences the full emotional impact of each. The digital-mechanistic life, on the other hand, clogs the conscious mind with superficial issues such as wealth, dominance, comfort, security, and status. These anesthetize the consciousness, leaving the digital person with only a vague, haunting uneasiness about life. The analog life is lived right-here, right-now; not over-there, or when-such-and-such happens. Analog passion versus digital compulsion.

On my bike ride today, a right-here, right-now experience, I pedal through farmland. The corn is just shy of knee high. The winter wheat has a soft, dusty green appearance and is pregnant with pods beginning to fill. The succulent first cutting of alfalfa is on the ground ready to be baled.

After my ride I relax on the back porch and discover that a pair of grackles have built their nest in the top of our pine tree. The cries of their hungry youngsters betray the nest's location. You can't really see the nest, it is too well concealed, but when a parent comes with a beak full of food, the chorus of hungry chirpers can be heard two houses away.

This evening, the beautiful half-illuminated lunar disc rides in mid-heaven at sunset. The more I look at it, the more I meld with it. Sister Moon is alive. (Touched by the moon = lunatic?) I am sure this is how our ancestors felt as they reverenced the moon and the sun as gods. We modern digitals look back at those ancient peoples and call them primitive, naive, foolish. Imagine worshipping a lifeless lump of rock or a thermonuclear power plant. But perhaps we are too quick to judge what we have neither experienced nor understand. Many contemporary people reverence lesser idols: Fashion, political affiliations, actors, rock performers; all in the name of being modern realists. Our contemporary lack of the spiritual mind, our lack of a passion for myth may one day be looked upon as the most primitive interlude in the history of humankind.

waxing gibbous₁

Comment:
You will find you need time to consider and then to re-consider the most important parts of your Portrait Journal. The themes that require more detailed reflection will continue to re-emerge until they have been sufficiently understood. This is one principle reason the Portrait Journal needs to span several months' time.

I have been thinking about death again . . . . and not feeling particularly comfortable. Does anybody ever *really* think about death and feel comfortable? Once over the idea of accepting death as inevitable doesn't do the trick. For a while during the past moon my fear was mute. But then, gradually, I became reminded of death whenever I saw a dead creature on the roadside or with every bite of meat I ate. The fear of dying is an instinct deeply ingrained in all animals' psyches, not just human beings'. We humans have no corner on that essential emotion. The animal whose flesh I eat, feared death and suffered, however briefly, to become my food.

It is this very fear of death which motivates us sentient beings to understand life and seek the Source behind life. It fuels our desire to get on the good side of that Source, hoping to succeed in receiving some special consideration regarding death or especially what lies beyond it. I wonder if humankind would seek God as fervently if death weren't the final common denominator for everyone. I don't know how to conceive of life without death as its absolute terminus. I do know, for myself, that life is sweet. I savor that sweetness when

I immerse myself in Nature or when I share the embrace of my mate. I don't want to lose these treasures. With each passionate contact, I only become more addicted to life. Attached. I am grateful for all five of my senses which provide access to the experience of physical reality. One day I shall die and experience the final and complete separation from the natural world and my loved ones. But for now, I will relish the marrow of life and continue to contemplate its mysteries.

waxing gibbous₂

My breakfast celebrates the arrival of summer; so many fruits are in season. I start with strawberries from our garden, and in honor of this moon I smother my toast with fresh dark honey. I need to find someone who has bees so I can participate in an actual honey harvest.

waxing gibbous₃

Des Moines, Iowa

I am here to present my travelling medical humor show to therapists who work with besieged farmers; hard working souls trapped by rising costs, falling prices, and too little rainfall. I remind them how humor helps people to cope with adversity and I weave in how altruism and spirituality form the critical groundwork for dealing with loss.

Though there are homeless here, I fail to meet any. Instead, as I walk down a quarter mile of highway to Denny's Restaurant, I meet couples on bicycles who smile and greet me as if I were an old friend. Friendly, comfortable people.

waxing gibbous$_4$

Home

On the way back from the airport I am treated to a sunset fit for the gods. I see gold oozing between the mountain peaks and the multi-layered clouds. The higher edges of the clouds define the standard for Transcendent White; a white beyond mere snow, more like the intense brightness of the first light announcing the dawn of creation. Meanwhile the lower billowy cloud bottoms settle in like gray goose breasts warming the earth at bedtime.

The air is laden with new-mown hay. I drive slowly, letting the speed freaks rush toward some meaningless moment in the near future that, once there, they will pass with equal abandon. I drive slowly so the air doesn't vibrate the inside of the car despite the four open windows.

waxing gibbous$_6$

Robins eat earthworms, right? Wrong. Robins don't limit their diet to meat, they eat fruit too. Our strawberries. We know they have families to feed, and our lawn has lots of worms. We don't eat worms. We do eat strawberries and we don't like finding them half pecked away when we go out for our cereal topping. I will buy a rubber snake for the strawberry patch, a non-violent alternative for protecting our strawberries.

FULL MOON

With Badger, the zen dog, at my side, I sit in front of the fire waiting for moonrise on the southeastern horizon. In the distance the others are playing *bed-sheet volleyball* with water balloons. Respecting my eccentricity, they leave me alone to my solitude. We are at Carl and Karen's house (out beyond where the paved road

127

turns to gravel) to dedicate his tepee; or as he says it is properly called, his lodge. Every summer he puts it up and decorates the interior with pre-1840 materials. Hides, bones of animals, Indian beads, Hudson's Bay blankets, and wooden trunks fill the lodge. The center has a circular fire pit with kindling and sage stacked neatly alongside, ready for the dedication ceremony.

How many millions of men have sat before a fire, with a dog at their side, waiting for the moon to rise and studying the infinite patterns of the fire? For the occasion I have broken out a very old friend. Twenty-five years ago John Kermott helped me buy this special briar pipe. I was a poverty-stricken medical student and he was doing well, building apartment houses. We went to Colorado for the first time ever and smoked our pipes around campfires. Good friends, we didn't have to talk much. It was a special time. We agreed Colorado would be a good place to settle. After that I went off to medical school in New York and he went back to Fargo to build apartments. A year later he was best man at my wedding. Two weeks after that, he was killed, the passenger in a car driven by an intoxicated freak. Tonight I smoke for John. Tonight I smoke with John.

Just as the moon rises, the group returns to sit around the fire. Carl lights his pipe too. Then I read poetry to the assembled friends. Toddlers on laps, teenagers, adult men and women; aged twenty-two months to sixty-nine years. We sit and listen and look at the fire. We admire the moon and reflect on the miracle of life.

After moonrise, the evening breeze grows cooler. We go into the lodge where Carl lights the fire and then dedicates the lodge by burning fronds of dried sage. We listen respectfully. First he gives thanks to the Great Spirit for life, love and friendship. Then he acknowledges of the four directions: North for snow and water, east for sunrise, south for warmth and greening of the world, and west for darkness. Then we remember the Native Americans slaughtered in the process of wrenching this land from them. We bless their memories, ask for their forgiveness, and pray for their peace in the after-life.

The younger ones rub their eyes. They are off to bed while the rest of us talk and continue to study the fire. I read aloud the words of Chief Seattle.

"This we know. The earth does not belong to man; man belongs to the earth. This we know. All things are connected like the blood that connects one family. All things are connected.

"Whatever befalls the earth befalls the sons of the earth. Man did not weave the web of life; he is merely a strand in it. Whatever he does to the web, he does to himself . . . . "

We light the pipes again, passing them one to another; each of us sharing the same air, the same spirit. The zen dog reclines belly-up on my lap, drifting into some canine reverie. Finally we sip a little brandy and go out one last time to savor the moon. Now riding high in the nighttime sky, its brightness illuminates the far hilltops and casts deep shadows into adjacent valleys. Light alternating with mystery. It is good to be outside by the lodge celebrating this full moon nearest the summer solstice.

---

waning gibbous₁

The summer lull has started. Psychiatry slows down when the weather gets nice. Abundant sunlight and nurturing breezes have a salutary effect on depressed moods and their associated neurochemistry. Lay persons are surprised when they hear there is a seasonality to mental disorders. But why shouldn't the movement of the sun and the moon modify these disorders and our brain chemistry? Their movements modify the growth and reproductive cycles of almost every other species on earth.

Despite the lull, this very hot summer afternoon has some interesting moments to offer. The FBI pays a call on me. A woman I saw several years ago, a rape victim, is seeking employment in a nuclear weapons plant. Not that I approve of her choice of work, I do attest to her psychological strength. Despite a brutal rape where she was assaulted at gun point in her own bed by a wild-eyed stranger, she managed to heal (albeit with considerable pain) and go on to trust men sufficiently to marry. The agent is an older gentleman and friendly enough. I don't talk to him about moon and Spirit, I just give him the facts, just the facts.

B* comes in looking vastly better. I reduce her medications which were nearing astronomical levels when she was in the grip of her suicide demon. She has separated from her spouse. "Just for a while." But I have my doubts. Whenever someone looks so much better out of a relationship, I have grave concern whether the marriage will survive.

waning gibbous₃

Thoreau had a deep love of nature, simplicity and solitude. And he detested people, avoided intimacy, and was generally disagreeable. He was pure analog with an arrogant personality-disordered twist. But in my heart I share a great deal with Thoreau. I love nature and solitude, and I seek ever increasing simplicity. But I have friends, family, patients and co-workers whom I love. I have obligations to them which I will honor. I have a career which, troubled though it feels at this stage of life, has been rich and meaningful.

And most importantly, I have a mate with whom I share a wonderful and terribly final love — a love so complete that if she were to die, I would not just lose the will to live, I would lose the very air that sustains life.

waning gibbous₅

Summer Solstice

"Good morning, Paul, what's up?"

"Congratulations, you're off the hook. They're not going to come after you. They weren't interested in you in the first place . . . . they just included you in the suit to stir things up. After I told them you never saw her and she broke the only appointment ever made with you, they decided to drop the matter. Anyway, the other therapist's insurance settled for 'eight K' to keep the suit from ever being filed. That's a hell of a lot cheaper than going through discovery and a trial."

"Thanks, Paul. I hope I don't have to talk to you again. Nothing personal, you understand."

That dialogue starts a day filled with the usual array of depressions, alcoholism, marital problems, and incest survivors. But it turns out to be a day that closes on a set of different notes.

After my office schedule, I go to the hospital for a CAT scan. My diseased sinuses drain without ceasing, leaving me with a constant sore throat. All traditional and holistic remedies have failed. I need surgery. Today the surgeon wants to look inside my head with a new digital miracle: Computerized Axial Tomography, the CAT scan. A million dollar machine to look and tell us whether there is anything more serious wrong, like a tumor or something.

I insert my head into a huge plastic donut. Lying on a table that moves in and out on some predetermined pattern known only to the brains of the machine, my neck is contorted to its most uncomfortable, hyper-extended position while the robot does its thing. I pass the time by visualizing my laughing place. The procedure lasts only a fleeting instant. The news is positive: No tumors, just thickened, infected tissue. With the radiologist, I look at the shadows on the film. He points to this and that, wondering how I breathe through my nose at all.

At home, Carol has prepared for our observance of Midsummer's Eve. We pack a picnic and head to the mountains. I had wanted to climb horsetooth rock and watch the sunset on this, the longest day of the year, but the cloudy, cold weather argues against such a plan. Instead we head up the Poudre to Young's Gulch and hike in a couple miles. The trail is deserted — just birds, columbines and an occasional raindrop. A fallen cottonwood crosses the trail beside a stream. It serves as our table. Facing one another, we straddle the tree trunk. We open the champagne and enjoy our special midsummer feast. A loaf of bread, a split of champaign, some shrimp, some fruit, some Swiss chocolate. . . . and Thou.

We see no deer until back at the car where a little velvet spike buck watches us for several minutes as we sit on the hood of the car and watch him in return. The day, the place, the deer, each other . . . . all gift.

Comment:

As you go along you will not just ask questions, you will answer them. This answer is not etched in stone, for time and all eternity. But you answer now for how you understand yourself and how you understand life at this time. Our understanding of truth is always relative.

I am beginning to understand the purpose of life — not the meaning of life, the *purpose* of life. *We are alive to experience, to appreciate, and to enjoy the gift that life is.* Our enjoyment, however, is never to be at the expense of others. *We are to appreciate our life and we must extend ourselves so others may appreciate the gift of their lives as well.* Nature, diverse, alive, transcending humankind's fleeting existence on this planet, is one gift we are to appreciate. Love is another.

Our work in life is to remove the impediments which prevent achieving our purpose in life. This translates into working at the prevention of hunger, fear, and disease *for all people.* Thereafter, our work in life is to create beauty and to practice love.

Spiritual development is simply seeking to come to know the Source of life, The Origin of The All, the Giver of the gift of life, God . . . . and to say, Thank you.

132

waning gibbous$_6$

Those of us who adore life, must routinely reckon with death as it hovers on the periphery of our consciousness:
    Just as all rooms are bounded by walls,
    yards by fences,
    continents by oceans,
    atmospheres by empty space;
    so are all lives bounded by death.
If we, attached and clinging to life, daily rehearse our death with its attendant terror, we succeed only in defiling our moments of fervent living in the present. If we, avoiding death's reality, try to escape into addictions or other forms of numbed-out living, we rob ourselves of life itself. If we, terrified at the uncertainty of death, seek to take control by choosing the mode and time of our death, we drain all passion from life and are as good as dead, even prior to our suicide.

To live without a constant dread of death, consider the infant who once craved his mother's breast. Upon growing older he drinks from the cup and explores a wider world. He outgrows his dependence on milk, naturally weaning himself from the breast. Death is the cup waiting for us. It holds a wider universe than our natural mother earth. Living life passionately, without reservation, will naturally wean us from our mother's breast. One day we will willingly leave this life, having outgrown it. We will exit with no remorse, no terror, only a bit of nostalgia for what was once very special, occasionally very painful, and, in the last analysis, very lovely.

LAST QUARTER

It is a clear, warm weekend day. We travel a hundred miles south to the annual Renaissance Festival. A rollicking good time, we enjoy the ribald humor of a pair of Shakespearean miscreants named Puke and Snot. We watch a joust that has all the suspense of televised wrestling, but then we are all surprised when the bad guy wins. Medieval cheerleaders try to get us to say *huzzah* but the audience starts its own cheer with "Tastes Great . . . . Less Filling." I am touched when I encounter a blind carpenter who builds exquisite wood-and-canvas chairs; he even runs my credit card through his machine. He carries on as though sighted until I ask, "How sighted are you?" His reply: "Three percent."

We arrive home after sunset to unpack and enjoy some time on the back porch. The moon rises too late to be any company at this time of month. The phone rings. It is the coroner. Do I remember a Mrs. L*? Well, yes I do. Haven't seen her in four years or so. Why do you ask?

She came in to the ER early this morning and expired on the spot. We suspect she took an overdose. The autopsy is pending but her husband said you had seen her in the past.

Yes, I remember her well. Obsessive-compulsive, she secluded herself in her house, endlessly washing her hands to avoid any contamination from the outer world. But with medication and therapy, she recovered. Last I heard, she had moved to the west coast and was doing well.

The coroner is pleasant enough and promises to get information to me as soon as he knows more. He apologizes for interrupting my evening. I hang up and go out on the back porch with Carol to enjoy and appreciate the gift of our life together.

waning crescent₁

Certain smells evoke certain feelings. Almost every poignant memory has its corresponding smell. I am taking care to smell my world, not just the aromatic, but the unsettling as well. Today was characterized by three distinctive smells, each of decidedly different character.

Trivial: As Carol and I pull into the garage after meeting for worship this morning, we encounter the smell of fermenting garbage.

The warm days and our enclosed garage create a rank, fetid smell. I comment to Carol about renaming this the moon-of-fermenting-garbage.

Tragic: I visit N* in the hospital. A life-long cigarette smoker, she had a panic disorder throughout her adult life revolving around her fear of not being able to breathe. Now she has lung cancer. On oxygen for several months, she has deteriorated to eighty pounds of skin and bone. She gasps with every labored breath. Her GP and the nurses are upset about the amount of medicine I have prescribed for her. I reason that if she is dying, who cares whether she is addicted? At least she is free of panic. Today when I see her, I smell death. She is not frightened of death, "It's the dying part that bothers me, not what comes after." I agree to keep her comfortable, regardless. She says she is counting on me. She foresees no after-life, just a permanent mindless sleep from which there is no awakening. For her this is just fine. She has weaned herself from life's breast.

Lovely: I take a long bike ride in the country. While the weather is so warm, I seize every chance to enjoy the summer air. A most sumptuous fragrance greets me — sweet clover. The roadside ditches are smothered with purple blossoms. It's nature's own very special perfume.

waning crescent$_2$

Last night I was awakened by a dry thunderstorm. Such an event is different from a thundershower because it lacks meaningful rain. We were asleep when the first flickers of lightening flashed over the foothills. Gradually, the thunder grew louder and there were shorter time intervals between lightening bolt and thunderclap. When the time between light and sound was down to two seconds, the flashes were intensely bright, lighting our bedroom with a thousand flashbulbs. I awakened enough to realize our house was right in the path of the storm. I didn't worry about fire or loss of life,

135

I worried that the lightening might fry the hard disc of my computer. I hurried down and unplugged the safety strip from the light socket. At that moment, the thunder crashed almost simultaneous with a lightening strike in the front yard. It didn't hit the house, but it was too close for comfort. My hair rose and stood upright just before the crash. The man at the computer store said the safety-strip was good for power surges, but he offered no guarantees about lightening. As I went back upstairs to bed, the storm furiously engulfed Warren Lake with brilliant white flashes and booming thunder. Twelve drops of rain fell.

This morning I read in the paper that a fire was started by lightening up the Poudre near Rustic. A small, intense blaze, the fire fighters don't have control of it yet. Two hundred and seventy-five acres of too-dry timber have burned.

Is this the way of the natural world? Death opening the way for new life. The eskimos spoke of the wolf being the friend of the caribou. Culling the weak, the sick, and the otherwise vulnerable caribou, wolves kept the herd healthy. The dry thunderstorm is a predator. It brings death to the too-dry forest and perhaps, in the long run, it is a friend of the forest, just like the wolf is the friend of the caribou.

I rarely look at any living creature anymore without reflecting upon its death as well. The Buddhists suggest that a deep appreciation of death on a daily basis makes it possible to live mindfully, conscious of the life process every moment. Life and death are flip sides of the same coin. There is no coin without two sides. There is no life without death. To be truly mindful of life is to be truly mindful of death as well.

When I think back over my life to those experiences of utmost terror, the memory of open-drop ether anesthesia is among the worst. At the age of ten, I had my appendix removed and then four months later my tonsils were summarily cut out as well. The appendix episode was not too bad since I was very ill, but the tonsil memory was terrible. One June morning I entered the hospital for surgery I did not want or need. I felt too healthy. Surgery was my mother's idea. She was tired of my always catching cold. (What else is there for a boy to do, growing up in a North Dakota winter?) I was physically restrained by heavy leather straps while they put me to sleep with the nauseating open-drop ether. Dreams terrorized my coma. As I awakened, I vomited blood all afternoon. Then I spent two weeks lying around the house while all my friends were outside playing. Ice cream was no comfort at all.

Once again, it is summer and today I voluntarily submit to surgery. This time on my sinuses. I like to call the procedure a ring and valve job. But what a difference the years have made. The digital advances in anesthesia are incredible. And my own knowledge of what is going to happen, coupled with my understanding of the absolute necessity for the procedure, make this much easier to accept. The whole process goes as smooth as can be. Upon awakening from anesthesia, my first words are a ribald quip to the nurses: "What did the elephant say to the naked man? . . . . Cute, but can you breathe through it?" Waiting outside, Carol is reassured everything is OK when she hears the nurses' laughter coming from the recovery room.

Now it has been two days of pain killing drugs. I can't read, write, or even watch TV. Instead, I have reflected on the remarkable ease of this whole process. How far medicine has come since I was a child! More efficient, more friendly, less painful, less drawn out. Terrific advantages that we all somehow take for granted. I prescribe antidepressant drugs that turn around the course of many adults' lives; medicines unheard of thirty years ago.

The digital world can be an immeasurable blessing. The only problem with its considerable success is its urging us to leave the analog world behind as if of no validity at all. I believe there is positive digital orientation and negative digital orientation. The positive solves problems; it is the language and process of science. A digital orientation becomes negative only when numbers are dealt with as if they alone represent reality. The analog orientation likewise may be positive or negative. Positive, it is the path of spirit, wonder, creativity and intuition. Negative, it becomes superstition and prejudice. The ideal balance would be a world of fifty-fifty. Currently the modern western world operates with substantial negative digital and very little positive analog.

They are called cottonwoods for very good reason. The female of the species produces her ovules in cottony profusion at this time of year. The Lakota prized this cotton using it for all sorts of hygienic purposes.

My swollen, painful sinuses dictate a slow careful stroll around Warren Lake, one slow enough for me to notice minute details I wouldn't notice when jogging along. The pods on the cottonwoods are breaking out, covering the ground downwind of the tree with a soft downy carpet. The geese are flightless. The little ones aren't mature enough to fly yet and the adults are starting to molt. As I walk towards them, they all waddle away, making no effort to fly. Adult killdeers scold me, bobbing up and down as they scamper through shallow watered areas. They must not have their young nearby, they don't play the old broken wing trick at my approach. It is a clear, hot day. No clouds. True summer. A good day for healing sinuses and taking the time to enjoy the gift of life.

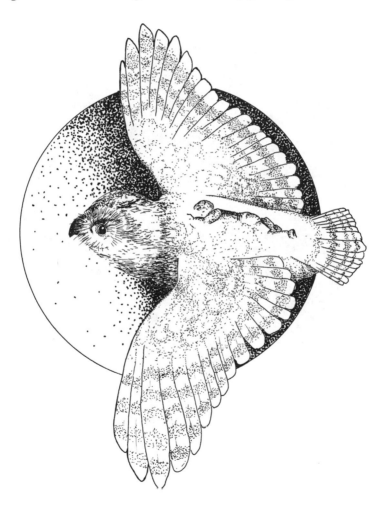

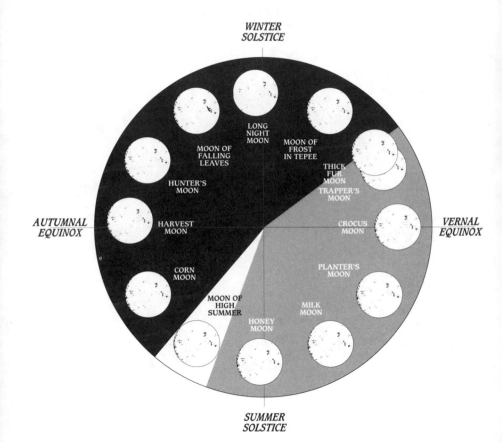

WINTER
SOLSTICE

LONG
NIGHT
MOON

MOON OF
FALLING
LEAVES

MOON OF
FROST
IN TEPEE

THICK
FUR
MOON

HUNTER'S
MOON

TRAPPER'S
MOON

AUTUMNAL
EQUINOX

HARVEST
MOON

CROCUS
MOON

VERNAL
EQUINOX

CORN
MOON

PLANTER'S
MOON

MOON OF
HIGH
SUMMER

MILK
MOON

HONEY
MOON

SUMMER
SOLSTICE

Chapter Six

MOON OF HIGH SUMMER

BIRDS DON'T SING much during these hot sunny mornings. I haven't heard the redwing's shrill *treee-treee* in a moon. The grackle nest is empty. The geese are molting and the ducks keep to the shallow edges of the lake, rarely flying around the neighborhood anymore. Our strawberry plants, supposedly an ever-bearing variety, are, at the moment, more of a never-bearing variety. We harvested only a single strawberry in the past week and it was pretty tart. Brown patches on the lawn demarcate the zones of individual sprinkler heads. The grass grows more slowly now, too. Out in the countryside, the corn is waist high, the second cutting of alfalfa is nearly ready, and the winter wheat is beginning to turn a pretty shade of chartreuse. Every day is hot; high nineties. Our dry air makes it comfortable to be outside despite the heat. And we are blessed with evenings that always cool off. No hot, sticky nights here in the high country.

141

Summer comes in several different varieties: Early summer, high summer, dog-days summer and finally Indian summer. The old colonial names for this moon include summer moon, buck moon, thunder moon, or hay moon. Somehow, summer moon feels the most accurate; but the word, summer, is a bit too general. This is summer at its summery extreme. This is *high summer*, a time of clear hot days offering the best summer has to offer. No one is bored with it yet. Almost no one complains about the heat except for those chronic complainers who complain every time they get the chance.

I love this time of year. It is a bit too hot and too sunny for my Norwegian phenotype, but I don't complain. I walk in the sun with my shirt off, getting my nordic version of a suntan . . . . . something resembling a light lobster color, but it doesn't hurt. No, really it doesn't. Just don't touch.

waxing crescent₂
San Diego, California

Here in Southern California, the crescent moon hovers in a blue evening sky. An astronomical treat is happening: Venus is very close to the crescent moon creating an image that makes even a non-Muslim smile. Beautiful, simply beautiful. It is free for the viewing, no charge. Appreciate life. Dance with it.

The weather is flawless and the variety of plant life is fantastic. And where else can you get such broad expanses of concrete? Eight lanes for motor vehicles going each direction and not even in the heart of the city. Because it is beautiful here, many people move here to enjoy the beauty. Because so many people move here, the beauty is being compromised. There is no place on earth so beautiful that it cannot be destroyed by the crush of too many people. Whatever the answer to our global dilemma is, one fact is clear: It will require that substantially fewer people be alive at any given time. That will require that fewer babies be born. We cannot count on morality or education to do the job. Each has failed miserably.

Religion is of absolutely no help at all. We will have to call on the best of the positive digital world to provide technology for that to happen and we will need fewer babies without resorting to scraping fetuses out of the womb to prevent their crowding the planet.

---

waxing crescent₃

As a boy I was cautioned about the dangers of *the dance*. Too risky because of uncontrolled sexual temptation. I was told to avoid it. I didn't. And as a consequence, I feel vaguely uncomfortable dancing; self conscious and a little guilty. Nevertheless, tonight we are dancing. The group hosting my workshop fills the room with families and guests. Coming from all over the country, there are single adults and married adults, assorted teenagers and sundry little children, people of all different colors. There is a DJ, a portable dance floor, and an open bar. Everybody dances, just as if we were celebrating a Polish wedding: Children dance with parents, children jump and play. Three single women unabashedly dance in a triangle. Young couples dance close with intense non-verbal eye contact. Older married couples dance further apart and laugh. We dance, we laugh, we dance, we sweat, we dance, we drink, we dance, we celebrate life, we dance.

There is a positive and negative aspect to almost every human activity. Sex can be used positively and negatively; as can anger, humor, and guilt. Dancing is positive when we celebrate living in our physical bodies. We celebrate movement, relationship, music. We celebrate life. Dancing is negative when it is competitive narcissism or one more way to promote pseudo-intimacy. I have seen people dance whose one intent is to bed the other. There is no joy in the dance, just a necessary stage to accomplish the sexual exploit. I have seen people dance as a way of showing off their superior coordination or their physically attractive body. They dance to put down their less coordinated or less attractive companions.

143

I have been up and down with dancing in my life — more down than up. Mostly, I feel poorly coordinated, not very attractive, and as if I don't quite fit in. When the Twist came in, I quit dancing much. I have taken some lessons, but dancing often seems like work. Then Theophane said to *dance with it,* dance with whatever gets in your way. Don't kick it away or avoid it, dance with it. OK, I will dance with life. And I will dance . . . the real thing. In the process of my dance, I accept the gift.

waxing crescent₄
Los Angeles, California

Making your way through the air here is like scuba diving a North Dakota pothole: Hard to see where you are going — thick, dirty, smelly. My sinuses cry out. I pacify them with a squirt of salt water. But for now, polluted air and forty bucks is the price we pay to see *Les Miserables* at the Shubert. The music, the dancing, the sets, the story; all blend, conspiring to play the full scale of emotions.

Jean Valjean, the protagonist of *Les Mis* lives a painful, saintly life. Our world needs more saints. But to be effective, saints need a better public image. After all, they do not seek to manipulate other people through guilt trips. They celebrate the dance in their special, total, joyous way. They relish life by loving God with complete abandon. Their privations are not felt to be privations, only necessary steps in the process of giving themselves fully to the natural expression of their love of God.

waxing crescent₅

Another day of crowded freeways, exotic food, and once-in-a-lifetime entertainment. At the beach, I get knocked over by a boisterous wave of the incoming tide. Not intending even to get my feet wet, I get soaked, clothes and all. Fortunately my wallet manages to stay dry (averting a mini-disaster). After a quick change of clothes, we are off to the Greek Theater to see Harry Belafonte. What music, what dance, what rhythm, what laughter. All six thousand of us, black, yellow and white, sing *Matilda, Da-a-ay-Oh, Hahvan-a-geela.* We sing, we clap, we move, we laugh. And we admire talent and physical beauty. How beautiful black skin is.

We not only need to dance more, we need to sing more, we need to whistle more, we need to laugh more, we need to clap our hands more, we need to howl more — alone and with all our brothers and sisters. Not just our White brothers and sisters or our American brothers and sisters or our Christian brothers and sisters, we need to celebrate with ALL our brothers and sisters: *All of them, everywhere.*

waxing crescent$_6$

Home

The Lakota called this the Moon-When-The-Cherries-Are-Ripe and they knew what they were talking about. For the last two evenings I have gorged myself on bowls of fresh, sweet, firm, succulent, perfect cherries. They are only around for a few weeks at this time of year. Canned or frozen cherries are OK, but nothing equals a fresh cherry for the absolute essence of cherry-ness. Dancing with fresh cherries is easy business.

waxing gibbous$_1$

I have come to the conclusion that my favorite moon phase is the waxing gibbous moon. Its light fills the early nighttime sky when I am most in the mood for moon watching. It's bright enough to illumine the landscape, etching sharply-defined shadows. It lasts so much longer than the full moon which is really only present for one night. It offers promise of more to come. It gradually reveals itself to us. It unfolds like the unconscious mind, slowly but steadily illuminating more and promising even more to come.

_____ *waxing gibbous₅* _____

Her name was pronounced hell-yoe, but I have never been sure how to spell it (Heljo?). I was only six when she came to live with us. Mom was back from the mental hospital for the first time and had just had a hysterectomy. We needed a woman to help out. Heljo was a DP, a Displaced Person. In return for helping us as a domestic, we sponsored her entry into the United States. I don't remember too much about her except she scraped the white of an egg from the eggshell to avoid wasting a single calorie. She worked hard and kept to herself while mother took her time to heal. We laughed at her fear of scarcity because we were rich Americans, the war hadn't brought my family much hardship. Dad's business was actually better, though toys were hard to get for me. The only toy I remember was a wooden model of an M-1 Carbine.

One day I came home and Heljo and mom were both crying. Heljo was telling of how the Nazis came to her farm and methodically shot her father and brother while they were working out in the field. Her father was an official in the Department of Agriculture of Estonia and the Nazis decided the simplest way to deal with such people was to shoot them and let them lay. A few remnants of her family escaped at the end of the war as the Russians invaded and promised more of the same. America was her dream. America is where she shed her bitter tears. America was where she started a new life. The last we heard of Heljo is that she married and her husband was attending medical school.

Now Deng is here. His friends and family advise him to stay here as long as possible. In fact he is trying to get his wife to come and join him here. But the bureaucracy both in China and the United States is a nightmare. He hasn't participated in any demonstrations, just stuck to his studies. He has smelled freedom

146

and he loves it. Many Americans take it for granted. Too bad. The framers of the constitution blessed humankind with a most glorious document. It makes so many of us safe. It gives us the freedom for our analog-ness to express itself in its own individual way. Tonight we go out for sushi. He had never eaten Japanese food in his life.

Comment:

It is as important in the process of self understanding to note what is positive as it is to note what is lacking. The same goes for the people you share life with and the institutions that govern you.

The Heljo's and the Deng's in this world are my teachers. They take totalitarianism from the abstract to the very real and the very personal. My one piece of advice for Deng and his countrymen: Bring about change, yes. But at all costs, avoid violence. Follow Ghandi and Martin Luther King, not Mao or Hitler. Violence only temporarily ends tyranny. It also fuels an inner rage and the new regime becomes despotic as well.

As I reflect, I am awed by how ignorant humankind has been about the limited effectiveness of violence — violence in raising children, violence in settling disputes, violence in reforming whole countries. If we only took *Thou Shalt Not Kill* and applied it to everyone, both enemy and friend alike, the world would be forever transformed. It's really that simple.

FULL MOON

Nothing can impede a contemplative more effectively than a too-busy life. The last two weeks have been on the shy side of chaotic. Principally, the problem is that of being on-call. We psychiatrists rotate call so each of us gets a week now and then. I expected the summer lull to be easy on me. But that hope was not to be. Last week I awakened several times in the night to respond

147

to the emergency services team. I visited the Intensive Care Unit regularly (a place where psychiatrists fear to tread). I talked too many people out of their intended self destruction. I admitted four people to the hospital as a result of suicide attempts. Only one was my patient. The others belonged to doctors who were out of town or had no previous mental health contact.

We have a suicide epidemic going on right here in river city. Nobody is quite sure why. Currently in our beautiful county nestled here in the foothills of the Rocky Mountains; our upper middle class community (a great place to raise a family); our lily-white culture without pesky racial or social problems, has a suicide rate three times the national average, almost the highest in Colorado. Why? No one knows. It isn't merely the climate; neighboring Utah has a very low suicide rate. It isn't the economics; other places in the country are more sorely depressed. It isn't broken families; we are on a par with other areas of the country in that department.

The beauty of nature here promises what life could be. The spirituality of the land beckons thirsting souls to contemplation. But the rat-race is no different here. Most people's attempts at spiritual answers fall woefully short of satisfaction. Some embrace the dominant religion hereabout, a somewhat fundamental protestant Christianity. Others embrace a generic New Age mysticism that flounders for want of real myth and jumps from one fad to the next (this year it's crystals). It has been remarkable to me how few lives are actually enhanced by one's spiritual convictions. The fundamentalists will proclaim a lot, putting God and man in little word packages, but they have the same neuroses, love affairs, and suicides as the rest. I know, I treat them.

The newspaper listed all the suicides so far this year with brief descriptions. Two were my patients. Interestingly, both claimed to be *born-again*. I can see why psychiatry became so atheistic. God really doesn't seem to make much difference to the vast majority. In fact, I often see God related to as if He were a transcendent Rorschach test; an amorphous blob of celestial ink in the unconscious onto which people project their hopes, prejudices, and unresolved feelings from early childhood. So few people honestly try to encounter God, trembling with the uncertainty of it, awed by the grandeur of infinity. Rather I see people most succumb to hard-sell evangelists or settle for some formula that, once accepted, allows them to live the same life while wearing a different label.

It seems to me that meeting God, letting the Source of all life challenge your innermost soul, should be a life changing experience. If God coincides too closely with my political affiliation or my nationality, I probably have a counterfeit God. Organized religion is a necessity. It has to carry on the business of marrying, christening, and burying in some sort of consistent fashion and teach about God in the process. But it frequently falls short. It somehow must provide for a moving deep internal experience of encountering God and being changed forever by that encounter. It must provide a setting for growing in the experience of God. For me, silence with its wordless prayer is the answer — silence and solitude. Followed then by study and learning from my life's companions. It must change me from my preconceptions, unless I want to believe that they were somehow pretty close to perfect to start with.

_____*waning gibbous₁*_____

I feel physically well and finally have enough time to run around Warren this morning. Looking more like a muddy bathtub than a lake, the reservoir is being drained of its inventory for the thirsty crops. It has been a dry time. Water is scarce. So rather than leaving water in the lake for city folks to look at, it is put to use.

I haven't looked at the moon much lately. I've been too busy. Last night when I left work at midnight, I paused and appreciated the sight. I have missed the moon and what looking at it symbolizes to me. Being busy isn't merely the devil's work, it is the devil himself. What better way to divert man's interest in uniting with The Origin than to make him think he's too busy? If I have one great flaw to mend in my character, it is the tendency to over-schedule myself, leaving almost no time for contemplation. Money is the excuse, four kids in college and all that.

Comment:

After you have been writing for awhile, you will begin to see themes recurring. For example, my continued complaint of being too busy. Watch for these recurring themes. They say much about you. And they are likely to be quite apparent to your companions in life.

---

waning gibbous₂

39,000 feet above Idaho

Looking from my plane window I see the faint glow of sunset on the horizon as we chase the evening star. Behind, darkness follows. The moon will not rise for another hour or so. The DC-10 on which I am flying is identical to the one which crashed yesterday in Iowa. There are many open seats. I presume frightened passengers opted for a different airline or a different aircraft.

Today before I left, I spent the whole day in the office. A busy time, but not overburdened with impending suicides (only one). B* came in looking more comfortable, even a little bit composed. Her depression is better, the obsession with suicide has abated for now, her medications are tapering back, and her relationship is all but over.

A new patient, a social worker from Denver, came to see me. The face sheet reported his age to be within a few months of my own. Why did he want to see me? "Chris, I have cancer." He knew I have worked with cancer patients, helping them cope with the threatened loss of life, easing the effects of chemotherapy through self-hypnosis, and seeking to influence cure by visualizing the cancer's destruction by the body's natural defenses. I never offer such interventions in lieu of traditional cancer treatment. I offer an adjunct, not an alternative.

I told him if visualization is to work, it will require consistent, passionate practice. Patients who perform visualization as if marionettes on my mental strings succumb to their tumors as rapidly as the average. Those exceptional patients who are successful in altering the course of their disease are passionate in their willingness to radically alter the course of their lives. Deep inside they *know* their mind is connected in some mysterious way to their body's defenses.

And then he offered more. "I have been in therapy for two years. Last year I uncovered the most horrible visions of childhood. I don't want to believe they are real. . . . . maybe I just made them up. I grew up in the deep south. My family was in the KKK. . . . I witnessed ritual killings of blacks. I think I participated . . . I . . . I was four . . . . I think. And I remember them abusing me, too. Anal penetration. They told me the seed was planted within me too. Eight months ago I actually saw the demon they planted in my belly. Now the cancer is located in the exact same place."

waning gibbous₄

Tacoma, Washington

She puts on her prettiest red dress and her new beige pumps. We aren't going anywhere. We are just going to spend the day talking. At ninety-two, my Aunt Pearl looks all of sixty; a full head of thick brown hair and all her own teeth. Her appearance doesn't betray her advanced age. Neither does her mind, it is clear and agile. Her laughter is full and fearless. She has a plastic hip and her eyes are distorted by cataract surgery. She needs a large magnifying glass to examine the photos I bring her. She was the youngest child in my father's family; too young to recall the family's migration to the North Dakota homestead in 1898. The only restriction in relating stories from her life isn't senility, it's her fear that she might bore me. Yet as the hours pass, we talk endlessly and I extract wonderful vignettes of pioneer life.

151

"Mama would go out in winter to gather sticks. We had no firewood in those days. Papa would get lignite at the mine and your dad and I would go down to the train tracks to pick up coal dropped by passing trains; that coal was the best quality, real hard and shiny. But Mama had it the worst, eight miles by horse-drawn wagon to the sand hills to collect branches from the scrub brush to use as kindling for starting fires. When she would return, she was so cold her hands wouldn't move. She didn't complain, she just moved stiffly, getting on with the never-ending work.

"We slept in one room, all eight of us. The whole house was only one room. We didn't feel poor. Everybody was in the same boat."

My Uncle Iver isn't well. His mind has deteriorated. Yet his remarkable sense of humor shines through. He always liked to tease and still responds with quips as he always did. It's just that he doesn't know who I am. No memory of my visits as a child, loaning me money for medical school, or going moose hunting with me in British Columbia. He sleeps nineteen hours a day. He spends his waking hours eating bacon and eggs, drinking coffee, and smoking Camel cigarettes. At eighty-eight, he is just a pup compared to Pearl, but his mind is gone and she cares for him just as she has cared for people all her life.

My only surviving aunt and uncle are exploring the alternative to death, they are growing old, very old. They don't go out anymore, didn't return to North Dakota for the centennial. "Everybody we knew is dead now. We wouldn't want to go, sit, and talk to people we don't know."

The isolation of age must be one of the ways we come to welcome death. Pearl has no fear of death. With a twinkle in her surgery-distorted eyes she simply states she can't go on forever. Wouldn't want to. I doubt Iver has the ability to appreciate what death may hold anymore, though he may be practicing for death with his long hours of dreamless sleep.

152

waning gibbous₅

Seattle, Washington

No bigger than a peanut when they were born, my sister's daughters are now mature women. One has a ten year old son, the other has a ten week old pregnancy. Their friends come in and out. The phone rings. Dogs bark in the yard. We barbecue salmon on the grill. We talk of family, hopes, dreams and plans for the future. We talk of problems with children and drugs and too little money. I manage to secure some special private one-on-one time with each of them. This time I am the uncle, the elder. I am the life-experienced one. I am quizzed about vague memories of early childhood and ancient history like The Beatles and John Kennedy.

We go to the Pike Street Market and shop. We taste the infinite varieties of honey, preserves, and vegetables. We watch as the fish vendors holler back and forth and throw a fresh salmon as if it were a slippery, deflated football. Street mimes, street musicians and street winos mingle with the crowd. We watch some and pretend not to see others.

Birth is easier to examine, accept and talk about. Filled with hope and happiness, birth is the one boundary of life filled with little anxiety once it is an accomplished event. My nieces and I spend the day talking about the beginning of life, filled with potential, hope and happiness.

Comment:

The various generations of our families help to inform us who we are and where we are in life. Your Portrait Journal will urge you to talk with your surrounding generations. The older members of your family are especially important. Spend time with them. Their memories are made of gold.

Snohomish, Washington

Prince Alexander Golitzin earns his living by making toilet paper. Descended from White Russian aristocracy, Al is a chemical engineer with one of the numerous paper companies in the Pacific Northwest. Needless to say there is no bliss in making a softer, whiter toilet tissue. Al's passion, inherited from his uncle Andre, is wine-making. It is not a hobby, not a diversion, not a whim. Al is committed to creating the finest Bordeaux wine America has to offer. Here is his bliss.

We go to the winery. I am blessed with perhaps one of the most graceful aromas I know: Cool oak, musty wine, a touch of mold. Al offers me a vertical tasting of his efforts since I last saw him four years ago. His son, though merely eighteen, has the interest and palate of a mature adult. We taste. We appreciate. We analyze. Words do scant honor to the complexity of the experience of taste. Yet we try. Al is getting close. One day he will have the finest Bordeaux in America.

The evening lingers over salmon, wine, memories and photographs. Where once they shared the experience of diapers, our children are now in college. They have few memories of one another. But we adults have reels of memories that entertain us through the evening. We talk of the past and we talk of the future. Al knows he won't make toilet paper much longer. He will soon succeed in making his sole living as a wine maker. I will not make my living as a psychiatrist much longer, I am a writer. (What courage, mixed with ego, mixed with deepest hope it takes to call myself a writer — having only published one book that has sold a mere five thousand copies.) Just as Al experiments one year to the next with fermenting methods and aging techniques, constantly improving his wine, I will do the same with my books. Without passion, there would be no great wine, there would be no great books. A writer must have a special passion for life; for observing it, for loving it, for writing it. I have no choice really. I must write.

way to spend my time before I become an Uncle Iver or his now-deceased contemporaries; writing, and savoring the gift of life.

Home

Among the many differences between Washington and Colorado, one of the most striking is trees. In his veritable jungle, Al sees them as pests to be chopped down when they grow and obstruct his view of the valley. I nurture each tree in my yard, seeking professional consultation when one doesn't look well. We value most what we have to work hardest to enjoy.

For the first time in a moon I heard geese flying this morning. It was not a long flight, just a simple cruise around the lake. The adults must be feeling very fulfilled, having raised their families and are now regaining the magic of flight. The young geese must be confused, wondering what it is that the big birds are doing. No doubt some teenage goose is terribly embarrassed by her parents' strange behavior: "I mean, Mother, how could you? How could you just leave the ground like that and move around. I could have just died. Brian's parents didn't do it. Why did you?" She wouldn't be caught dead doing such a thing herself. Parents can be so stupid. I look forward to watching the goslings as they learn the wonder of flight.

The workdays have been steady since my return; full but not overflowing. No imminent suicides knocking at my door. I wonder about N*; the last time I spoke to her husband she was not doing well. I had smelled her death a moon ago. He promised he would call if anything happened. But we psychiatrists are usually the last to know about death, as if *real doctors* don't think it makes much difference to us. I call the nursing home. N* died last week. Hadn't I been informed? Hers was a death in the fullness of time of a woman who was fully ready for an everlasting sleep. I don't mourn her passing, but I am touched. She was a cantankerous and completely delightful woman. I will miss her.

155

I start my day with a quick run around Warren and an even quicker shower, then off to the hospital to see a patient. She is dressed and eager to see me. Now in the middle of a transference neurosis, she idealizes everything about me. I am attractive, athletic, deeply spiritual, competent, wise, loving. She sees me as the perfect father, saint, and lover. I know this is part of the process. I have long ago learned never to get my own ego involved in such idealization. When the idealization turns the other way, look out. And turn it will. Freud called this the transference neurosis. He believed the patient could work this neurosis through and in the process recover from the one that has gripped her since childhood.

A childhood more awful than most I hear of, she had no father and an alcoholic mother who subjected her to unbelievable abuse. Her marriage to a man whose only passion in life is rebuilding '56 Chevys has left her continuing to starve emotionally. Neither she nor her husband holds a job for any length of time. They are penniless causing her to worry about a roof over her head and food to eat as well. They have one child; I worry about her too. But, the situation looks a little less grim today. I think the meds are helping, but I'm not sure yet.

The office day passes as a standard sort of day: Nine patients and several long-distance phone calls as I play telephone tag with some folks in Tennessee who are trying to arrange a humor workshop.

I finish on schedule, eager to get to my sinus doctor when Carl stops me going out the door. It's an emergency he says. His pallor bears witness to the truth of his words. (Darkly complected Italian men don't exhibit pallor particularly well.) A woman he saw a year ago had done well with antidepressants and therapy. She is in his office. She is suicidal. She has a gun.

"Loaded?""

"Yes."

156

"She still have it?"

"No."

"What kind."

"A revolver. I unloaded it."

All therapists should have some familiarity with guns. These sorts of events happen with a too-regular frequency.

I meet a middle aged woman who wears a forced smile, but her puffy eyes and her tear-streaked face speak more loudly than her smile. In the interview, I find she has recently re-entered a major depression. She has all of what we call *vegetative signs*, evidence of altered brain chemistry. She needs antidepressants again. Carl has worked out a plan for using a network of friends rather than the hospital. She works for another therapist in town and would be mortified to have to stay on the psych unit. I suggest a hospital in another community, but she declines, saying she has passed the crisis, proof of which is her bringing the gun in. She won't do anything to herself now. If she feels worse, she has contracted with Carl to call him, or me, or the on-call psychiatrist. I am satisfied with her contract. I give her a prescription and arrange for her to see me again in two days.

waning crescent₃

Heidegger suggested there are two fundamental ways of being in the world: First, a state of forgetfulness of being; secondly a state of mindfulness of being. This idea didn't have much impact on me as a young man, it just seemed like so many words. It does now. Looking death squarely in the face, not pretending it isn't real or avoiding the very thought of it, causes me to be constantly mindful of life. So many people are absorbed in idle chatter living, or quick-fix religion. They remain in a perpetual state of forgetfulness of being, never awakening to taste life; the good, the not so good, the awful. The blessing that comes from facing my own death, the very real possibility that my existence may cease completely forever, is that I

157

become more alive. Rather than grieving for myself or cursing God, I delight in the gift that I have life today. I experience the consciousness of my own being. Either I look at the wonder of Nature or I turn my consciousness inward; both special places where I encounter God. And say, *Thank You.*

---

waning crescent₄

I love these rare Saturdays when I can sleep in. This morning I awaken to Carol's fresh strawberry waffles topped with the darkest maple syrup known in the free world. I take a half hour for prayer. I am becoming more comfortable calling it prayer rather than silence. After all, that is what it is, only I don't pray with words all that much. Words are often overrated as a form of communication. Interestingly, the words of a hymn I used to sing as a child flow through my mind, *Sweet Hour of Prayer.*

Then I take a four mile run. I shower and go to the hospital to see my most difficult patient. We have much work to do — therapy, intense stuff, seven days a week.

Then Carol and I drive to Cheyenne a mere fifty miles to the north to see the Frontier Days Rodeo, *The Daddy of Them All.* Saddle broncs, steer wrestling, calf roping, horse racing, bull riding. Our favorite is the wild horse race. Four year old horses that have never seen a halter are saddled by groups of three cowboys each and then the best rider races it around the track. Early in the afternoon, the announcer pauses to remember the professional rodeo cowboys who have died during the past year. All rise. Men, hats off, please. Let us bow our heads . . . . listen to the list of names. I notice the absence of any Jewish sounding names. Then a prayer about death and about how cowboys find their church in nature with only the sky over their heads. I wonder how many people are mindful of life at this moment and how many are just being led through a quaint ritual. How splendid it is to consider death right in the middle of this rodeo, so pungent with life.

After the rodeo events, we dine on barbecued ribs (what else?) and American beer ("We don't serve no imports here"). While we eat and try to manage the gooey finger problem, a young mother from Dallas sits across from us and proceeds to breast feed her six month old baby. She apologizes. We say none needed.

We finish with a visit to the High Plains Indian Village. There are Kiowas, Apaches, and Comanches dressed in remarkable feathered costumes. Several wear face paint. More wear glasses. Three Indian men of considerable girth chant and beat a large tom-tom. There is a circle dance and all are invited to join. White eyes with their children, clad in tee-shirts and running shoes, dance with the Native American men and women. Much laughter, good vibes.

We get disoriented in the parking lot and find ourselves in the midst of the real cowboys, the ones who compete. We can tell; they still have their numbers on their backs. There are Winnebagos everywhere, families with small children, and diminutive barbecue grills. They look at us in a friendly sort of way but offer no greeting. They are off duty now — no time to chat with city folk.

waning crescent

Tonight Ron comes over and we watch his new video, *Twelve O'clock High*. (Black and white sure beats color.) Friends for over twenty years, Ron and I met in the Marine Corps when Viet Nam was at its hottest. He had just returned from a tour of duty in-country. I was lucky enough never to have to go. No one ever shot at me. We bonded by our mutual love for the out-of-doors and the fact that each of us had just lost our best friends. Ron's friend, Duncan, had his life cut short by a sniper's bullet in Viet Nam. My friend, John, died at the hands of a drunk driver in Detroit Lakes, Minnesota. Through the years we have enjoyed a friendship that has spanned differences of vocation, location, and education. We have remained addicted to talking about the Marine Corps and military things. For my part, I flew in some pretty hot jet aircraft and

159

brushed close to death on more than one occasion. Ron got seriously shot at on several occasions but never saw an enemy to shoot. Though neither of us believes in war for settling disputes and neither would ever want our sons to go to war, we enjoy talking, reminiscing, and reading about combat and military exploits.

Why do we enjoy talking about the military, about war? Why do we enjoy watching *Twelve O'clock High*? Why do we drink cognac and swear frequently as we re-experience our past military ventures?

I think I know why. I think I know why men enjoy war; why they enjoy guns and mountain climbing and bull riding and fast cars and so on and so on. Getting close to death makes life come alive. Never are men so aware of being alive as when they are on the edge of not being alive. I have known many fighter pilots and combat veterans who find peacetime life dull, hum-drum, boring — something to be endured. Why are there soldiers of fortune? Because such men only become alive when they court death most closely. I used to think it was an addiction to excitement, but now I realize it is the sense of being very much alive by being close to death.

Women are different. They don't value such brushes with death. They come very close to the other boundary of life, one of which men are incapable; they give birth and suckle a child. The thrill of feeling alive comes with pregnancy and delivery. Many women enjoy being pregnant. They experience a special magic forever denied to men. They feel life come alive within their very bodies. The pain of labor is forgotten, while the wonder of birth remains forever. How sad that doctors often have deprived women of the experience of ushering a new life into the world by narcotizing them out of awareness of that special moment.

Men can enjoy childbirth vicariously, but that is all. Women don't need war or life-threatening sports to experience the full awareness of being alive, of living mindfully. They have pregnancy, childbirth and suckling to do it for them.

160

This morning I read that a young bull rider in Cheyenne was gored by a bull Sunday and died. (We were there on Saturday.) I talk to a patient who knew him. A very fine young man . . . . . the best. I talk to a friend who witnessed the ride and the attack. The bull had it very clearly in mind that he wanted to kill the young cowboy. He thrust a single large horn in the rider's back as he attempted to run away. He knocked him down and then sort of stirred him about on the ground breaking several ribs which in turn severed the aorta. The young man lived for bull riding. The young man died by bull riding. He must have felt very much alive for each of those eight second periods astride two thousand pounds of heaving flesh fueled by pure testosterone.

We cannot be mindful of life without being mindful of death. They go together like the proverbial horse and carriage. You can't have one without the other. The terror and the reality of death serve to get our attention. How many neuroses will we spare ourselves if we but only take the time to be properly fearful about our own death, to contemplate the complete cessation of our own existence? What comes after death remains an ultimate mystery. No one really knows. Only the dead . . . . and God.

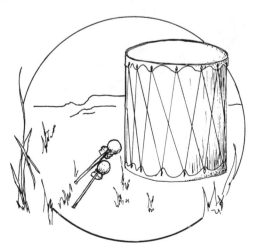

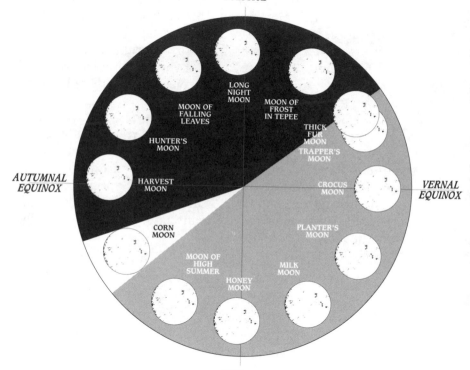

Chapter Seven

CORN MOON

Home

IN THE OLDEN days they called this the dog days moon or the woodcutters moon. But dog days require a soporific combination of humidity and motionless air. And woodcutting is only necessary now if you rely on a wood burning stove. I have a stove but I also have an ample supply of very dry wood left over from last year. So I won't be involved in any woodcutting and it is just too dry here in Colorado to create a dog days atmosphere. At dinner tonight Carol has some of the sweetest sweet corn. The Cheyenne call this the moon of the new ripened corn, the obvious choice of a name for this moon.

Digital pace. Rapid pace. No-peace pace. I haven't prayed as I would like and I haven't exercised. Last night I didn't sleep. Insomnia is God's way of telling me I am getting out of balance again. I am like a little kid who is slow to learn. I know what I need to do, I like doing it, but somehow I let it get crowded out of my life. Well, I won't beat myself over the head, I will just settle down and for the umpteenth time get back to basics.

D* is settling into the therapeutic process. The issue has changed from preventing her suicide to how she has become the way she is. Trusting me more, finally believing I won't abandon her or reject her if she discloses some particular misdemeanor, she is recalling memories from the shrouded mists of childhood.

Today she recounts a dream of an animal being sliced open from the genitals to belly. It looks at her with plaintive eyes before it dies, pleading with her to do something, anything to save it. She does nothing and as the animal dies, she abruptly orgasms and then suddenly experiences cold metal sharpness in her pelvis. I ask her to relax and close her eyes. She follows my suggestion and then she senses the presence of an adult figure beside her crib. She cries muted baby sounds to no avail. Then she feels a sexually arousing massage where she shouldn't be touched, followed by the feel of sharp cold metal objects inside her body. I ask her how old she is, she replies, "young, very young . . . she don't know how to talk yet."

Weekends help. This afternoon we go to Carl and Karen's. We take a hike in steep, rocky country looking over the destruction wrought by last week's thunderstorm. Rocks and even small boulders have been washed by the torrent down the normally dry creek bed. The rain also has reawakened the grass. Hills now kelly-green contrast sharply with the red canyon walls. On a steep game trail I discover a soft-blue egg shell. Far away from any trees or obvious nests, another beautiful eggshell. My third. I carry it for awhile, wondering why I am singled out for such subtle signs of affection. Then I leave it on another hillside as we return to the lodge for dinner by the fire and another chance to commune with Badger.

FIRST QUARTER
Yellowstone Park (A year after the great fire)

Carol and I look out on Yellowstone Lake and savor a flawless first quarter moon suspended in a blue evening sky ever folding upon itself with changing patterns of billowy clouds. This day has been a full and varied day.

This morning started with the news that my back-up would not be able to see D* while I was gone. I had to scramble to find another psychiatrist, one who would see her and be willing to forego payment. Fortunately, I was successful. While I was at the office tying up loose ends, Carl came in with the news that P* died last night. This is not a surprise, but clearly a tragedy; a youthful woman in her mid-thirties succumbing to cancer. Our efforts at holistic supplementation of her therapy failed. Though, as Carl and I reflected, maybe not. We can't be sure we added an hour to her life, but her quality of life was exceptional these past two years — especially so within her therapy group during the last four months when the brain metastases became evident.

On the highway crossing Wyoming, I find I am unable to read, to write, or even to feel remotely creative. I sit numb and sleepy, watching the land flow along the sides of the car. About midway across the state we come to the Basin of the Great Divide, a high desert area encircled by the continental divide. Were it not for sagebrush and antelope, we could have been on the moon. Stark, rocky beauty and a seemingly uninhabited mystery. By the time we reach Lander and have lunch at McDonald's we are returning to the real world. A round faced Shoshone teenager dressed in brown

165

polyester is behind the counter working for minimum wage like a million other such kids around the country. When we sit down my attention is seized by a hunched over gaunt man in dirty blue clothes and a blue baseball cap. His face never stops grimacing except when he sips his giant glass of water or when he pulls on his cigar. In a world by himself, he looks like a person with sticky stuff caught on the roof of his mouth, licking, licking, licking but never stopping. He has tardive dyskinesia, a disorder that comes as a result of being on large doses of major tranquilizers for several years. His is the worst case I have seen since my mental hospital days. Here in rural Wyoming, there are schizophrenics too. No place is immune. In San Francisco he would probably be on a park bench, in Wyoming he is here at McDonald's. And to finish the scene, two Indian children peer at him through the etched glass like all children do when they see a person who is funny to look at. He doesn't seem to notice either them or me. I am staring too, only I remain cool and am protected by my dark glasses.

Then on past Dubois and to the Grand Tetons. The roadside is flooded with teeming millions of blue, pink, and yellow flowers. As far as I know they only exist for the sheer beauty of it all. As we approach the Tetons, their purple jagged peaks tease the cloud bottoms. Aaron Copeland's *Appalachian Spring* hits the tympanies right at the precise moment the Grandest Teton of them all spreads itself across our windshield.

Yellowstone is eerie. There are stands of dead timber everywhere. Occasional patches seemed spared for no particular reason. In some places the grass is reappearing. In others the soil was killed by the searing heat, so the ground remains black and lifeless. It is all a part of the natural cycle — growth following death. Fire creating a mosaic on the mountainside, soon to provide new pastures for elk, deer, and bison.

Corn Moon

On the road, Montana

As we drive through the never-ending variety of mammoth hills, granite mountains, pristine valleys, tumbling streams, and golden grasslands we listen to music, eat black licorice, and drink diet pop. I see a unicorn lying in a field next to a red horse. I tell Carol, but she doesn't believe me. She is driving and doesn't have the luxury of examining the fields as we drive along. Of course unicorns are rare. She has reason to doubt me. But this sighting is clear — a solitary gray unicorn. There it was, lying in the pasture. I estimate its diminutive single horn measured about five inches long. It was located on its mid-forehead right between its ears. It was lying quietly, seemingly unaffected by the passing traffic. I doubt anybody else looked closely enough to see it was a unicorn and simply not just another horse.

I explain to Carol that I have read a book about unicorns and fancy myself well-versed in observing them. She chides me by saying that I probably believe in dragons too. Wrong question. I tell her how it is that certain flightless dragons have been thought to breathe fire. They have a rumen which has, as a byproduct of the bacterial action, the flammable gas methane. The same process occurs in occasional human flatus, thus rendering it flammable with a blue flame. When excited, the dragon clicks its teeth together and belches at the same time. The sparks of the clicking teeth ignite the methane producing a flame. Actually, I explain, there are no fire breathing dragons, they are actually fire belching.

Convinced of my expertise, Carol suggests I visit the Montessori school and teach the children what I know about both unicorns and dragons. I'll be glad to, providing she will pay my speaking fee.

waxing gibbous₁
Kalispell, Montana

As a boy I caddied to earn money. I hated the work but it was all a twelve-year-old boy in Minot could find. It left a bad taste in my mouth, carrying golf bags for rich people. We had no clearly defined minority, so those of us who had to work the most menial jobs felt like the oppressed. When I became a physician, I vowed never to own a Cadillac or belong to a country club. My sports have been more related to the out-of-doors and physical fitness than to being part of a rich elite. Now here I am vacationing with Carol's parents. Her father is a retired minister. Not part of the rich elite, he has golfed all his life and knows how to teach the game well. I have been unburdening myself of old garbage, so why not my ancient dislike of "the golf?" Today I learn how to hit the ball, rather than the ground around it. To my amazement, it often flies straight and far down the course. For once in my life I am having fun on the golf course. I am dancing with it. It? Golf, having some money, not analyzing all the time, vacationing with family.

waxing gibbous₂

Guilt has bad press. In our recent past, guilt was a primary technique for obtaining compliance and conformity in religious life. Guilt was also found to be a successful parenting technique; especially by those who detested physical violence and didn't recognize the damage of psychological violence. Little wonder, then, that psychotherapy found itself up to its armpits in unnecessary, neurosis-inducing guilt. So, with zealous agnostic enthusiasm, therapists set about freeing everybody of guilt. What we succeeded in developing was an amoral generation with empty, meaningless adult lives filled with competitive narcissism and revolving door relationships.

Guilt feels bad. That is why so many of us want to avoid it. A problem I want to understand is why guilt need always be satisfied by punishment. There is a curious eye-for-an-eye mentality persistent in the world in general and Christianity in particular.

Humans are directed to practice forgiveness, that is to let the other guy off without punishment. And in the process, we hope to experience such a treatment from God. Forgive us our trespasses as we forgive those who trespass against us. Hence I see well-meaning people forgive others in order to gain an advantage.

Little wonder that guilt has bad press, it can be so misused. Little wonder therapists have stomped out guilt wherever they find it. But I am beginning to think of the process of guilt another way. I am not interested in cheap or quick forgiveness to avoid a painful feeling or forgiveness as some sort of cosmic bargain. I am interested in guilt serving as my teacher. I am no longer seeking to distance myself from my guilt and at the same time I am not feeling hurt or pained by it as much. The wise counsel of my personal guilt can be very helpful.

---

waxing gibbous₃

Flathead River, Montana

Brother osprey. Fish hawk. What shall I call you? We enter your domain where your sentinels mark their territories along the river. There are so many of you. You must eat well, you have many children here. Fishing must be good. When you do fly, you treat us to such a display. One of you, so bold, chases a bald eagle. What a display of aerobatics. What courage! The big bird was fleeing, yet you dived on him time after time. He rolled to his back. Talons and beak directed skyward, he threatened, but you pulled up leaving him empty taloned and falling. And you chased him relentlessly till he crossed some invisible boundary and then you retreated. Thanks for the show. I think it is a rare human who has witnessed such a display.

But that is not all; within another mile, two of you engage in a second dogfight with yet another eagle. I remember how, in my past life, I thrilled to the excitement of air combat maneuvering. You do it so well. The two of you coordinate your sequenced attacks with such precision. Have you practiced this before? Do you train your young in these skills before they get their wings? You must really hate bald eagles. I hear they steal your food. Do they also harm your young?

I see that humankind has fouled your river. Along the bank are rusted auto bodies, half-submerged in the water. People say they're there to prevent erosion of the river bank. But how about the centuries before humankind had cars to use for such a purpose? The river bank seemed to do well without them. I suspect humankind is protecting the river bank from itself and what people do to the river with their power boats. I see fifty or maybe sixty of you today. You ospreys look particularly splendid when you soar above. The white diagonal markings on the underside of your wings are no accident. They are a gift for those of us who see you.

I see you dive for food, splash in and disappear. When you emerge, you shake like a wet dog as you take to flight again. Seeing how you fly so well, I know you enjoy the dance.

waxing gibbous₄

Condon, Montana

The Swan highway is an aisle through wilderness; lakes on one side, mountains on the other. We drive to the Raptor Room, an analog place dedicated to extending humankind's best effort so other creatures might experience the gift that life is. We meet two eagles, a red tail hawk, two horned owls, an american kestrel and a fawn. We only peek at a young bald eagle about to be released. We don't want him to become familiar with humans.

The most common problem bringing these birds to this hospital is collision with automobiles. The birds are attracted to the dead animals lying along the roadside. While gorging on the carrion they become victim to the fast-moving automobiles themselves. These creatures have no defense in the human world of high speed vehicles. I am most touched by Sheba. A three year old golden eagle who is blind, her retinas were detached by the impact of a car. I ask if she relates to the male eagle perched fifteen feet away. No, I don't know if she knows he is there. As she looks our way, she twists her head halfway around, staring at our sounds with unseeing eyes.

Sheba, life was a gift to you when you were born. Is it a gift anymore? Or has it been ruined? Sheba, is there any dancing left for you sitting there, sightless on your perch, not knowing your own kind perches nearby? You don't answer, but you do eat the food offered you. Is that your answer? Do you meditate? Would I live your life if offered? Maybe. I'm glad I don't need to try.

_waxing gibbous_5
Kalispell, Montana

When I was in Florida it was gardenias. Here in Montana it is raspberries. To say they are abundant is an understatement. Carol's parents have raspberries everywhere, just waiting to be picked. We eat fresh raspberries with almost every meal and Doretta prepares raspberry pie, raspberry preserves and packages of raspberries for the freezer. This morning I go out with my first cup of coffee and pick a quart of raspberries (and eat an additional pint in the process). Then I come in for a breakfast of oatmeal and raspberries. Raspberries are quintessential gift. They come off easily when ripe. If too green they won't come off. If over-ripe, they fall to the ground before you pick them. The bushes aren't thorny, so picking is no problem. Ants like raspberries too. I eat several this morning. I hear ants are good survival food if you are starving, high in fat.

Today we play more golf. Patients try to intrude into my consciousness but I don't let them. Last night, some tried to sneak in via my dreams, but I just looked for the message and then forgot them. This is vacation.

_____ *waxing gibbous₆* _____

This process of remembering my past failings, mistakes, sins, shortcomings, ego escapades, and so forth can be dangerous damn business. As each unrepressed memory emerges into consciousness, the guilt washes over me like a wave and I feel a fleeting stomach-rolling nausea. Then I try not to run away from the feeling. Instead, I stand bowed before the Eternal, naked, my sins in my hands, and say *this is me*. The reflex is to anticipate punishment or to punish myself with a most deserved depression. Yet I feel, or more accurately, I hope, this repentance process need not result in either punishment or depression.

Carol and her family have no idea that I am up to anything in particular. There is no need to drag them along, wear a long face, or otherwise involve them in what is a very private process. As far as they know, I am a happy camper learning the fine art of hitting a golf ball with the sweet spot of my club head, and not becoming angry when I fail to keep my head down for ten shots in a row.

Patients and friends who have gone through the Twelve Steps have historically had the greatest problems with this searching moral inventory. I suspect the depression and self-loathing are the hard part — enough to drive them to drink; often the very reason they drank in the first place. And then making amends, except when to do so would hurt the other person, is no picnic either. Usually, I have been careful to make my amends as I have gone along. Unfortunately that process has not always been welcomed as I had hoped. The offended parties not only wanted my amends but a pound of flesh as well. In some cases they have achieved their aim. Those events have tested me and taught me both about myself and about human nature; lessons not taught in a psychiatry residency. Amends are not always welcomed with open arms. I hope the

Eternal isn't the same as people I have known, or we are all into it up to our very armpits.

Repentance (Guy calls it a Godly sorrow over sin) is the first step of purgation, emptying myself to become open enough to be filled and illuminated. I suspect this process may last a very long time. Repentance may be more an orientation in life rather than a one-time event. But I remain genuinely frightened of the prospect of this culminating in a depression. Being a psychiatrist gives me an advantage mystics haven't had, the knowledge of brain chemistry and how depression becomes a downward spiral that feeds upon itself. Once the chemistry is badly disturbed, pulling yourself up by the bootstraps is next to impossible.

I will keep the flip side in mind:

> . . .*whatsoever things are true,*
> *whatsoever things are honest,*
> *whatsoever things are just,*
> *whatsoever things are pure,*
> *whatsoever things are lovely,*
> *whatsoever things are of good report;*
> *if there be any virtue,*
> *and if there be any praise,*
> *think on these things.*
> *Philippians 4:8*

Comment:

For those so inclined, the Portrait Journal will depart from simple psychology and enter a distinctly spiritual process. For those not so inclined, a new way of understanding will nonetheless develop. It is important to understand that your Portrait Journal will be unique to you. Though my Portrait Journal has taken this direction, it may not be the same for you.

FULL MOON

This is our last day of visiting *The Folks*. It is an interesting experience to be called *The Kids*. It makes us feel younger than our near mid-century marks. It only goes to show that age and youth are relative. We golf at Eagle Bend, a beautiful place that charges an amount corresponding to its beauty. Golf is funny, you pay for a beautiful setting and then focus your attention on this little white ball and remember the basics, hoping to hit it right. I would like to take a walk here or maybe jog. Of course, that is not permitted. I play terribly and sacrifice a few balls to the water gods. But I remember to *play* golf. I refuse to work at it.

Tonight the full moon fails to rise. The broken clouds don't help. Still an hour after scheduled moonrise, there is no moon to be seen. Finally when I check two hours later I see a half-disc of the moon as it emerges from a total eclipse. Something I have never seen before, the moon rising in full eclipse. We won't have another lunar eclipse for three years. A nice show. But I'm chilly and tired, so I go to bed, throw on an extra cover, and let the eclipse finish its display without me. There are no dog days here in Kalispell. It is almost cold. The thermometer says high forties. How cold is it? It is turn-on-the-electric-blanket-if-you're-going-to-keep-the-window-open cold.

---
waning gibbous₁

Highway 2, Montana

As soon as we leave Glacier Park, the terrain becomes flat and agricultural. We pass through towns named Cut Bank, Shelby, Havre, Chinook, Malta, Glascow, Wolf Point and Culbertson. This is a sparsely populated land, rich in wheat and barley. The harvest is in full swing. Stately combines march with military precision through the fields. We have seen no black people since leaving Colorado, but plenty of Indians though. This highway passes through numerous reservations. One place we see a funeral platform hoisted above the ground on wooden stilts. I don't know whether any person occupied it but it causes me to wonder. Why not let my body be consumed by the birds of the air and other creatures rather than encasing it in concrete or burning it. In this cycle of nature this seems so much more reasonable. I will ask about that some day. Of course, I am sure there are rules against it. What would happen to some poor person who stumbled upon you serving as dinner to a dozen crows. Anticipating that law enforcement will be spread thin, I choose to drive faster than the double nickel. Too bad. A very polite highway patrolman has me pegged with that digital gadget, a radar gun. His reading of seventy-two coincides with my speedometer. He asks for five bucks and gives me a ticket. I ask whether my insurance will find out. He says no, not to worry, but don't speed anymore. I recall as a boy that the speed limit in Montana during the day was _safe and reasonable_. He remembers it too when I mention it but it doesn't change a thing. I drop him five and leave doing fifty-five. He was friendly enough. I let Carol drive after the next town, the better to spread the wealth around. In the next fifty miles we come across two more highway patrolmen giving tickets. In Wolf Point when we stop to eat, I meet another highway patrolman in the men's room. Very friendly as well. He smiles when I mention meeting his colleague. He is eager to know who it was and speaks warmly of the guy. Along Highway 2, no place is safe from the watchful eye of the police, not even the men's room. I imagine this stretch of highway is pretty profitable. More so if they charged twenty a pop. And it would be a bargain at that price, too. There are white crosses in the ditch marking past fatal accidents. It is sobering how many people have died on a flat straight stretch of highway in the middle of nowhere.

175

Minot, North Dakota

One score and ten years ago I left this place to seek my future. Unknown ideas beckoned. I knew I must go. I had loved the land and respected many of the people. I loathed the winters and thought the rest of the people petty, backward and narrow minded. I have returned from time to time and watched the town evolve and the people age. Now with both of my parents dead, there is little to draw me back. But here I am at my thirtieth high school reunion. I expect a competitive environment where we all try to make it look as if we have arrived. Recognizing one another is a trick, but we are assisted by buttons bearing the image of some person we once seemed to have been. Some are easy to recognize, while others bear little resemblance to their former selves. It turns out that there is less competition and more curiosity: Where are you now? What do you do? Kids? Do you remember the time that . . . ?

I remember myself as an immature appearing, un-athletic kid, hovering somewhere on the periphery of the in-group; subsisting on compliments about braininess and always wanting the cute girl who would rather be with the more mature and virile athlete. The feedback was interesting. Most remembered: Braininess and a gift of gab. Some remembered the physical immaturity with peach-fuzz face and alto voice. There were girls I dated and never kissed. I asked them if they remembered those occasions when it felt to me I was stupid, awkward and slow. They remember laughter and feeling respected, happy to recall such a time. I wonder if I could enjoy such conversation with the women of my past adult relationships. Such women and I are happier steering clear of one another. It is almost as if not getting sexually involved permits such an uncluttered past that you welcome a visit any time.

Most of us were just a touch too old to get very involved in Viet Nam. The least likely of our classmates did — the artist, a man short in stature, gentle in temperament, and given to appreciating the beauty of life. He was drafted into the infantry and was among the first troops in country. What did he remember? Not much, a few snipers. Basically he succeeded in forgetting those two years of his life. The Most Likely to Succeed disappeared in East Africa many years ago. It is rumored he is dead. Some say he went crazy. None of us knows for sure.

I take time to drive around, see the old haunts: The asphalt slab where my home used to be, the hill where we parked but didn't kiss, the old high school, the park, the zoo. Carol and I walk around the periphery of uptown. It takes twelve minutes. Then we visit Marge, John Kermott's mom. Thirty years ago I was like a second son. Today as I return, she is starting her decline into terminal emphysema. John has been dead for twenty-three years, Henry for seventeen. Only Oz survives. He is teaching biology at St.Olaf. We talk and reminisce. Her once very sharp mind has lost its edge for lack of oxygen. I give her a copy of _A Laughing Place_ with page 129 highlighted where I refer to talking with her following John's death. As we talk we both know this will be our last conversation. She doesn't travel anymore and I have little reason to return to Minot again. As I depart we hug. Half laughing, half choking back tears, she tells us to be on our way or she will cry. As we drive away she is out on the lawn. She waves. I say "Good-by, Marge." Carol hears me, but Marge is too far away.

---
waning gibbous₃

waning gibbous$_3$

On the road, North Dakota

Clouds merge into a soft gray comforter spreading from horizon to horizon. We travel in silence, savoring the simple, austere beauty of the countryside — mile after mile of rolling farmland. Potholes are everywhere — _The Great North American Duck Factory._ How many years as a boy I watched those potholes and dreamed of the coming duck season. Often my dreams were partly realized, though more often the four greenhead mallards I hoped to bring home turned out to be a pair of teal and a mud hen.

More missile silos mark the thermonuclear holocaust waiting to happen. Here, concealed in the peaceful silence of wheat and barley, are dragons waiting to awaken — sleeping, waiting for Armageddon. The locals see them as boons to the chronically-struggling economy and as the patriotic way to keep the peace. It is un-American to see them as our own death as well. Don't think of them that way. If you do, you will become weak and finally turn Communist.

Rather than eating anymore licorice, I turn to sunflower seeds, the ideal addictive food for this country. We see sunflower fields everywhere. I entertain Carol by stuffing twenty in my cheek and then with tongue and tooth nimble as can be, shell them and spit the shells and swallow the seeds with a single chew.

Here and there, on strategic hilltops, are occasional ancient threshing rigs or too-old silver rusted combines. Mute monuments to the industry of a generation, they are now properly seen as art. Windbreaks stripe fields with green and gray: Pine trees, cottonwoods, Russian olives. Windbreaks exist primarily to control erosion and give snow an occasion to drift somewhere else than the highway. They are also art.

waning gibbous₄

Highway 85, South Dakota

The land is desolate. We stop at the Oasis Cafe in Buffalo for a cold drink before the seventy mile section with NO SERVICES. A cafe, a bar, and a four lane bowling alley; the Oasis has it all. The pie is homemade. Then we travel on in silence. When we turn west to Wyoming to see Devil's Tower, we again are confronted by more missile silos. Armageddon waiting. The dragon sleeps. Deer who never learned about cars lie dead along the highway, dinner for crows and magpies. We drive on to see the volcanic core that is now thrusting eight hundred feet above the surrounding forest. We walk around it, pausing to watch the young and strong scale its sheer walls. The older and obese sit with binoculars watching and commenting on the mistakes the climbers are making. Ugly teenagers walk near us, fighting with parents and belching so loudly I fear they might wake the dragon. The fire-belching dragon that sleeps nearby is not a fanciful one of my imagination, it is thermonuclear-powered and all too real. That's the problem, it's all too real and no myth. What ever happened to counting coup as a manner of warfare?

waning gibbous

Mount Rushmore is myth embodied in granite. Myths of presidents and myths of sculptors. The air is pungent with patriotism. And for the first time in my life I think I understand patriotism in its deepest sense. I have been patriotic since my earliest years, thanking God for letting me be born an American. Of late, like so many of my generation, I have been disillusioned with America's behavior and feel compelled to call her to task. Now I understand, patriotism is the passionate belief in the *ideals that underlie the formation and purpose of our country.* It's not the country itself, but its ideals: The ideals of Washington, Jefferson, Lincoln and Roosevelt; the Constitution; the Bill of Rights; the Declaration of Independence; the Emancipation Proclamation. I believe! I am a patriot and I will be one forever. Whenever the contemporary practice of our current collection of politicians or special interest groups runs counter to those ideals, I will protest. I must if I am a patriot. America is not passe. It is only coming of age. It need only remember its founding principles and start to apply them to all of earth's people, every one of them.

Next stop is the Crazy Horse Monument. Not completed, it is a private project dedicated to the ideals and spirituality of the Indians who first inhabited this magical land and then had it stolen from them. No man can look at nature with loving eyes and not feel a brotherhood with the Indian peoples. Of course today, they suffer a depression of their whole culture, stemming from the loss of everything they held dear; left instead with welfare, alcohol, and government bureaucracy. (The latter would be enough to depress anyone.) We linger long and I get lost in the bookstore. We finish with lunch of buffalo (what else?) and then drive home.

LAST QUARTER

Home

2798 miles. 108 gallons of gas. The Volkswagen served us well. Travelling by car is a special way to vacation, none of the abruptness of air travel. We had hours of semi-monotony to allow our spirits to return home as well. I remember how the Viet Nam vets suffered because of their abrupt return. Saigon to San Francisco in seventeen hours. The military should have put them on slow ships that took fourteen days to return home. If they had, we would have fewer of them in therapy today. Our spirits don't make journeys as quickly as planes do.

waning crescent₁

No dog days in Colorado — the nights are ideal for sleeping. Where we were punished by nameless winds in the spring, we are now blessed by gentle breezes. We sleep under the covers, cool and easy. The days are blue-sky clear, decorated with ice cream castle clouds and absolutely dazzling sunsets. I love the leaves on the trees, now so mature, deep green, ripe. I go for my run and once again mallards are flying eye-ball high right down the middle of the street — speeding as before and seeming to enjoy it. The geese are flying too. Not in high V's, but in low irregular strands, honking and cackling to one another. The young are becoming accomplished fliers, they cup tightly in the slow flight mode for landing. Others have even taken to a modified split S for tumbling from the sky in a near stall, only to recover a few feet above the water and land with both feet extended and tail rudder down. These are good days, warm and filled with every sort of blessing.

Carol and I dine on the back porch. This evening we are entertained by a sunset so dazzling that I am sure God squandered one of Her best just for us. As we sit fumbling for words that could somehow encompass our experience, a pair of industrious yellow jackets come to scavenge the remains of our trout dinner. For the first time in my life I see them as part of the system. They probably feel the same way I do about this evening. We watch as they wrestle a small fragment of trout free from the skin and then fly off with it. They drone around us for awhile. I don't fear being stung as I so commonly have in the past. I let them do their thing.

But all is not peace and love in our home. We are still victims of certain prejudices or passions. We have had an influx of mice recently. I am sure they have been at least as prolific as the ducks and geese. And the mice have no predators here, no cats, no dogs, no owls. We draw the line on mouse feces where we keep food and dishes. We have put out D-Con for them. Tonight the pile which we replenished for the previous two nights remains untouched. I am afraid somewhere in our walls some mice have died, stuffed with coumarin, a drug we sometimes use for heart patients. A little is good medicine. A whole meal is deadly. The mice are gone for now. Somehow poison is easier than using a trap in which we would be confronted by death with its abruptness and totality. We would have to take more responsibility for it also.

---

waning crescent₂

Purgatory is a metaphor. Being raised Lutheran and now a practicing Quaker, I have never been troubled by purgatory as a real place waiting to burn the evil out of me. But now as I contemplate purgation, I realize that purgatory is a state of being, somewhat like repentance is an ongoing approach to life. In purgatory, I purge myself of all those polluting attachments which get in my way of experiencing the underlying Reality that gives birth to all life and exists beyond death.

The word, God, is so woefully inadequate for describing the Source of our being. The more we use the word, God, the more we trivialize it. Perhaps this is what the second commandment is about. Speaking the word, God, only lulls us into an ignorant frame of mind where we trivialize God and reduce God to almost human proportions. And of course language is woefully inadequate regarding gender of God. In order to have a sense of the closeness and lovingness of God, Jesus suggested the term, Father. I don't take that to mean that God has a specific gender at all. But now we are stuck with calling God Him or Her, not liking the impersonal word, It. I will go on alternating the gender when referring to God only to remind myself that God is beyond gender.

But back to purgatory. I am now in purgatory. I am purging myself of all attachments. I am trying my best to appear before God in my primal essence. How am I doing this? In my silent time I am moving beyond guilt. Purging myself of my guilt and my shortcomings is only a part of the picture. Now I let go of being a psychiatrist, an educated man, a father, a husband, an American, a Quaker. I give up my dreams of being a great writer. I give up my hopes to travel widely and speak to large interested audiences. I give up my future, I give up my past. When I let go of all of these and stand in silence in the presence of God, I say, "Write on my soul. Let me melt into You." I surrender every expectation I have for however short a time I succeed in this meditation and then emerge with no knowledge of what has happened within me. And then through the day, I remind myself of that moment. I am not good at giving up, at surrender. I guess none of us is. But it seems clearly the way to go — a way in which God is immediately at hand, around me and in me. I remove my prejudices, mistaken projections, or whatever gets in the way of experiencing God in the present — right here — right now.

And then I return to life, a husband, a father, a psychiatrist, a writer. And I trust something is happening within me that I may not understand. I look at Nature and see a capital N.

Corn Moon

Goatheads are nasty. Unless you have direct experience with them, you probably don't care much about them. But on the Montessori playground, they are deadly. They are small weeds that fan out over the ground with fern-like leaves and subtle yellow blossoms. But underneath, look out. The goathead! Less than a centimeter in size, this hard little nubbin has several sharp points intended to help the plant procreate. Unfortunately, they stick preferentially into socks of little children and poke so severely as to make them cry. Carol has tried to pull them, hoe them, spray them; all to no avail. They only get mad and become all the worse. We survey the situation and call in professionals. Their decision: Roundup, the complete herbicide. It plays no favorites, kills everything in sight. Oh, and it will cost a couple of hundred dollars, too — all part of running a school.

Beside the goathead problem is the new carpet. The old one fell apart when threatened with another shampoo. And finally, the last straw, a number twelve bulb in the fire alarm system needs to be replaced. Only it is now obsolete. We can't find one anywhere in town. The fire code is specific, if this can't be restored to complete full *original* functioning condition, a new fully integrated system will be required . . . . to the tune of three thousand dollars. Digital obsolescence! All this for a small building with only three rooms and about twenty kids at a time. Goatheads are nasty, but digital obsolescence is nastier.

I sleep well. I dream. Most are sweet dreams, some are wonderfully metaphorical. They tell me that the warhead isn't large. Our sophistication has provided for tiny, but effective thermonuclear devices; about twice the size of a grapefruit and pointed at one end.

They operate on me, inserting a warhead from a Trident submarine into my left upper abdomen. I accept it and marvel how small it is. They are doing this for secrecy and storage. They will know where to find it in the event of war. Then I get a great idea. Everybody opposed to war needs to take one of these devices inside their bodies. Then when the time comes to use them, we simply refuse the surgery. A way to prevent Armageddon. I awake feeling pleased. There is a way out. My abdomen isn't tender, but I feel anyway to see if a warhead is there.

waning crescent₅

Purgation has become part of my silence. It is never the same process, it varies depending on what is on my mind. Today it goes like this:
Relax deeply into silence.
Breathe slowly and deeply, relaxing all my muscles.
Warm my hands, relax more deeply.
Wait awhile, experience the moment.
Experience silence.
Purgation:
I let go of today,
I let go of my worries,
I let go of my plans,
I let go of my writing,
I let go of my degrees,
I let go of my education,
I let go of my guilt,
I let go of my anger at others,
I let go of my past,
I let go of my children,
I let go of Carol,
I let go of my dreams,
I let go of my future,

184

Corn Moon

I let go of my body,
I let go of my ego,
I let go of my expectations of God.

I experience be-ing.
  Just spirit in the presence of Spirit.
  Our only connection is compassion, love.
I take time to experience this, as long as needed,
  I have let go of time, too.

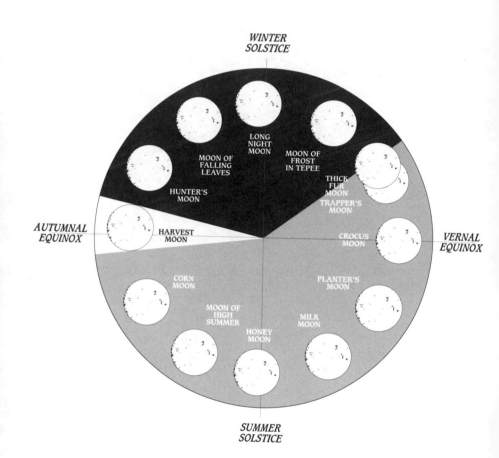

WINTER
SOLSTICE

LONG
NIGHT
MOON

MOON OF
FALLING
LEAVES

MOON OF
FROST
IN TEPEE

THICK
FUR
MOON

HUNTER'S
MOON

TRAPPER'S
MOON

AUTUMNAL
EQUINOX

HARVEST
MOON

CROCUS
MOON

VERNAL
EQUINOX

CORN
MOON

PLANTER'S
MOON

MOON OF
HIGH
SUMMER

MILK
MOON

HONEY
MOON

SUMMER
SOLSTICE

Chapter Eight

HARVEST MOON

COMMON ADULT COMPLAINTS: The summer has gone too fast. Time goes too fast. As we age, a year occupies a progressively smaller percentage of our life history and so it seems to pass more quickly. Now here it is, the Harvest Moon: The full moon closest to the fall equinox.

The days continue to speak only of summer. No birds gather in flocks. No leaves are turning. I don't count the mourning doves, so plentiful along the roadside, as birds flocking. They are just in two's and three's. I am kidding myself. It is like not wanting to get up in the morning: Just a couple of minutes more, then I will get up. Just a few more days, or weeks, and I will admit fall is starting.

The days are shorter. I watch the stunning sunsets and notice the sun is creeping southward back towards Horsetooth Rock. Perhaps I will see it juxtapose the rock this fall. I missed it last spring due to clouds. It has been wonderfully clear lately; we will see.

The mornings are ideal for jogging — cool, a light breeze, ideal. A sign of the change of season is obvious: Children line up at the school bus stop at the corner. Mothers hover nearby watching their first graders, partly to see that they get on the bus safely, partly to savor this brief vignette, a bittersweet moment of life. Some hold video cameras to save the images for the future. Of course when the future gets here, video tape will be obsolete. Only twenty years ago, I caught my children on super-eight movie film, and now it has gone the way of the DoDo bird.

Fall is my favorite time of year — ideal weather, wonderful colors and aromas, and sports of every outdoor variety. It is a time of anticipation; the completion of Nature's cycle and the beginning of human cycles, e.g. school. The psychiatry business usually picks up a little, now that people are finished with the summer entertainment. It is a time for more mood swings in the manic depressive population. But overall, depression is not as prevalent; not like the spring equinox when depression reigns with its tyrannical drive towards self-destruction.

waxing crescent₁

All drugs are not created equal. Some are safer than others. Some are popular. Some are not. They have a place, even the odd ones. The art of medicine is knowing the time and place to use even marginal and sometimes risky drugs. Many physicians simply avoid marginal drugs and stick with the tried and true, thus depriving their patients with the most difficult problems a chance at recovery. In psychiatry the most scary drugs are a group of antidepressants called the monoamine oxidase inhibitors (MAO-I's for short). They frightened me when I learned of them because of their potential interaction with other substances, both foods and medicine. But in my desire to help those unfortunate few who fail with conventional therapy, I have tried my hand with MAO-I's. And they have often caused worse problems than they solved. Worst of all, I have been

188

a victim of malpractice litigation because of their side effects. Most doctors never admit to malpractice suits. They would rather talk of the devil himself, necrophilia, or even their income tax, but never their personal malpractice suit. Such talk is always in the abstract and liberally sprinkled with epithets regarding lawyers. In any case, D* is still struggling on the edge of suicide. She has failed with hospitalization, intensive therapy and a whole host of different medications. Friends and support group are in place, but she is tortured by depression, panic and a deep nameless terror. Despite my past failures and real fear of MAO-I's, today I have started her on one. I feel unsophisticated, childlike, and more dependent on Heaven.

waxing crescent$_2$

What a wonderful name for a place to live, Love-land. Just down the road from us is the Sweetheart City, a place that loves to send valentines. But a name is just a name. To our high school football team, they are the adversary, the team to beat at the start of the season. Birds may not be flocking yet, but people are. They are flocking to the football field. Tonight, Fall starts, the first high school football game of the year pits Fort Collins against Loveland. For the past four years Carol and I have had sons playing on the team. Tonight we go for the nostalgia. We are fans. We dance. Not as intense as the pros or as colorful as college, high school football offers us a chance to see old friends and watch their children play. Ex-montessori students are here and there. They don't recognize Carol, but she recognizes them.

We win tonight, the first time in four years. But the victory is marred by a Loveland player who doesn't get up after a play. I predict he'll be up in a moment. But no, he lays motionless. The ambulance comes, picks him up on a rigid board, and then drives off slowly, too slowly. We don't want that. Nobody does. We only want to win a game. We want to see old friends and their children. We want to hear the band, watch the cheerleaders, and eat some pop corn. We don't want to see any boy hurt. Especially we don't want to see any boy not move. Tomorrow we will read the paper to find out how serious his injuries are.

Fort Collins wins. We drive home, welcoming the fall, but in the back of our minds we wonder what happened. Will he be all right?

waxing crescent₄

Ben died. He was seventy-three as I figure it. When he was young, his face was disfigured by a terrible infection. Yet he remained outgoing, robust and even a bit aggressive. I often thought he was too protective of his family, especially the way he reacted to the sounds of fireworks on the Fourth of July. His last years were marred by an undiagnosed neurological disease that made it hard for him to walk straight. Near the end, he had to ask for help just to stand up or go out in the yard. He was stone deaf too. That made conversation very hard, though fortunately he was never prone to being paranoid as often occurs when one becomes deaf. Ron was going to put him down on Tuesday. It was going to be very hard to do, but Ben was failing so badly. Then, in Ben's own special way, he walked out in the yard by himself on Monday afternoon and lay down quietly and died. It is as if he knew what was coming and he wanted to spare his family the anguish. Maybe he wasn't too overprotective after all.

Comment:

Something as common at the death of a friend's pet has meaning for your life. Not just when writing your Portrait Journal, but every day. The journal process makes you focus and reflect. In the common and ordinary, the marrow of life is found.

Harvest Moon

waxing crescent₅

D* is back in the hospital. Suicide demons were demanding their due. So while we are waiting for the MAO-I's to kick in, I explain to the hospital that she has no money. They understand and agree to minimize her charges. As they say in the health care industry, the costs of her care will be shifted to those who can pay for their hospitalizations. While at the hospital, I check on the boy injured in the football game. He went home; a bruised spinal cord they say. He will play again.

waxing crescent₆

Dr. Osler thinks he has broken the law. He calls asking my opinion. It is one of those ethical dilemmas suggested but not discussed in medical school. His patient came to see him over a year ago complaining that she kept hearing the word *devil* in her mind ever since she got high on pot.

Her complex history started long before. Like so many women who present for therapy, her problems started with sexual abuse by an adult male when she was five. Of course, being "a good little girl," she never told anyone. At fourteen she acquired an abusive boyfriend who held guns on her, forced intercourse and finally impregnated her. When the pregnancy was discovered, he disappeared. Then, all alone, she went for an abortion. Her years thereafter were consumed with obsessions and compulsions: Endless hand washing and bizarre counting rituals, pulling out her hair a strand at a time, checking curling irons and stove burners ten times to make sure they were off. She managed to graduate from college, but then succumbed to this latest obsession. She failed at her career and returned home, convinced her only hope was to commit suicide. Dr. Osler tried all the conventional therapies including psychotherapy, hypnosis, antidepressants, electro-convulsive therapy, and long term hospitalizations. She remained a basket case.

191

As a last resort, Dr. Osler discussed a drug with her family which is available in most of the rest of the world and is specific for obsessive compulsive disorder (OCD). But our FDA is slow and painstakingly methodical. The drug company decided not to fight the battle in the U.S., assuming the demand for it would be low and the profit meager. Now, however, it is clear how prevalent OCD is and the company is scurrying about to get it licensed. The young woman is penniless now, her funds depleted by her past care. To get in on the humanitarian program to obtain the drug legally would cost her a minimum of three thousand dollars and numerous trips of several hundred miles every week to be tested. So her family went to Mexico and obtained the drug. Dr. Osler supervised her receiving it and low and behold, she has dramatically improved. She is back at work and ninety percent symptom free. Unfortunately, two weeks ago, the family's contact said no more medicine. It is too dangerous to get it across the border. So they faced the prospect of the OCD recurring. That is when Dr. Osler decided to break the law. He called a doctor in Canada, explained the situation, and now is obtaining the drug and seeing that his patient gets it. He realizes he is breaking the law. His question was if I would do the same thing in his shoes.

FIRST QUARTER

Forrest's uncle got married. Forrest, being forty-one moons old, was ideal for the ring-bearer. He is cute, outgoing and a bit of a ham. At the rehearsal dinner he was overcome with excitement so his nanna had to teach him some rules. When the preacher talks, everybody has to be very quiet and listen. At dessert, Forrest stood on his chair, gestured for everyone to listen to him, and announced in a serious tone of voice, "Listen everyone, listen. When the alien starts talking you all have to be quiet."

Needless to say, the group was amused and a bit confused. Nanna asked, "Where did you hear that, Forrest?"

Disgusted, he said she had told him only a couple minutes ago, "When the *creature* talks everybody has to listen."

Comment:
There is nothing like the wonderful quotations of a child to keep you from getting too serious. If you don't have your own children in your life, borrow some.

waxing gibbous[1]

I awaken to cool clouds and thunderous rumbling in the distance as if a mountain giant has indigestion. Gradually, the thunder and lightening draw closer. By the time the coffee is brewed we experience a full blown spring thundershower. The day is cool and wet. We turn the heat on and don warmer clothes for the first time this fall.

The morning offers me a chance to do something I do well, but loathe: Testify in court. I spend two and a half hours on the stand as an expert witness. Thankfully, I am not a defendant.

Finished with court, I eat my brown bag lunch in the office and spend the afternoon seeing folks. I am particularly disturbed by the first visit of a Viet Nam vet whose non-verbal expression clearly communicates his disgust at psychiatry. In fact, he looks like he would like to murder someone, any one, except he knows he would end up in jail. He drank a six-pack before coming in and glowers in stony silence for the first half of the session. I admit I am scared of him and then reminisce about my times in the Marine Corps back during Viet Nam. He softens enough to curse society and anyone who never served in the military. He blames Viet Nam for all his problems. I inquire about his life before he went to war. He says it was never-ending parties. Booze? Of course, what's a party without booze? Fights? Of course, all teenage boys fight when they get drunk. I ask if he thinks he is alcoholic. No, he only drinks to relax. I tell him I think he is alcoholic. He defiantly shuts up and glowers

193

the rest of the hour. I ask why he is here. He pops his wife when she doesn't mind him; after all he is the primary authority in the house. The kids? They fight all the time too. They drink a little too, but all teenage boys do that. I agree to see him three times if he would like. He says he'll return; he's not scared of anybody. I tell him I might not be able to help him. He smiles a jackal smile and departs saying his wife will pay the bill; it was her idea to come. The last person I met like him is in prison for attempting to murder his therapist.

waxing gibbous₂

On my morning jogs this past week I have been swarmed by gnats. On the far side of Warren they are so thick they get in my nose, eyes, mouth and stick to my perspiring body. Where's a gnatcatcher when you need one? But now the weather is changing, the rain continues and it is cool enough to demand a warm-up suit on a run. The honey locusts are the first trees to express the fall; most are very yellow and even beginning to shed a few leaves. The highest boughs of the cottonwoods show yellow patches and our vine maple in the front yard is reddening up a bit.

On the back porch a small nighthawk has taken up residence. Sitting motionless all day, he looks as if he is meditating. There is little reason to be active, the cool wetness has cut down on the flying bug population. His gray feathery body contrasts with the wet redwood planks. I pause to look at him, wondering if we will see much of him in the coming days. I hope so. He could teach me a great deal about meditation.

waxing gibbous₃

I am amused by how ingrained habits become. When I was a boy, I learned that if I was going to be a good citizen in a democracy,

I had to stay informed about current events, both local and national. So I dutifully read the morning paper every day, I listen to the news on NPR every morning and evening. And I check out a news magazine from time to time. OK, so I am a good citizen, but what does the morning barrage of bombings in Lebanon, drug wars, murders, stock market fluctuations, hostage-taking and airline disasters do for me? They jade my thinking. They depress me. They invite me to hopelessness. They crowd out my time for contemplation. The news is like a cowbird egg. Once hatched it kicks the songbirds out of the nest and starves the parent in its demands for nourishment.

Now I awaken to the clock radio to check on the time and local weather. Then I turn the radio off and go downstairs for breakfast. I bring the morning paper in and set it aside. I don't have to read it right now just because it is here. I put on some meditative music and mindfully go about breakfast preparations. I reflect on all the hands that labored to get the food to me. I look out upon the morning and study the sky, the birds, the foothills and my own inner landscape. Carol and I talk quietly over breakfast and I feel peace fill me for the day. I follow that with prayer and if time permits, a run and some writing.

It is interesting how much better a therapist I am when I start my day this way. It is interesting how much more love I have available to share with the world. It is interesting how everything seems to take on a simpler perspective. It is soothing how much peace follows me through the day. I think I may be a better citizen of a democracy this way. I can read the news in the evening when my workday is over.

Comment:
Your Portrait Journal may bring enough awareness to your life that you will begin to change habits — some habits you didn't even know you had, until you look carefully at your life.

195

waxing gibbous₄

If you draw a line straight east from Horsetooth Rock, it goes down Horsetooth Road, about a couple of blocks north of my house. So now, I look out my bedroom window and see the sun set right behind the rock. A couple of days ago the sun was setting a finger's breadth to the north of the rock. And now we have had four days of rain. I think I have missed my sighting. This morning we are greeted not by more rain, but by snow. Here we are, still officially in summer. But for all intents and purposes, if you look outside, it is winter. The vast majority of the leaves haven't even started changing. I hope it doesn't get so cold that the leaves simply fall without showing us their best colors. Don't judge. Dance with it.

Get out the herringbone jackets, start a fire in the fireplace, and enjoy some homemade chili. This cold snap too will change in a couple of days. As the Buddhists say, the only thing certain in life is impermanence. I will simply have to move my point of observation around to see the sun set behind Horsetooth. I sympathize with ancient astronomers who waited a year at Stonehenge or at a pyramid for some special celestial event, only to be put off by clouds.

waxing gibbous₆

I sleep well; some dreams sweet, some dreams not-so-sweet. I awaken to clear skies and frost on our once-again-emerald-green lawn. The day warms quickly as I voyage down to see Mary Luke. Cloudless, crystal blue skies above snow-dusted mountains delight me. But, more striking than the view, is a dream looming at the edge of my consciousness, demanding I share it, demanding I write it.

Scenes flash on the screen of my mind. John, as a little boy, broke a bone in his foot and, oh, how he cried. It hurt so very much. A couple years ago, Carol broke her hand. Though she didn't cry, it hurt most exquisitely. Then I see Nazi soldiers breaking hands of musicians whose crime is being Jewish. I have treated many broken hand bones, metacarpals — tender, very tender.

And then, in some mystical way I am with a dear friend. A loving young man, a teacher who only wants people to let go of their attachments, whether they be wealth, fame, or bigoted religious convictions. He only wants love to spread further than our own kind, beyond our own country, beyond our own religious beliefs, beyond our own color. He wants love to spread everywhere, for without it, our species will die at its own hand, our planet will become a waste land. He has a simple message: Admit your shortcomings, God is right here, even inside of you. But deaf ears and arguing factions misconstrue his teachings to their own ends.

And now they drive huge, rough iron nails through his hands. Each nail crushes two metacarpals — tender, so very tender. And then his feet too. They drive a single huge nail high up on his instep, through the bones of each foot and into the wood. Then the wooden structure is raised and his weight pulls on the fractured bones, each fragment screaming with agony. Breathing comes so very hard; the weight of his body pressing the scapulae and compressing his rib cage, suffocating him. Every breath pulls at the wounds, more pain. But not to breathe is to die and so some deep reflex demands breathing as long as possible, regardless of the pain. I not only observe, I feel with him. I am with him and outside of him at the same time.

Support yourself, partially on the nail through the feet for just a few minutes, breathe more easily. When will it be over?! Crowds and faces press in, some jeering, some crying. Mumble, pray, escape, but no . . . you must stay here with the pain and await death, too slow in coming. You are so innocent. Only love you taught. Not pain. Not violence. Only love. Healing, a few miracles, even some wedding wine. Finally your senses dim. Death welcomes you. The strangers on either side are taking too long to die, so the soldiers crush their tibias with blows from rough wooden clubs. There, they will not support themselves on their feet any more. No more room to breathe, they will suffocate in a couple minutes. But you? They

197

are unsure about you. Not supporting yourself with your feet, but are you still breathing? To speed the process along, they stab a spear into your upper mid abdomen, piercing your stomach. The water you sipped through the day to soothe your cotton dry mouth pours out with a little blood and you feel nothing any more. It is finished.

They just don't understand, do they? Not then. Not now. They don't understand. In other faces, in other places, for other reasons, they continue to practice violence fueled by religious bigotry and fear of differences. Teach love. Teach compassion. That is the only way. Teach love and compassion for all; not just our country, our color, our religion, *but for ALL.*

He is gone. Alone, but not really alone, I feel very heavy . . . very sad. Yet I feel as if he, free of attachments, continues to be. And I feel very honored to be given such a dream.

I tell Mary Luke my dream and she tells me that today is the Feast of the Holy Cross. I never knew that. Not being Catholic, I don't follow those sorts of things.

Comment:

Dreams that break in on you demonstrate the participation of your unconscious mind in your Portrait Journal. Such dreams are gifts; perhaps they are the closest moments you will experience of the Transcendent speaking in your life.

---

waning gibbous₁

The step beyond purgation is illumination. Having freed yourself of attachments, fears, guilts, and expectations, you are ready to be filled. The glass needs to be emptied of water before it is filled with wine. In silence I become empty and then after a long time (I don't know how long, time is not linear in silence) the wish rises within me: Make me a more loving person. The wish becomes an ocean and I immerse myself. I go beneath the surface trusting I can breathe. I don't think about what is happening. I don't anticipate.

I don't analyze. I don't wonder how I am doing. I simply exist in The Great Sea of Silence and breathe the wish to love well, to remain empty and free of attachments.

This transformation won't be complete any time in the immediate future. It will take time to season. I will repeat the process of purgation over and over again, perhaps daily. It's not something you do once and then are done with. But time is something I have, a whole life worth. And in the meantime I have so many gifts to enjoy.

The full Harvest Moon rises over the high school football field where we watch the young people dance with life. We are warm, comfortable, and involved. This is living. The fullness of a season, good friends, my soul's companion by my side, and a quiet conviction that I am on the right path.

waning gibbous₂

I awaken to Bach's B Minor Mass. It is First Day (in the Quaker vernacular). Sunday to the rest of the English speaking world. Today I partake in a different sort of harvest. There are many crops to be harvested at many different times; calling this the Harvest Moon made sense when only one or two crops prevailed. But nowadays with our varied food sources, harvest has been going on since the Moon of High Summer and will continue well into the Hunter's Moon.

Colleen invites me to help with her honey harvest. So I drive to her place out in the country. On my way there, I pass through Severance, past Bruce's Bar. It is a bit of a task, the road is blocked by about two hundred Harley Davidson Motorcycle riders sporting black leather pants, large stomachs and black tee shirts. They drink beer as women walk about in small leather bras exposing colorful tatoos on their shoulder blades. Driving through the sea of bodies in my VW reminds me how birds must feel to be the guest of honor at a turkey shoot.

199

At the farm, I don a white bee suit and enter into the process. It is scary standing there with about twenty thousand bees swarming around your head (not unlike driving through Severance just now). I know they aren't supposed to sting, but it seems to require the same kind of faith; the kind when you first fly in an airplane, your intuition says you should fall. My intuition says there must be a secret passage into my suit and at any moment I will be attacked and punished for my thieving ways. We lift out white wooden racks laden with honey. Once in the house, we unceremoniously remove the last few bees with the vacuum cleaner. Then we use a hot knife to cut the caps off each comb and then extract the honey in a big centrifuge. Finally the reward, catching the fresh honey as it comes out and licking it off our fingers. It doesn't get any better than this.

waning gibbous₃

Summer has reasserted itself. The snow of a week ago is a bad dream. The trees kept their leaves and a slow color change is starting. Again the day is crystal blue, clear and warm. On my run this morning, I watch the gibbous moon suspended in the blue western sky. Amazingly, it is setting two fist-breadths north of Horsetooth. That moon certainly has a mind of its own. Darned if it will follow the sun in its measured and predictable path. The moon is like my unconscious. It stays close, but listens to a different drummer. At home I am delighted to find some late appearing strawberries. There are just a few, so I sit in the patch and eat them right off the plant. It doesn't get any better than this.

waning gibbous₄

The answering service has an unsettling message for me, an anonymous female voice just called and said Dr. Hageseth needs to go to his office immediately. But it's early morning, nobody should be there. This is my time for silence and writing. What's happening? Why do I need to be there? And why an anonymous voice? I admit to Carol I feel more than a bit unsettled. Will I discover a body there? Is some violent family member from some past abuse case waiting to get me? Carol is concerned too and so we drive over in separate cars. I consider calling the police, just in case, but then decide not to get so theatrical.

What do I discover? Toilet paper, everywhere; on the trees, the shrubs, the walks, the parking lot, everywhere. I've been *TeePeed*. There is a big cardboard sign on the door: "Thank you for saving my life. I've decided to lighten up and live a little." And it is signed, R*.

---
waning gibbous₅

The Great I AM uttered a word, or some such metaphorical act, and the Big Bang banged. His knowledge so total that each microsecond's intimacy was known. In the process, I AM created time and space as boundaries to creation and, as their Creator, exists unencumbered by neither one.

Better to be nameless, than to be reduced to a mental construct, a linguistic convenience for the projections of human minds. Yet we fumble with words like God, Universal Spirit, Yahweh, Allah and then foolishly argue among ourselves. No word encompasses. No gender suffices. No culture has exclusive rights. But still we venture discourse to gain understanding, to grow in wisdom, perhaps to experience the I AM more completely, more personally. I find using different words for the single Creator keeps my consciousness aware that no word really suffices.

Today, here in this chair, *God is* — within me and everywhere I am not, at this moment and at all other moments as well. That makes sense, considering that time and space are irrelevant to Him. At least our minds, limited as they are, have evolved to acknowledge that God is not an old man, far away in some distant sky.

201

If I quiet myself, let go of my attachments, and then wait in the Presence, uttering only a simple *yes*, I believe God will mold me to express Her more clearly here in this time and place. I have the freedom to ignore God; even to say no. Our evolution from this point in human history hinges on more people sitting in silence, letting go of all attachments and saying yes — a *yes* that ascends in the great ocean of Silence and swells angelic choruses singing Hallelujah. Or so they say Way To Go?

Why do I do this? Why do I contemplate, seek, pray? I don't know. I was called, I guess. And when I become quiet, when I say yes, something very right happens. And it is not hypnosis or biofeedback; I have experienced both and this is radically different. And it is not psychosis; I know that subject well. I know there is no separation, no distance between my Origin and myself. That idea, once an abstraction, has become an experience. I can't say I worship Allah. I do recognize His great magnitude: Infinity compared to some tiny minute fraction. And in that recognition, I experience awe. Maybe that is what worship is, I don't know. I exist solely at Her pleasure. I choose to say yes, not to gain favor, not to gain heaven. I simply say yes as a lover responds to the call of the Beloved.

I look back at my fear of death a few moons ago and I smile. It was necessary, I guess. Who knows? I will probably walk over that path again.

waning gibbous$_6$

Autumnal Equinox

The dawn, quiet. Low clouds muffle the sun. The morning darkness suggests we lie in bed a bit longer. We are rising before the sun now. It changes how you feel when you feel you have to get going before the sun does. To influence how I will feel, I am beginning to practice a pleasant Buddhist technique. On awakening, I become mindful and offer my attention to the Great All and smile; not just a half smile, but one that twinkles, that gives me crow's feet.

202

My morning jog takes me by the junior high school. The kids going out to the athletic fields wave and a couple even invite me to join. I decline saying they are too fast for me. The lindens, the honey locusts and a few green ash are painting a pretty scene, presenting bright yellow and bright green leaves on the same tree. In one case, the leaves almost alternate throughout the whole tree.

On my return, I harvest the plum crop from our single dwarf plum tree. I wipe some of the dusty purple fruit with my sweaty shirt and eat them on the spot. And then I smile. Gift. Thanks.

The disappointment of the equinox is that standing on Horsetooth Road and looking up to the rock at sunset does not give the juxtaposition I had hoped for, the sun is already a fist-breadth south of the rock. Either I am not due east or there is something I don't understand about this whole idea. Now I have to wait for the vernal equinox again. I hope it isn't as cloudy next year as it was this past spring.

LAST QUARTER

Rabbi Bob calls. His news: They don't want us on the show. For the last four moons I have waited to hear whether *The Phil Donahue Show* wanted Rabbi Bob, the Reformed Rabbi turned stand-up comic, and me, the psychiatric humorist, to present a program on positive humor. Seemed like a great idea to me; not to mention an ideal opportunity to publicize *A Laughing Place*. But no, our proposal was too up-beat. Bob suggests they wanted a group of hermaphrodite wife beaters to keep their ratings up.

I confess I was looking forward to making entries in the Journal about my appearance in New York City. I thought it would be a nice contrast. Well, real life is happening; no big time in the Big Apple. Little wonder our world is spiritually bankrupt. Rather than celebrating love and laughter, the common mind wants to be titillated by the extremes of human pathology; not unlike the crowds in Rome going to the Coliseum to watch the gladiators duel to the death. I think it is possible to get very distanced from the common mind as I live my life appreciating Nature, reading books, praying and teaching people how to love and laugh.

waning crescent₂

I have not been faithful in appreciating this particular lunar phase. I seem to have overlooked that the moon can be watched in the daytime too. In the morning, after my breakfast and silent time, I go out and look up and _voila_, there it is: A perfect crescent moon about half a heaven away. Its rounded porcelain shoulder gestures back to the sun. Contemplating the crescent moon in the blue daytime sky presents a wonderful aesthetic experience, one more subtle, one needing more care than studying it in the black nighttime sky.

waning crescent₃

Ever since my crucifixion dream, I have been troubled by dreams of dreadful boredom or disquieting ridicule. Last night hyenas came after me, chasing me from sleep. I awaken with pounding heart. In spite of thinking in an optimistic and even joyful way, in spite of remembering to smile and twinkle; my mood is somewhat down, one that I would like to change. Or better yet, understand and then change. I preach against what I call _the tyranny of feelings_. There are more guides to my understanding than my feelings alone. Where, in past generations, feelings used to be ignored and were forced to live underground, causing great upheavals from the subterranean unconscious, nowadays they cause great turbulence on the surface consciousness, existing in full view for all to see. Feelings are one important barometer of how we interpret life, but only one. Thinking, behavior, feedback from others, and successes and failures all guide my interpretation of life. I caution my patients with biological depressions that their feelings are not accurate guides to reality. They must rely on other data to assess their lives, not their feelings which are chemically distorted. My thoughts are positive, my behavior directed to right living, my feedback from colleagues, patients and family is good, and my future is bright. But my mood is down, my dreams uninspiring or even frightening. All I can do is watch my mood, take time to understand my unfolding life. I will draw no conclusions yet. I will take my time.

Comment:
When you watch yourself closely you will discover that your mood changes independent of outside events. There is an internal cycling to our moods. This is useful information for those people who look about seeking some outside person or event to blame their bad mood on.

waning crescent₅

D* has overdosed again. This time her intent wasn't to end her life, rather it was to challenge the medication — just how sick would it make her? Suicide has a younger demon-in-training named self-mutilation. But the MAO-I is a dangerous drug, not one to be trifled with. She has been very sick with tremulousness, nausea, weakness and marked sleepiness. Has she learned? Perhaps. For my part, I intend to make this lesson one that sticks. If she abuses any drugs I give her I will be forced to refer her to the state hospital. She seems to like the limit-setting and agrees, even asking to sign a contract. And to be doubly sure, I now dispense her medication one day at a time. It is still touch and go.

This harvest time provides unique payments from my several non-paying patients: Vegetables. Several folks are so disabled that they cannot work outside the home. Their garden is therapy, a job and an economic necessity. At this time of year I have lots of tomatoes, green peppers, corn, carrots and especially zucchini. I believe the secret to solving our energy crisis is zucchini. Take that vegetable that grows from carrot-sized to watermelon-sized overnight and turn it into gasoline. *Voila*, no more fuel shortage. In fact, they are issuing warnings in the newspaper never to leave your car unlocked at this time of year; if you do, you may come back to find somebody has filled your back seat with zucchini.

I find the payment-in-vegetables arrangement more satisfying than relying on Medicaid. For years, I participated in that bureaucratic nightmare. The forms on which we submitted billings were always changing and if you made a single mistake, it was kicked back to you two months later. When you resubmitted it, they said it was too late to claim payment. And then they arbitrarily reduced your fees, covertly suggesting that you had fraudulently billed for excessive services. Finally, the payments were late and almost every year they ran out of money. I decided to provide medicaid on my own. After all, the cost of billing almost equalled what I earned from them. So now I see a number of patients for vegetables or whatever else they can pay. I get the drug companies to supply me with a liberal number of drug samples and then supply them to my economically deprived patients. Medicaid is too digital for me. Every person and every transaction is reduced to a number. No thanks. I choose my analog way, I will give my services to whom I please. Anyway, I need the zucchini.

waning crescent₆

Phoenix, Arizona

It appears I visit here around each equinox. Last time it was spring and Easter, the vernal equinox. Now it's fall and football season, and the autumnal equinox. I take time to see the boys. I go to classes with them, help them shop for new underwear, watch as they get gussied-up for a formal, and I drink beer with their fraternity brothers. We go to football games and once again I feel some of the comraderie of my own college days. But much has changed. The talk now is of safe sex. The talk when I was young was sex or no sex.

206

Now the girls reserve rooms at a local hotel for after the formal. When I was young the girls had to be checked into the dorms by two a.m. Now the five-year-plan is the rule. Back then the draft hovered over our heads precluding any leisurely semesters off. In some respects these young people are less mature; in some ways more worldly and experienced. I don't know what it all adds up to for their futures. I think I better reserve the all-too-easy snap judgement and watch what they do with their world. I do worry about young people's materialism and seeming obliviousness to matters beyond their own immediate world. I avoid preaching. But I do offer my reflections on the need for more contemplative time, the value of silence and solitude, appreciating the gift that life is, and the importance of consistently following a spiritual path. They listen politely, even respectfully. They are fine young men. I content myself with planting some seeds and modeling an analog life in this digital world.

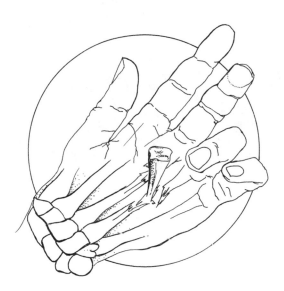

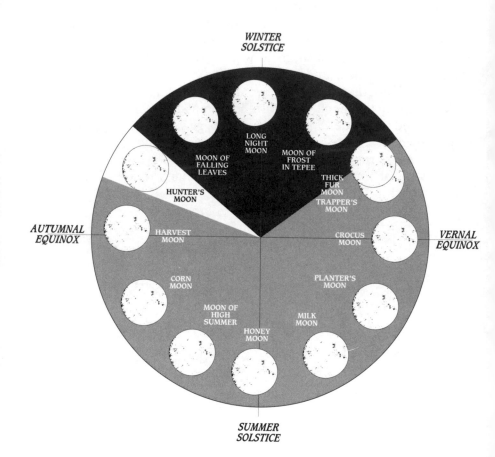

WINTER
SOLSTICE

LONG
NIGHT
MOON

MOON OF
FALLING
LEAVES

MOON OF
FROST
IN TEPEE

HUNTER'S
MOON

THICK
FUR
MOON

TRAPPER'S
MOON

AUTUMNAL
EQUINOX

HARVEST
MOON

CROCUS
MOON

VERNAL
EQUINOX

CORN
MOON

PLANTER'S
MOON

MOON OF
HIGH
SUMMER

MILK
MOON

HONEY
MOON

SUMMER
SOLSTICE

Chapter Nine

HUNTER'S MOON

Home

WHEN I WAS EIGHT, my father introduced me to an experience which radically altered my life. To the urban mind the event may seem callous, barbarian, violent. To the rural mind the event is ordinary, just the thing any father would share with his son. When I was eight, my father took me hunting.

He carried an old twenty-two pump in his car. Gophers weren't plentiful that Sunday afternoon, so we shot some empty beer cans. When I held the rifle, when I pulled the trigger, when I watched the tin — not aluminum — can flip, I felt a power never experienced before in my life.

Growing up in my family had been difficult for all of us, principally because of my mother's very real mental illness and her very imaginary physical illnesses. She constantly threatened us with her death from heart disease. She passed her time lying on the sofa with a headache, often in a morphine induced stupor. She was finally committed to the state mental hospital after attempting to shoot my friend's father with a shotgun; though actually she knew not a whit about guns or shooting. Dad saw that she remained appropriately ignorant. But Dad was a travelling salesman and was often gone a week at a time. That left us at home alone to contend with Mom.

A rage grew within me; one that had no acceptable means of expression. And then Dad let me shoot the twenty-two and I felt strong; I felt a release. Under the influence of the frontier, nature-is-ours-to-dominate mentality, it was an appropriate sublimation to re-direct angry impulses at crows, blackbirds, gophers, rabbits, (they ate our crops); foxes, coyotes, hawks (they ate our chickens); ducks, geese, partridge, grouse, pheasants, rabbits, and deer (they were our food). The government provided bounties for foxes, coyotes, and certain hawks. At one time pennies were offered for gopher tails. So with a frontier sense of righteousness, I displaced my hostilities and grew up hunting North Dakota's prairies and wetlands.

Not exactly a party animal in high school, I found myself drawn to the solitude of the plains more than the roughness of teenage competition. My best friendships were forged out in the country. I grew to appreciate the stark visual beauty of plains and marsh. I picked up a camera and began shooting in a different way. My deepest insights came when I was alone or with John. My passion for hunting also transformed into a love for dogs as I trained Midge, my runty labrador, to flush birds and retrieve them. I experienced a special joy then; one I have rarely recaptured in my adult life.

But something nagged me, something didn't seem right. Coming home from a hunting trip, I often had headaches. I somehow needed to block out the reality of killing to continue hunting. Redirected rage no longer fueled my passion. I found, instead, a love for the animals I pursued and guilt for causing their deaths. A love grew for all of Nature, a reality which became a proper, not a common, noun. I asked my pastor about the morality of hunting, about the commandment *Thou Shalt Not Kill*. He assured me the commandment only applied to human beings. And only to those with whom we weren't at war. Otherwise, the earth was ours to have dominion over, including the beasts of the land and the birds of the air. I was not to feel guilty.

I went to college and my days of hunting ceased. Life was too busy to allow for thoughts of the out-of-doors, let alone actual time for hunting. Yet I could hardly tolerate the congestion of eastern cities and their urban social problems. I longed for open land and simpler ways, but my intellect was being fed a different diet. When I returned to my rural roots, I was disappointed to find no kinship there either. The ultra-conservative attitudes, unquestioning pseudo-patriotism, and the raw callousness towards Nature left me with almost no place to call home.

Later in life, I tried to introduce my sons to the joys of hunting. I doubt I succeeded. Though each has bagged his own big game animals under my careful tutelage, I doubt either has any passion for hunting. I doubt they will ever be hunters. It is just as well. No person should ever be forced to hunt.

But the headaches I felt as a boy continue in the form of doubts about the rightness of taking any life at all. I cannot hunt unless I come to terms with taking life. The ethics concerning wildlife have changed so greatly. No longer are there bounties paid for so-called predators. Better there should be a balance as originally ordained. Better such a balance than the disequilibrium caused by killing those creatures seen to compete with us.

The wolf was perceived to be a terrible threat. So people massacred wolves, pushing them to the point of extinction. There are no wolves left in the lower forty-eight states. No wolves free to roam and sing at the moon. In the past, cougars and bears have been on our hit list, too. But now they are being seen in a different light. No more pennies for gopher tails. Even crows are seen to function as valuable carrion eaters. Much has changed.

Joseph Campbell suggests three elemental human bioenergies: The need to survive, which means living off other life; the drive to procreate (little needs to be said about that); and, if history is any guide, a drive to dominate, to pillage and destroy.

Clearly, hunting started out manifesting the first bioenergy, the need to survive. Until very recently our ancestors relied on hunting for a large bulk of their food. A hunter in Native American villages was respected as a good provider. But with the dominance of technology, hunting has become for too many Americans an expression of the need to destroy, to pillage, and to dominate. It provides a convenient outlet for aggression — hence so many red-necked hunters; men who equate the gun with freedom and The American Way, and who spend a substantial amount of time hating Communists and itching for the day they can get one in their gun sights. In the meantime, deer will have to do. And the food is too often wasted. The animal frequently is relegated to a locker to succumb to freezer burn and then be discarded.

Campbell suggests another bioenergy, weak in its first manifestation and carefully modulated by one's culture and religion: *Compassion*. It can be a threat to a culture. What if we develop compassion for Communists, Arabs, Indians or other *"savages?"* Compassion starts in the loving bond between mother and child and grows to love of family and finally loyalty to tribe or country. It becomes risky when it starts to spread to all people and even to all creatures on the face of the earth. After all, look at the hopeless mess of the Hindu cultures.

But my analog strivings pull me toward compassion for the All, and I must answer for my passion for hunting. What will I do? Will I continue or will I quit? In my compassion for all creatures must I then become vegetarian? It may be the only ethical response. After all, meat doesn't come from grocery stores, it comes from animals, killed by people to whom we pay a union wage to act as executioners in our behalf.

It is the new moon. I have anticipated this moon, knowing my reflections would confront my life habits here. The fall continues to be slow moving, giving me time to reflect on this topic, giving me time to decide about hunting and my willingness to grow in compassion. Fall has always been special for me. It was fall when Dad first put a gun in my hands. That act created a special bond between us and with it a special bond forged between me and Nature as well.

Comment:

Introspection requires examining your life-long assumptions. It means being willing to face yourself honestly and become congruent in thought and action. Your therapist is your own unconscious. Providing that you don't succumb to self-shaming, the process provides you the opportunity of becoming integrated and whole. The process is, however, painful; one we often avoid in normal, waking life.

waxing crescent₁

The mornings are darker and darker. The rate of change in the length of day is at its maximum. Just two weeks ago we awakened to a sunrise of reds and yellows. This morning we get up and it is dark. My sleep is progressively deteriorating and I don't know why. When I had my heart-to-heart with the boys this weekend I surprised myself when I described my current feeling state as *content*. Though I have a great deal on my mind, it is the kind of thinking that I am at home with. My silences are rich and renewing. So *content* fits and I like it. Why is my sleep becoming more shallow, my dreams so disjointed and superficial?

Birds don't sing the morning to life anymore. The only avian sounds come from the geese flying low over the house and they are more quiet than usual. Perhaps they have a premonition of what next week holds for them.

waxing crescent₂

The question she asked is one I have heard before and routinely dismissed as clever or rhetorical. But her manner urged me to stumble through an answer. She asked, "What is love? I mean,

213

really, what *is* it?" I scanned my memories for notable quotes or some pithy one-liner but only succeeded in mumbling a few unintelligible words. Then I lapsed into silence. After a while, I'm not sure how long, I found myself talking without hesitation.

I think like a psychiatrist so please excuse me, but it comes so naturally. When a mother holds her infant in her arms, she experiences love — unconditional, boundless, ecstatic, emotional love. Not because her baby is pretty, though she sees him that way. Not because he will bring her wealth or prestige, quite the contrary. Not because he has not caused her pain; the painful work of labor is still fresh in her mind. She loves him, she just does. Just because he exists and came into life through her.

And then there's Dad. He enters the picture and the love expands. Not as naturally as for mom, but nonetheless a profound experience; a child of his flesh, and he grows to experience a love similar to mother's love. Then the family comes to love this little one and the circle of love expands.

Such a love experience is infectious and will spread around if not inhibited; if nobody says *no* to it. Not as intense, but in its essence the same, the love spreads to the community, the tribe, and the country (where it becomes labeled patriotism).

For many, the love spreads to creatures whose cuddliness reminds us of our human infant; kittens, puppies, the young of other species. The love spreads. Then a radical leap may happen. When unencumbered, love encompasses the land, the sky, the waters, the whole earth. Love goes beyond being a feeling, an emotion; it becomes a perspective, a way of being in the world.

With grace, luck, or I don't know what, some souls achieve the experience of love extending not just to all of the earth, but to all those who are different — different colors, different cultures, different religions; even to those we call enemy.

Then the love may become total and the mystery of the Origin of The All becomes infused with and blended with this love. An awareness opens between the God and the person. It is not made of words, but rather it is love. All is seen to be worthy of love and the person blessed in this way becomes a saint.

Where does this love come from? It comes from the Origin of The All. We are not responsible for it. We did not create it. We merely discover it and are responsible for saying *yes* to it.

I can't say what love *is*. I can say what love *does*. Love is like electricity. Physicists can tell you its properties and how it seems to work, but they cannot tell you precisely what it is. We can't create electricity, we only discover and use its properties. We use electricity all the time without understanding it. Not knowing electricity's essence doesn't stop us from turning on the lights. Not knowing love's nature in no way prevents us from seeking to let our love spread throughout the world.

And then she asked if it is possible to prevent someone from becoming loving. Can a child be so abused or neglected that it never develops the capacity to love?

A painful question, but one that has to be asked. There is so much pain and evil in the world. I see its damage in my office every day.

Yes. I have seen it. There are many ways in which you can deny love. But our work in life is to remove the impediments to love's natural expression. Those who neglect or abuse little ones so badly that they snuff-out love in its infancy; they who kill the capacity to love before it gets its start; those persons are better off having a great millstone tied around their necks and being cast into the deepest part of the sea. And I don't mean that I recommend capital punishment. I mean it as a metaphor for how far they should be separated from those they have harmed and how they should be banished to a place where they can cause no further pain.

The business of psychiatry is removing the impediments to love; the biological ones and those caused by neglect and abuse. It is impossible to practice proper psychiatry unless one realizes that principle. A further development, a natural extension of my spiritual process, is creeping into my morning silence. I am reviewing my list of patients for the day, one by one. I picture them in my mind's eye and I intone a very special word, *loving-kindness*. I guess you might say I am praying for them.

_____ *waxing crescent₄* _____

Fall is modifying moods. My patients with recurrent depressions are beginning to lose it. Several are becoming psychotic once again and the community depression index is rattling its way up. Many well-informed patients call me knowing that medical modifications are needed to keep them functioning. It is interesting how it has all seemed to happen in the past couple of weeks. It isn't the moon that troubles chemically-disturbed minds. It's the sun. The days are rapidly shortening, depriving us of nurturing sunlight. Some yet-unravelled neurochemical mystery is being triggered and those susceptible are descending into the abyss. I am grateful to have some tools to help. Not enough, but some — certainly better than in ages past.

My own sleep continues to deteriorate. I wonder if it is the change of season, sort of a little brother phenomena related to seasonal depression. I am now awakening shortly after midnight and the rest of sleep is disturbed; superficial dreams, no wonderful visions, just junk. My mood remains good and even optimistic. Reality checks with Carol and my friends are consistent: I don't appear down, but I am getting more fatigued. I am afraid I will have to start medication once again. "He who has himself for a physician has a fool for a doctor." So be it. This phrase is intoned by all physicians, yet I know of no one who does not treat himself for something. A terrible confession to make about our profession; kind of like letting out a great fraternity secret. But it is true. I don't want to explain all this insomnia to some colleague. I will take a mild sedative. I have done it before. I will achieve some semblance of normal sleep and I will continue on with life. If I become truly depressed, I will run, not walk, to my nearest trusted colleague.

Hunter's Moon

Tonight Carol and I eat the last of last year's venison steak. It remains as sweet and delicious as it was last year. We have wasted not a single bite.

The crescent moon, the evening star, the muted pinks and purples of sunset, the dry leaves crunching underfoot in the yard. Gift. All gift. Thanks.

waxing crescent₅

Almost a perfect fall day. I run farther than usual, cheered on by some avian friends. The meadowlarks sing, though not as robustly as in spring. The geese cackle and honk from on high. They are flying much higher than two weeks ago. One or two have a couple of primaries missing, testimony to the start of goose season. A single raven perches atop a real estate sign and *awk-awks* as I pass. I have never learned the language of ravens, but no doubt he was commenting about the splendid day or just offering me a bit of encouragement.

Carol and I busy ourselves with fall's work, cleaning, sorting, shopping, putting things in order. While downtown, we happen upon the local Oktoberfest. Bratwurst and beer and wonderful music that calls a polka from the feet of every passerby. The band consists of two accordions, a hammer dulcimer, a trombone, and a bass guitar. They don't make bands like that anymore. Young parents dance about with their toddlers astride their hips. Older couples who obviously know the steps remember times past when the polka was a way of life and not a museum piece. The man across the table from us doesn't polka, not even with his eyes. He sits stony-faced; his oxygen measured to him through a green plastic cannula. He leaves after listening briefly; his expression never changes once. I think he has stopped dancing with life.

217

waxing gibbous[1]

Cougars aren't all that common; at least they are rarely seen even if they are in an area. In the last day, I have had three cougar conversations.

We are not exactly on the edge of nowhere. Fort Collins has ninety thousand souls and a series of similar cities extend all along the front range to Denver. But the mountains start on the west edge of town and rapidly blend into wild country. Fifty miles farther in, wilderness.

Ron works for the Loveland school district. There is a rural school at the mouth of the Big Thompson canyon presenting him with a pair of unique fencing problems. The area has been home to a generous local population of rattlesnakes, requiring a creative fencing scheme to keep them from wandering onto the playground. But such a diagonal three foot fence does nothing to deter a local cougar who has been seen roaming the school yard. That will take an eight foot fence and some government trappers. Cougars don't attack people. But then again, as this one gains familiarity with human dwellings, who is to say a child might not look like a Big Mac to him?

Carl was jogging on his property this morning and came across a cougar kill. Deer are the natural prey of cougars. He said the destruction was unbelievable. The process of the kill covered nearly a hundred yards and left little to the imagination as to the cougar's tremendous ferocity. A necessary process for the cougar to eat. And eat he did, about a third of the deer in one sitting. When Carl came across it, the carcass was still warm. Undoubtedly, the cougar wasn't far off, watching Carl with a very full stomach. It is unusual for a kill to be so close to a road where a human could see it.

Then I talked with a local wildlife biologist about the front range deer population.

What would happen if deer hunting ceased?

More road kills would be the first thing we would notice.

How many were there last year?

Twelve hundred in our immediate area and we suspect for each one counted, another is injured by a car and drags off into the brush to die.

Are the dead animals put to any use?

No, we just dump them in the landfill.

If we didn't hunt would the natural predators ultimately become plentiful enough to control the population?

No. The urban public does not tolerate cougars in their back yards killing deer and their dogs.

Are cougars plentiful?

No one knows, they are almost impossible to count. I've been a biologist for twenty-one years; I have never seen one in the wild.

If we don't hunt the deer what will happen besides more road kills?

They will exhaust their food supply and then by mid-winter, their semi-starvation will lower their resistance so that many will die of illnesses which, in a healthy state, wouldn't bother them.

Is hunting by humans necessary now that there are too few bears and cougars?

Definitely.

What is the biggest problem with hunting?

People. Greedy, selfish, unthinking people who are out for the fun; who kill the game with no respect for the law or the game. Animal control is simple. People control is the problem.

waxing gibbous$_2$

When I was a boy, my neighbor, Jimmy, once shot a pigeon with a BB gun. The pigeon was big and the gun weak. After he had shot it six times, Jimmy's mother came out and was horrified at seeing the pigeon's suffering. Jimmy wanted to shoot it some more, but she asked me to take care of it. I took it down from its perch and placed it on the ground. It was shivering, weak, but very conscious. I picked up a big metal pipe and with one blow, stopped its agony. I was ten at the time.

As an intern, I was covering a floor with several terminally ill children. One, abused and brain damaged from birth, was in renal shutdown and obviously near death. A senior resident wanted to keep him alive to complete an experiment studying how a failing kidney handled the blood levels of certain drugs. Not part of a systematic study, it was more for his own information. When the child suffered cardiac arrest, I was summoned to resuscitate. I paused, looked at the child and then placed my hand on his shrunken chest and let him die. I was called on the carpet the next day. Though the professor respected my values, he said I had no right to interfere with the resident's experiment.

------------------------------ *waxing gibbous₄* ------------------------------
San Isabel National Forest, Colorado

I sit twenty feet from an enclosure intended for monks of a different kind. We have travelled two hundred miles to be here for this special moon, for the flaming fall colors, and most especially, for the music — sacred music performed in no concert hall anywhere in the world. Last evening when we arrived, they were already tuning up. By nightfall we had pitched our tent and were ready to attend vespers. The mature gibbous moon dazzled the wilderness scene, creating sharply defined shadows with a light so intense the aspens looked midday gold. Single file, four of us entered the enclosure behind Dana, a young blond woman with gray feral eyes. Quietly and emphatically, she convinced us of one proper attitude in the sanctuary: Respect.

They will know how you feel. This is their space, we are their guests. When we enter, we will sit on the wooden bench near the gate. We will wait. It is their choice to greet us. It is their choice to sing for us.

Once seated on the plain bench, we waited but a few moments when Lucas appeared from the shadows. He greeted Dana, but startled when he saw us. Stiffening, he disappeared silently back into the darkness. Next came Nikkolah, a gray cloaked monk. He studied us from midway up a pinion pine and then he too faded back into the shadows. We continued to wait. This sanctuary was so different from the one at Snowmass, and then again, so much the same. The monks were different too, and then again, so much the same. We drank in the silence and the peacefulness. Inside we felt a tinge of uncertainty. We sat, knowing many eyes watched us from the darkness and we continued to wait. Time counted for little. The moon angled higher, casting new shadows, banishing old ones. I settled into meditation. Becoming simple awareness, I existed as only my spirit would exist, following my transition into death. I waited and I breathed and I smiled.

Then one by one, the monks slowly emerged, each from a different shadow. Carefully examining us as they approached and greeted Dana again. She touched them affectionately, speaking quietly to each by name. Then they became more active, more bold, moving silently between shadow and moonbeam. All but Nikkolah wore black cloaks, making them especially hard to see even when standing in the bright moonlight.

Finally, Dana encouraged them to sing. She intoned a low rising note of encouragement and then suddenly, as if on cue, they broke forth into song, each coming in sequentially, developing some primeval fugue. The monks surrounded us at various distances, booming a wordless and ancient chant. Nikkolah's bass resounded so deeply, the ground itself shook. The chorus rose and fell existing outside of time. Then other monks from other enclosures up the valley joined in the response. A primal delight, deeper than language; my tearful smile stifled any sound I may have wished to make. I was in a sanctuary I have always longed for, one I have dreamed of for years. Here I listened as monks prayed in their unique way — monks misunderstood from time immemorial. I sat, a guest, at midnight vespers of a pack of wolves.

Comment:
Your Portrait Journal will influence you to act on your dreams. You may find you finally do those things you have never seemed to find time for in the past. It is as though your Portrait Journal comes alive and counsels you to experience the reality of your dreams not just the fantasy.

This monastery is a mission of sorts, a sanctuary for wolves, *Mission: Wolf*, a non-profit organization dedicated to convincing humankind to respect all of Nature. *Education vs. Extinction.* The wolf is a metaphor for the dying wilderness. The near extinction of the wolf, an example of humankind's propensity to dominate, pillage and destroy any creature too much like itself. Wolves have been portrayed as vicious, wanton killers, stopping short of nothing; devil dogs coming straight from hell to torment humankind. Isn't that the way to justify genocide? Claim that the target of persecution is the personification of evil.

These particular wolves have been rescued from thoughtless humans who believed genetics counted for naught and that raising a wolf in the city would be an interesting idea. These creatures cannot survive in our square fenced, digital cities. And now, they cannot make it in the wild either. So here is *Mission: Wolf*, a sanctuary for wolves with no other place to call home. A spacious, fenced-in valley in the remote Sangre de Cristo mountains where they can live in packs and experience the uniqueness of being wolves. It is not exactly like living on their own in the wild, but close. Just as so many analog people have had to compromise to survive in the digital world, so too have these wolves had to compromise to live at all. Trapped by overpopulation and the human bioenergy of domination and destruction, wolves are analog creatures, one hundred percent analog. Rather than being demons from hell, I see them as messengers from the Origin trying to live out the principles of familial loyalty, respect for elders, and lifetime monogamy. They kill only what they need to eat and celebrate the gift of life in their chorus to the Origin of all life as they chant in the moonlight.

Our campsite was situated on a dry grassy bluff above the mission; there Carol and I dined on venison stew and then we fell off to sleep. All through the night we awakened at intervals as the monks prayed their various offices. Just as at Snowmass, they have set times for prayer — times determined, not by the clock, but by the moon and the first light of morning.

Now it is mid morning and we are waiting to enter the enclosure again. In the daylight the scene appears remarkably different. I can see the wolves gamboling about their spacious grounds, alternately playing, watching and then resting. Never quiet for more than a few minutes, they appear to dance with life; sensual and aware of the gift that life is.

Once again, we enter the sanctuary. This time they seem more accustomed to us and dance with Dana. Unashamedly, they leap up, kiss her face, jump about, and establish, with throaty growls, the dominance of who gets petted first. They still don't approach Carol and me. They appear disinterested in coming to know us better. They pay us scant attention, behaving in exactly the same manner as the monks at Snowmass.

I think our world needs fewer people and more wolves. More precisely, I wonder if our world wouldn't run ideally with about one tenth of its current human population. Of course, that would require humans control the second bioenergy, the drive to procreate. Wolves manage that very well. Only the alpha male and female mate, the rest of the pack does not. During periods of starvation, they have been known to omit mating entirely for a year. In unusual cases a female, once impregnated, has actually reabsorbed the developing fetuses within her own body. As a species, I wonder if they aren't considerably more advanced than humankind.

waxing gibbous₅

On the road, Colorado

Our trip takes us through towns with names like Fort Garland, Alamosa, Monte Vista, Del Norte, and Pagosa Springs. Each community proudly spans the main street with a banner rarely seen in urban America, _Welcome Hunters_. Tomorrow is the beginning of hunting season. Hunting is a mainstay of the economies of this area. Motels and restaurants advertize special rates, free coffee and other enticements to lure hunters from their pick-ups. These hairless bipeds are the necessary predators, now that wolves reside in sanctuaries, grizzlies are relegated to the wilderness, and cougars too rare to make a difference. But do these men know the sanctity of killing game? Do they reverence the taking of another animal's life? Do they pause prayerfully after the kill, promising the animal's spirit that its flesh will be well used — that its death will not be meaningless? Will they refuse to give in to the celebration of the bioenergy of destruction? Will they kill to eat and to reverence the created order? Some will, I am sure. Unfortunately, many more will not and therein lies the tragedy.

Where are Carol and I off to? We are shifting gears to become average, everyday parents once again. We are going to visit Steve at college for Parent's Weekend.

waxing gibbous₆

Durango, Colorado

Few towns are more western-flavored than Durango. The Durango & Silverton narrow gauge railroad station is just behind our hotel. The steam whistle and chugging black smoke harken back to my early childhood; a time when my usual lullaby was the sound of The Empire Builder on its way to Seattle from Chicago. A festival for cowboy poets and a mountain rendezvous draw more tourists than the college homecoming. Carol and I drop in at our hotel's watering hole, the Diamond Belle Saloon; we find ourselves in the midst of honky-tonk music, gun-toting cowboys, and scantily clad barmaids. The latter, looking like a blend of Calamity Jane and a Playboy Bunny are competing in a saloon girl contest. I feel like my psychic needle has skipped a groove. I begin to lose contact with my body in the whirl of the noise and garish color. My soul longs to be back with the wolves. The contrast is more than I can tolerate. But this is life, too — at least my life, here and now. Dance with it. But it is too difficult. Instead, we leave the din. We go outside and greet the moon. We stand, unmoving, and listen. Could it be? There . . . in the distance. Could it be? The monks singing vespers? Or is it the echo in my soul? No matter, we listen . . . and I smile once again. We walk the streets holding hands and stop to buy some chocolate.

FULL MOON

The day is filled with campus tours, football games and dinner with Steve. Visiting a son in college is one of the rewards of being a parent at this stage of life. But, one event early in the day leaves my stomach turning, haunts my peacefulness. It demands I do something, but I am at a loss what. Before the game, Carol and I visit the fairgrounds to look at the wares of the local western festival. All sorts of arts and crafts are for sale: Beads, buckskin, silver, books of poetry and audio tapes of cowboy songs. Fine, no problem. But there, next to an Indian lodge, is a man of opulent girth (a charitable observation) selling furs. My heart sinks as I see gray monk's cloaks, tanned and hanging there for sale for a mere hundred and fifty bucks. I ask whether the fur is wolf. Yes. Where from? Northern Canada. He had several furs, six to be exact. I want to cry. I want to scream. I want to grab his scraggly black beard and spit in his bloated face. Is a hundred and fifty-bucks to this beer-distended savage the proper reward for killing a monk who sings to the Origin of The All? As if this noble cloak could serve as a proper trophy for some digitally stressed yuppy to hang over his fireplace! I consider making a statement to convert him from the bioenergy of destruction, but realize I could not do so non-violently. He does not look ripe for conversion. Instead I content myself with a promise to see these words make it to print.

_____ _waning gibbous₁_ _____

Long streets with tree-lined central boulevards are meant for one purpose: Pleasure, pure pleasure. And in the fall especially, the pleasure is multiplied by the yellow and orange leaves overhead, the dry brown carpet of dried leaves on the ground, and the spicy aroma as they crunch underfoot. I take a long, easy morning jog along Third Avenue. A pristine place, there are few cars to pollute the air. Several churches line the thoroughfare calling out to dark-suited parishioners with their tolling bells. Another perfect morning to celebrate the gift of life. I jog down to Main Street and past the railroad station where the 9:30 train is getting ready to depart with a load of multilingual passengers. German and Japanese are every bit as common as English. How nice. When I was a boy, I was taught to fear these people because they were the personification of evil, the enemy, straight from hell and should be removed from the face of the earth.

As I walk to cool down, I encounter Durango's schizophrenic representative. I have met him in so many different cities, San Francisco, DuBois, Fort Collins. This time he is short, talks wildly to himself and, as I pause to wait for a traffic light, he pauses too, looking at me strangely while carrying on a conversation with some indecipherable neurochemical entity in his brain.

Then I meet Carol crossing the street with our morning cup of coffee. We go down next to the railroad tracks and watch the train pass, belching its dark smoke and speckling us with small flecks of soot. Those old locomotives were pretty polluting machines, a fact you forget when wrapped up in nostalgia.

In my mind, I am never more than a few seconds from the recalled thrill of the monks' chorus. Brother Wolf. Yes, Brother Wolf and Sister Wolf — Lucas, Nikkolah, Cyndar, Jordan, Raven. Names of very special, holy individuals.

On our drive back, we see no animals strapped to the sides of vehicles, no horns or feet protruding from the backs of pick-ups. We see one elk hanging in a hunting camp and we count four deer, dead along the roads, victims of collisions with cars, not hunters.

---

waning gibbous$_2$

Home

It couldn't last forever. Our splendid lingering fall is giving way to winter. I awaken to two inches of wet snow and more falling all the time. Everywhere, soggy piles of wet leaves surround the bases of balding trees. I decide to go for a jog. This is no time to become timid in the face of the weather. If I do, I might just stay in all winter and curse the cold.

My mind still mulls over the hunting issue. Two years ago I hunted with a friend of Alan's who is a wildlife biologist working for a large eastern city. He passed up a shot at a fine bull elk because it was next to the road, and then went through the rest of the hunt never getting another chance. He said he was a hunter of elk, not a killer of elk. Unfortunately for him, his job has degenerated into being an executioner of deer in order to assuage the feelings of the urban public. His city has many large woodlots, small forests often measuring a section or more. Having no natural predators, the deer overpopulate. A vast number succumb to automobile collisions (their most common cause of death) causing insurance companies to demand something be done. But hunting is not an option since the urban public can't bear the idea of these animals being shot. On occasion, disease wipes out large numbers. That is easier for the public to handle, since the deer die off in the woods where nobody notices.

227

My friend's job required he be the population control officer for the deer population. The only solution which seemed humane was to harvest the excess population of deer, but do so without the public seeing it. So he and other officers go out at night with spotlights and shoot the deer to keep the population in check. They are the deer's only predators. I asked whether the meat of the deer was then donated to the homeless or the Salvation Army. No, the department of agriculture would have to pass on the meat before it is offered for human consumption. An expensive process and one lobbied against by the meat industry. The animals are taken to the landfill and dumped.

The tragedy: In a city where hunger runs rampant, a natural and healthy food source is thrown in the dump to rot. The conscience of the urban public is not disturbed. They don't know about it. Out of sight, out of mind. The whole affair is wasteful; a desecration of the gifts of life. Hunting, when accomplished for obtaining food, is a natural way of life. Killing and wasting animals, be it by automobiles, trophy hunters, or surreptitiously to assuage the urban public who wants to believe that all deer, like Bambi, should die of natural causes violates the purpose of life. In the pursuit of Disney, Kafka lives.

It is only two days till my hunting season is here. I have contemplated my role in the process. I am a predator. No intermediaries will kill food for me, enabling me to ignore the reality of an animal dying for my food. In the animal's death, I will be reminded about my own death. The kill will be swift and compassionate. I will make complete use of my prey. And I will remain on my path and I will continue to adhere to principles of non-violence. At least for now, I can remain a hunter and lovingly attend to life.

LAST QUARTER

The half moon presides just south of the mid heaven as the first light of day subdues all but the most prominent stars; Orion, the hunter, dominates the quarter heaven from north to west. I meet Carl outside his lodge. He has a fire prepared. Badger smiles and sneezes his special greeting. Leaving hunting attire and rifle outside of the lodge, we enter to share the pipe, bless the hunt, and promise Wakantanka we will hunt with care and use the flesh of the four-legged creatures with respect. Carl lights the pipe, offers the first draw to the Great Spirit, thoughtfully pulls on the pipe himself and then offers it to me. I savor the aroma, watching the smoke dissipate heavenward, up through the smoke hole; the perfect metaphor for the spirit's migration at death — a trip which I, one day, will make; a trip which, today, an animal will make in the process of becoming my food. Badger, in the manner of countless generations of canine forbearers, lies between us and the fire. How often have hunting companions sat before the fire with their dog on the morning of a hunt, reflected on friendship, the bounty of Nature, and the reality of death for the prey?

We linger a while. There is no hurry. The sky lightens. It is time. We go out and don our blaze orange, yielding to the digital reality that other hunters are afield with powerful rifles and eager expectations. Better not to be a target for fools. We walk mindfully, drinking in the colors of the sunrise. Our first sighting of deer is at a range my rifle is capable of shooting but I am not. I pass, waiting for a better chance for a merciful kill. Further on, Carl and I separate. He encounters deer at close range, a simple shot, but I cannot see them. Finally by mid morning, I do have a shot. I take my time, but my heart beats so intensely that my sights move up and down with each heart beat. I wait, aim, shoot and miss. They move downhill into trees. Again, with as much care as my excitement allows and with full knowledge of my act, I fire and miss again. Finally, my shot is true. Death is instantaneous.

We make our way to the fallen deer. We pause kneeling before it. We place our hands on its side and promise its spirit we will use it wisely. I look up and it is as if the smoke from the ceremonial pipe wafts heavenward. Then we get to the task of caring for the meat, being careful to dress the carcass so no contamination of the meat occurs. I obtain a test tube of blood for a Wildlife Department's survey of brucellosis among deer where overcrowding is a problem. Then we carry our prey to the pick-up and transport it home.

The proper preparation of venison is simple, but virtually unknown among most hunters. Such ignorance probably accounts for a vast amount of meat wastage. Hanging and aging the meat have nothing to do with assuring tenderness or good flavor. The issue is cooling the meat, avoiding contamination, and eliminating all fat. The tallow of venison is virtually indigestible by humans and is the source of the pungent, so-called wild taste. I carefully bone out all of the meat, trimming all of the fat. Carol helps me weigh, wrap and label. We prepare steaks, jerky, stew chunks, and ground meat (one hundred percent lean, lower in cholesterol than turkey). The entire process is complete and the meat frozen by nightfall. Our venison is ready for another year. I take the hide to be tanned. Allison has plans for it.

In the evening, Carl and Karen join us for dinner and we talk of the hunt. We eat our first meal of this year's venison with particular reverence. We talk of the morality of hunting. Why is it that some primeval force still exerts its will inside our psyches? It seems to be present more frequently in men than in women. I believe we are more closely connected to our ancestors than we want to believe. Men did hunt. Women did stay home and care for the children. However, nowadays, we could just buy the food from the grocery store. But, no, somehow I feel compelled to understand life at a deeper level and in the process I come to feel more humble about our role in life. Meat does not come from the grocery store, it comes from another creature who died, becoming food for us. The creature came from the land. The land is gift from the Origin of the All. We give thanks to Wakantanka.

True Indian Summer, a time of exquisite days, following the first hard frost. The trees shed their leaves, some bare, others full gold, and a few still dusky green. I drive to Denver to meet with Mary Luke. All along the way I survey the harvest. Corn is nearly complete, leaving an uneven stubble where the tall dried stalks stood at close ranks only a week ago. Along a train siding I discover a huge hill of sugar beets; at least two acres in area and taller than a railroad car. There is enough sugar to keep an army of dentists in business. The winter wheat has sprouted uniformly, and appears well prepared for winter's dormancy. Fall is a fluid time.

As usual, my time with Mary Luke is like visiting an oasis. But, together with her usual refreshing support, she voices a caution: Beware of spiritual narcissism. Beware of thinking that your spiritual development is somehow a product of your own effort. It is all gift, _all gift_. About all you can take pride in is saying yes to the process. And even then the word, pride, is risky.

I offer her some venison and suggest she not eat it until she has read my Hunter's Moon draft. Many people have been turned-off by wild tasting venison. Mary Luke too, has tasted ill-cared for venison and cannot imagine how any person could enjoy it.

We talk about ecology as I share my understanding of deer populations and my struggles over continuing to hunt. She suggests that to be informed spiritually we must be informed ecologically. If earth and life are gift, we must take care of them and use them wisely. We must know and apply ecology. We both wonder if some way couldn't be worked out for venison to be made available to those who go hungry. The concept is simple enough; of course the digital application of this altruistic notion would probably be a nightmare.

waning crescent₃

Feeling more like I am back in the routine of things, I dwell in silence to my heart's content this morning. There is nothing to hurry me. The jog around Warren is brisker than usual with a wet, north wind and scattered rain drops stinging my face. Despite the cold, I take my jacket off and let the raw coldness turn my skin red. Running in the wind has a special vigor about it. You can't help but feel very much alive when you meet the wind head up, chest out, and smiling.

A theme rambles around in my mind:

The world doesn't need more intelligent people.
The world doesn't need more clever people.
The world doesn't need more activists.
The world doesn't need more soldiers.

The world needs more deep people;
spiritual, compassionate, analog people.
People with humps, accents, curves, warts, disabilities;
people with strange ideas;
people who will join together with other people;
people who will not require conformity to a creed;
people who will simply choose to join together
in an ever-widening, accepting circle called community.

And then, an imp whispers in my ear: And avoid straight lines wherever possible.

waning crescent₄

Grand Forks, North Dakota

Forty knots of wind out of the north. Dusty sky, flat gray landscape. Here I am at a place that was home for me for two of the most intense years of my life. I am returning to present a paper honoring a professor who not only taught me biochemistry, but more importantly, taught me the importance of respect. Respect by the professor for the student. I'm reminded of Dana and I wonder if the world would not thrive if more respect was shown and less cynicism. After all, people, like wolves, respond to the expectations of those around them.

I walk around the campus and discover wonderful sights. And then am chagrined to realize my discoveries are not new at all. They existed back while I was in medical school; I simply never took the time to look at them. How much beauty do we fail to see because we simply don't take the time to look?

I run into Dr. Cornatzer in the University Bookstore. He is autographing his book. A heavy biochemical tome, it costs a small fortune. I buy it and ask him to sign it. He remembers me and we talk. In an instant I am the student again and he, the professor, excitedly talking about chemical moieties, free radicals, and molecular medicine. We talk, time passes and I remember what it feels like to feel respected by my elder. That was his most important lesson. The biochemistry came easily, a cinch. Anything would come easily in that relationship.

waning crescent

I offer my paper on humor to the assembled medical alumni and faculty. Received with warm, if reserved, compliments, it is a topic seeming to be more fluff, not the real meat of scientific endeavor. Many papers are presented and I am impressed with the scope and depth of the research. It is true, my humor material is not as scientific as most of the presentations.

One presentation stands out to me about how one disease can affect a single culture. A bombshell: In 1837, ninety-six percent of the Mandan Indian Tribe died of smallpox in one winter! Between white man's diseases, hunger for land, and drive to pillage and

233

destroy, it is a wonder any Indians survive at all. He showed paintings of these noble people, now effectively wiped from the face of the earth.

Wakantanka, why?

I hear no answer, only the sound of the steady North Dakota wind. There is no "because." It's too late. About fifty percent of the surviving Indians in North Dakota have diabetes. Their bodies evolved living on game, not fattened beef and sugary foods. They weren't diabetic before the coming of the whites. I think to myself: Give them better land, let them raise the buffalo. Give them back Wakantanka to replace Jim Beam. Heal their spirits, so long deprived of their spiritual food, and their diabetes will take care of itself.

The rest of the day is filled with football games, banquets, meeting old classmates and reminiscing about times twenty-five years ago. One classmate dead of AIDS, another blown apart in Viet Nam. As I go through the day's activities I wonder: If the Mandan cannot be resurrected, can their spirituality be salvaged? Doesn't their path to the Origin of the All have something important for all of us? Or is spirituality, like history, written by only the winners?

_waning crescent_6

My final day here, the end of the Hunter Moon. It is fitting, I think. Here, the state of my birth, where hunting first came to me. Here, at this school, where my roommate and I ate venison for a whole year, thankful we didn't have to go out and buy food. Despite scholarships and working in the library, we were very poor.

I consider taking a run, but the gale force winds and twenty degree temperatures discourage me. It's wear-your-ski-parka-cold. Instead, I stay in my motel meditating, writing, reading and reflecting. Next door the Tomahawk Cafe has a special luncheon offering intended for only the truly Scandinavian: Lutefisk and lefse. Lefse, the Scandinavian version of a tortilla made with potatoes, is no problem. Lutefisk is a different matter. Most people don't like lutefisk, a cod fish which has been pickled in lye, transforming it into a translucent, pale yellow, shivering mass with a fibrous, jello-like consistency. If you eat it with real *silver*ware, it turns the silver black. Consumed with cups of melted butter, it was once the staple for the old Norwegians deprived of refrigeration. Nowadays, it is a curiosity, a food reserved for special occasions and jokes: "Lutefisk: The piece of cod that passes all understanding." The cafe bustles with the rush of a New York deli, the courtesy of a Mississippi barbecue, and the white food only a Scandinavian could love. The customers have white hair, white skin, and unmistakable Scandinavian twangs. All, except my waitress, she is Filipino. Needless to say I eat lutefisk. My grimacing waitress fails to contain her aversion to this culinary delight. But, no self-respecting Norwegian boy can pass up good lutefisk. You ask, do I like it? There are some questions too personal to answer — even in one's journal.

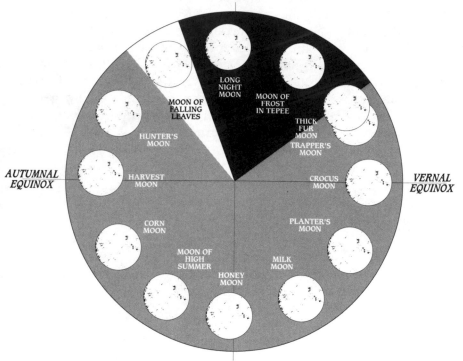

WINTER
SOLSTICE

LONG
NIGHT
MOON

MOON OF
FALLING
LEAVES

MOON OF
FROST
IN TEPEE

HUNTER'S
MOON

THICK
FUR
MOON

TRAPPER'S
MOON

AUTUMNAL
EQUINOX

HARVEST
MOON

CROCUS
MOON

VERNAL
EQUINOX

CORN
MOON

PLANTER'S
MOON

MOON OF
HIGH
SUMMER

MILK
MOON

HONEY
MOON

SUMMER
SOLSTICE

Chapter Ten

MOON OF FALLING LEAVES

Home

BETWEEN PHONE CALLS, I catch a glimpse of
Barbara visiting Lowell. I wave and she comes in for a hug. When
you hug someone whose life is hanging in the balance, who is ill and
apt to be a whole lot more ill, a person for whom you can do almost
nothing but express concern and boldly risk influencing God to do
things your way; when you hug such a person, you hug long, aware of
one another's breathing, savoring the moment, fearing there may be
too few left. Barbara's cancer is getting more active. Now her skull,
pelvis, and ribs all are being eaten away — more radiation, more
chemo, more nutritional involvement, more visualization, more time,
more hope, more not-giving-up. We hug, our bodies saying what
needs to be said, words not counting for much. She will lose her hair
again, get weak again, and maybe, just maybe, go into remission,
again. It has been ten years; her cancer was metastatic when first

237

discovered. She has outlived all predictions, and the quality of her life exceeds that of most; she's still concerned about foster kids, the homeless shelter, and her children. Like so many exceptional cancer patients, she has much to live for and gives herself fully to life.

This moon has several colonial names: Beaver moon, snow moon, or frosty moon. Indian names include killing deer moon, corn harvest moon, or the Lakota name, moon of the falling leaves. Few of those terms fits our particular situation. Beavers are uncommon. Snow, frost, killing deer, and corn harvest have all come during past moons. But the leaves are still falling. Some trees are bare, others remain colored and are dropping their leaves in a leisurely way. By the end of this moon, all the trees will be bare. So the most fitting name for this eleventh moon of the year: The Moon of Falling Leaves.

The trees and the earth have a lesson for us humans who curse winter. Just prepare for it. It is inevitable. Like death, you can curse, but it will do you little good. Just become quiet, meditative, and accepting. Anger is folly. Fear, the beginning of wisdom. Acceptance, the freeing of the ego to fly. The cycle continues, dance with it. A slower step perhaps, but dance with it nonetheless. Barbara hangs on to her leaves well. One day winter will come for her as for each of us. For her some leaves are dropping, many are still golden yellow. The seasons of life follow a pattern, but are not locked in by the sun and moon. Other mystical rhythms prevail, I do not know what. For now we hug. And in our own way, we dance. And one day, surely we will weep.

waxing crescent₃

Why this emphasis on Nature? Why the constant imperative to *dance with it*? Why so little talk about the practice of psychiatry with its daily parade of stressed and broken people wanting solutions, relief from pain?

Because focusing on my work *alone* starves my spirit. If I am to give of myself, if I am to approach my patients with love and understanding, if I am to prevent my descent into the abyss of frustration and despair, I must nurture my spirit.

Academic withdrawal? Too sterile. No nourishment.

Searching out the novel therapy strategy, the new in-vogue terminology? The foolishness of the dilettante.

Taking my patients home, carrying them in my dreams and worrying about them throughout all my waking hours? An exercise in futility.

My pursuit of life for its own sake, my seeking unity with the Origin of Life, my dwelling on the beauty of Nature; all are necessary for me to grow into the person Wakantanka would have me be. It is in my silence and reflection that I find peace. It is there my psychic battery gets charged. It is there I discover the joy of being alive and then carry that joy out to share with all I meet, be they patients, friends, family, or the woman who takes my money at the gas station. Am I passing on peace and joy well? Not very. Do I need to work at sharing love more effectively? You bet! (*You bet* is a Scandinavian's response of unequivocal affirmation, actually quite an enthusiastic response.) Do I feel guilty for not loving well enough? Yes.

waxing crescent₄

Contrast. Days of stark contrast. Days filled with a special richness, variety. No doubts about being alive, fully alive. I awaken early and head to the hospital without breakfast. One of my long-term patients has descended into her recurring catastrophic depression. By experience, we know these kind of melancholias develop into a very special personal hell. She and her husband called yesterday. This one is too deep, much like the ones before. Tired of medications, tired of hoping some new drug will do the trick, they ask for ECT. I agree. We saw it coming, but then again, we always hope that perhaps this time the depression will remit without the ultimate antidepressant. In the treatment room, she smiles and asks to hold my hand as she goes to sleep. The treatment goes smoothly. I talk to her husband afterwards; he is hopeful too; hopeful now that she will start to sleep again; hopeful that she will once again stop feeling pain everywhere in her body; hopeful that she will stop attacking him and their fourteen year old son.

I go home for a quick breakfast and then off to Loveland for a day-long workshop on humor. Mark is there with his magic and the day is a ten. I don't just talk of humor, I talk about love, altruism, wolves, respect, and courtesy. The workshop just evolves by itself. It started out being *Humor and Health*, then it grew into *The Art and Psychology of Positive Humor*, now it's becoming *Laughter, Love and Altruism*.

I return home tired and elated to share dinner with my best friend; a simple meal, but topped off with perhaps the most perfect chocolate chip cookies ever to grace the face of the earth. Carol and I hold hands in silence. We savor our love and the Presence witnessed by the single candle on our table.

Shifting gears, I make ready for elk hunting tomorrow. Carol has prepared the food and will come along as camp cook. Actually it's a time for her to read undisturbed. She has some knitting, too. For Ron and I, it's a time to walk snowy glades seeking a chance to fill the freezer for the winter. We pack the car, fill the gas tank, and then go out to listen to Mark for just one set. A young blond vocalist with a wispy voice sings with the group tonight. We drink in the music and choke on a nearby smoker's discourtesy.

At the break, Mark and I talk about creating an album of words, music, and wolves' singing. I suggest a title like, *Courtesy and Respect*. He likes the idea. He has the recording gear and can hardly wait to enter the enclosure with Nikkolah and friends. Then Carol and I return home for an early bedtime. I have two workshops in the morning before I can head to the mountains; one for professional businesswomen, one for teenagers against drunk driving.

240

They want to hear about positive humor, but I will weave in some respect, courtesy, and wolves too.

waxing crescent₅

Routt National Forest, Colorado

Powdery snow muffles my step but the wind at my back bears my scent to all creatures ahead of me, so there is little chance I will surprise an elk. I walk the dark timber, barren aspen groves, and open brown meadows. Each different, each offering a new chance, a new discovery. I walk slowly, listening often. I hear trees creaking against each other, squirrels scolding, and then, off in the distance, the unmistakable sound of a rifle shot. Nothing in nature duplicates that sound. Not frequent, not like warfare, just occasional focused explosions, letting the wild creatures know that man, the prime predator, is in the woods and is harvesting. The wind rushing high over head sings an eerie obligato. Studying the snow for tracks, I discover rabbit, mouse, and coyote, but no elk or deer. Ron and I hike through sunset. After dark we return to the car tired, invigorated, and almost grateful we didn't see anything. We return to Sam's cabin for a warm fire, homemade stew and chocolate chip cookies. Carol, Ron and I spend the evening around the fireplace talking of nothing too serious.

waxing crescent₆

Real winter: Snow, boot-top deep, wind drifting and packing the snow behind bushes and rocks. Trees snap with the cold or moan and creak in the wind. The terrain is ideal for elk. We hike, watch, listen, scan and . . . . nothing — no game, no tracks; just a few hunters here and there. At midday, I discover a fresh track and follow it, feeling more Lakota than Norwegian. Over an hour of

241

painstaking attention to tracks, broken twigs, the pungent aroma of the scat; expecting to discover the elk any moment, perhaps just over the next rise. But then, much to my disappointment, human tracks join the elk tracks and I become second fiddle. After a bit, I break off and hike down along a giant staircase of beaver ponds; white, silent, fully prepared for the winter. I wonder where the beavers are and what they are doing. After all, this is the beaver moon.

Reaching the road, three blaze orange men in a pick-up offer me a ride. First, as one gets out to rearrange his rifle in the window gun rack it accidentally discharges into the forest. I pause, standing behind their vehicle as they laugh at their careless companion. Their bumper sticker proclaims a revolutionary new discovery about human physiology: Human excrement occurs. I decline the ride and continue my walk back to the car. A mile and a half extra hike is a vast improvement over that trio's company.

By the end of the day my feet are damp, my body pleasantly fatigued, and my gun unused. Another day and no sighting of game. Hunting often is this way. At least I am not struggling with the morality of the hunt any more. I am hunting with a friend and enjoying the outdoors. Simple enough.

First Quarter

More snow. A lot more snow. Deep, dry, powdery. Driving off the highway requires chains and then some. Towards the top of The Medicine Bow Range (10,000 feet) our ancient Toyota pick-up (180,000 miles) groans under the strain, threatening to throw out its rear end or give up the clutch if we push it one inch farther. The over-the-knee snow is pushing ahead of our trusty steed and, like a twenty year old horse, it is just too old and too tired to push any more. So we turn back and hunt the lower country. It's another day of long hikes up steep mountainsides and through pensive, dark timber. Still no sign of our quarry. We pause at midday, overlooking an old abandoned gold mine. We wonder about the life and work this remote valley has witnessed. Finally, sun angling down westward towards the Zerkel's we call an end to the hunt. A note about predators. They are not always successful. I understand that wolves are successful only about one out of eight times they pursue a caribou.

We pack the car, shut down the cabin and return home. We drive down from high winter through late fall and back into Fort Collins with its green lawns, a few trees doggedly hanging on to their brown shrivelled leaves, and some color here and there from summer's last flowers.

But homecoming is not simple. We unpack and I head to the office to catch up on calls and mail. One call changes it all. One call and my mood transforms from a tired, but happy, outdoorsman to concerned brother. "Call Bev, your brother is in the coronary care unit in North Carolina." How quickly one piece of news changes life's perspective. I set about a vigorous telephone work-out and in thirty minutes am talking to Gaylord. His spirits are up. No heart damage detected but he has experienced the abrupt onset of high blood pressure and angina. He wonders about our family history. Grandfather Andresen died of a stroke. His first cardiac problems coming on at age fifty-three. Gay (as he prefers to be called) is fifty-three. I offer my presence if he wants it. I am flying to Philadelphia tomorrow and will be nearby. He says he will think about it. There are some times a person wants to be alone with his illness. Maybe he will want me to come later.

When your own flesh and blood hears death's knock, you hear it too. I am grateful for having contemplated death a few moons back. Somehow death seems a little more familiar to me. But how about the potential loss of a loved one? Contemplating death, your own death, doesn't cover all the bases. I sense a terrible chance of a great potential loss.

waxing gibbous₁

My silence evolves with some difficulty. For the past four days, between workshops and hunting, I have scarcely taken the special time needed to nourish my soul. And now, a swirl of ideas clamor for my attention. After several minutes of giving each idea a little attention (much like a parent listening to each child before getting on with important business) I succeed in relaxing. I systematically purge myself of the attachments which keep me bound. I let go of each concern pressing for my attention. I let go of Gay, of writing, of my education, of all labels and titles, my gender, my name, Carol, my future, my past, my expectations about what God should be like.

OK. What if God is not all good? What if God, like the human beings supposedly created in his image, has a shadow side? How do you account for evil without inventing a devil? The shadow side of God . . . . I wonder. Maybe not necessarily evil, but dark, unwanted. I will not reject this troubling concept out of hand. Neither will I embrace it. I will let the concept season in my unconscious. Lately, in spite of depressions, suicides, molestations, drugs, bombings and starvation, I have looked around and seen beauty and wonder. In the process, I have felt especially loved and have wanted to become especially loving in return.

I am reminded of my theory that evil is like a parasite living off whatever attention is paid it. I don't choose to be so naive as to live pretending evil does not exist. Yet I feel motivated towards devoting my energy, my creativity, my life to the nourishment of that which is loving, that which is uplifting, that which draws on the best of humankind's potential.

14,000 feet above Pennsylvania

Terribly digital. Here we are in a holding pattern, our landing delayed by bad weather. So it's in-flight movies and headphones for all. Ignoring the offers, I write on my trusty lap-top. I call Gay on the airborne phone, only to get a busy signal. Planes and all their sophisticated gear are so totally digital. And I depend on them. Yesterday morning it was coyote tracks in the mountains. This evening it is an imaginary race track pattern in the sky over a cloudy eastern seaboard.

_____*waxing gibbous₃*_____

On the train, Delaware

Another day, another humor workshop. I spend some time with Rabbi Bob and then Elaine chauffeurs us around the big city. The weather: Gray, rainy, and raw. The highways are packed with cabs and garbage trucks. Carol and I jockey on commuter trains through unfamiliar surroundings connecting to the Amtrack train heading for Washington. I talk to Gay. No longer brave or strong, he says simply, I'd love for you to visit. That's all it takes; I'll be off to North Carolina tomorrow. Silent time is snatched here and there; in a cab, in the train station, in moments looking out a window.

_____*waxing gibbous₄*_____

Washington, D.C.

Carol's sister and brother live here. Analog, loving people, they have committed their lives to serving the poor of the Washington ghettos. *The Community of Hope* appropriately names their facility where they practice what most altruistic people simply preach. Worn out from the day's variety and travel, we spend an exhausted night on Lois's sofa bed. She suggests I might like to jog around the Capitol, about a three mile jaunt. I know better. My inner self says slow down, you're going too fast. We opt instead for oat bran muffins, orange juice and coffee at the corner bakery. I have a couple hours to kill before my plane leaves. Instead of rushing about, we visit the Botanical Gardens. I leave Carol and Lois to sisterly conversation.

They leave me with the orchids. How aware you become when you smell the perfume of orchids with every breath. Now I feel ready to see Gay, who I just found out has re-entered coronary care.

If I let go of all attachments, if I even let go of all expectations of what God is like, I still find myself not letting go of one expectation: Trust. Regardless of what I release, trust remains. Because when I hang on to nothing at all, what am I doing but trusting that the Origin of Life will not mistreat me? Like an infant falling asleep in his mother's arms, I trust I shall not be dropped. Somehow I do not know how to let go of trust. Letting go is an ultimate act of trust.

I board the plane and watch Washington disappear under the wing. The trees, like so many muted clumps of earthen-colored cauliflower, carpet the valley. Colors are no longer vibrant, but instead soothing, seeming to accept and trust the coming of winter.

waxing gibbous₅

Greensboro, North Carolina

Trees enjoy a longer fall here in the South — interesting trees: Sweet gum, black gum, dogwood, willow oak, pin oak, water oak, live oak, ordinary oak, magnolias, myrtles, maples, sycamores, poplars. Some leaves are shiny green, some multi-colored, some dried and on the ground. I jog, soaking up the oxygen-laden air of sea level. When I come to drifts of dried leaves, I slow to walk so I can kick my way through — nice sound, nice aroma.

I spend several hours with Gay. His diagnosis isn't clear; chest pain, some heart blockage, but more pain than the heart problem alone suggests. I find myself, like other family members in the hospital, waiting long hours for the doctors to appear. I don't exert my influence as part of the medical fraternity. I wait my turn. They send assistants, nurses, chaplains and insurance clerks, but no doctors. In the meantime, Gay and I talk. We talk as brothers talk when life seems more precious; speaking of important things, remembering

246

shared memories, clearing up past business, laughing, telling jokes, being frank, talking of death. I help him shave. I carry his urine bag as he hobbles a short walk to the door of his room. I read to him and then write as he dozes. Fear isn't the issue, uncertainty is.

I wait for the doctors. And I wait. Don't I belong to that fraternity? I try never to keep my patients waiting. Maybe being analog means being courteous, being concerned.

FULL MOON

Two days and still no confirmed diagnosis. Two days of close talk with Gay, with Ann, and finally with doctors; all kinds of them now. Love, if it is genuine, easily translates into action. Love is not just a state of being, a manner of feeling; *love is a state of doing.* In past generations, love was translated into action while few words were spoken. Nowadays, love is spoken of but fails to translate into action. When you live out your love, you somehow do not become depleted. You may become exhausted, sleepy or dull, but you do not feel empty, depleted. I am glad to be here with my brother. I am glad he is alive. But I am troubled, I am so uncertain what is going to happen. Therein lies the rub. Tests, tests, and more tests. And still no definitive answers. My vigorous big brother can walk twenty steps and then stops, pale, sweating and exhausted. Returning to bed he falls off to sleep. Yet the heart tests fail to demonstrate any damage, only a seventy per cent blockage in one artery.

We talk of his intensity, his need to excel, his compulsive need to achieve perfection. We wonder if he were less driven whether he would be in this situation now. There is no way of knowing. We just wonder. I caution him against his tendency of self-criticism, fearing he will blame himself as though his condition is a result of some deep character flaw.

247

Finally I need to leave. Back to Washington to meet Carol and fly back home. I leave with a promise to return on the next plane if he needs me.

waning gibbous₁

Home

I awaken to a warm, heavenly morning. Before sunrise a snow white moon relaxes above the western horizon about three fist breadths north of Horsetooth rock. The eastern sky, painted by a clown, dances with the oncoming morning. It is warm, warm enough to jog in shorts. If the trees weren't bare, it would be hard to know how late in fall this morning was. Few birds call, just an isolated redwing and distant honking from a lone goose.

Home is where I experience silence most easily. Home is where I get the best breakfasts, the ones tailored just for me. Home is where the candles seem to pray just a bit more clearly. My home is my monastery; always a good place to be.

I'm home, ready to get back into the swing of things. Tonight I will find out more about Gay. Today I will see how my friends/patients have fared in my absence. I will try to scale the mountain of waiting phone calls. But first, I will start with my morning silence, a familiar run around Warren, and some nourishing contemplative reading. So far this moon has been a very busy time.

waning gibbous₃

Busy, busy, busy. My time for writing, my time for contemplation, each is inversely proportional to the demands of my practice. For the past several days, those demands have been intense — an overflowing schedule, more and deeper depressions. D* is not wanting to commit suicide, merely wanting to mutilate her body. Each evening I call for the medical report on Gay. More negative tests. We know many dread diseases he does not have. But still, no clinching diagnosis. Medicine is like that. We want it to be scientific, molecular, precise. We test with million dollar gadgets to pinpoint esoteric diagnoses. Yet, in many cases, we don't know for sure. We settle for a combination of causes in some odd mixture that seems to best explain the problem. Anyway, he is feeling stronger and more optimistic.

Piercing dry cold coupled with more wind has finally stripped all the trees. Few birds expose themselves. Yesterday I saw a large magpie, all decked out in his tuxedo, picking seeds out of some pine cones. I never knew they ate pine nuts, but then again, they are adaptable birds and know how to survive. A week ago, the finest crystalline ice formed lacy margins around the lakes. As I drive to ECT the morning sun reflects off hard mirrors of ice. Only the very middle of the lake still exposes water. It steams bright gold and red.

waning gibbous$_6$

Warm again — in the seventies. Today is Saturday, a day to be outside. Carol and I awaken slowly, ease our way through some waffles, linger over coffee and our morning reading, immerse ourselves in Bach's *B-Minor Mass*. I retire to my chair where my silence deepens and I continue the process of letting go. Back when I started this journey, I had no idea where it would lead. Would I find myself hanging out on a tropical beach? Would I become a hermit living in a mountain cabin? Would I quit my job? Would I relinquish being a parent? Would the whole process be a flash in the pan and would I continue living life, unchanged?

My meditation this morning: I center, relax deeply, paying attention to my breathing, assuring myself of silence. Carol, busy in the kitchen, respects my solitude.

I let go of my writing.
I let go of my education.

I let go of my need to be liked, respected, admired.
I let go of my worry, for Gay, for Barbara.
I let go of my children.
I let go of my patients.
I let go of being right.
I let go of my past.
I let go of my future.
I let go of all labels and titles.
I let go of Carol.
I let go of my gender.
I let go of my self.
I let go of my body.
I let go of the natural world.
I let go of my life.
I let go of what I expect God to be like.

Then . . . . alone, I trust in the Silence.

Living God . . . . God with me, Light within me.
Loving God . . . . God loving me, loving all.
Mystery God . . . . daring to trust what I do not know.
Shadow side of God . . . . trusting what I cannot know.

Trusting, trusting, trusting, trusting, trusting.

LAST QUARTER

Warren is full to the brim. The ditch company must have decided to store their water here for the winter. No wind, so the surface mirrors thousands of geese. The northerners are arriving, crowding the place. Quickly they accustom themselves to being in town, away from threatening shotguns. I jog past a small assembly of Canadians, they just waddle away. Midway around the lake, they all decide to take the afternoon air. What a commotion! Geese, thousands of them flying in ribbons or families or pairs — all different directions, all different altitudes, all cackling and honking at once.

When I complete my run, I climb on my bike and ride the circuit. All the crops are in. The soil is turned over and ready to soak up winter's moisture. Cattle glean the cornfields while sheep nibble the last of the alfalfa. Farmers are burning ditches, smudging the air with smoke here and there. Coming home, I remember a promise I made myself. I get a garbage bag full of leaves and take it to the abandoned dog/bunny kennel. Carefully, I mound the leaves and then, in full knowledge that I am breaking the law, I light them on fire for the aromatic joy of it all. Carol and I sit in lawn chairs smell the aroma and say good-by to the last remnants of fall.

For many falls as a boy, I smelled burning leaves and it brought a special sense of peace and rightness. So now, while the farmers smudge the sky, burning their ditches, I too smudge the sky, just a little bit, in a ritual celebrating the turning of the season and the bare tree moon.

Just when I am feeling the mellowest and waxing poetic, Trudy peers over the fence and exclaims "Thank goodness! I thought your house was on fire." I explain the ritual and she adds her memory of childhood. Raking the leaves into imaginary floorplans of the ground, then piling the leaves high and jumping in them, finally piling the leaves in the street and burning them. The whole generation since the time when John Kennedy was shot has been deprived of the fall ritual of burning leaves.

The sunset is a dazzling pink and periwinkle blue. I watch the sun disappear a full four fist-breadths south of Horsetooth. The smell of burning leaves lingers.

I really want his opinion; after all, he is an expert. For several days we have played telephone tag, now we are having breakfast and he presents me his glossy, bound marketing proposal.

I love speaking to groups, the bigger the better. I feel I have something to say about laughter, about love, about living in the midst of a digital/materialistic world. But my speaking engagements have leveled off. I want to go for it. One hundred percent, a life of writing, speaking, meditating. A life that will leave time to sit with wolves in the moonlight.

He suggests thirty thousand in venture capital, more pizzazz in my brochures, and videos costing eight hundred dollars a minute to be sold for twelve hundred a set. Then try syndication on cable television, columns in trade magazines, contacts with the Fortune 500 companies. Your potential is only limited by how hard you want to work. You are a good product, we just have to get you out there.

I like him. He is sincere, hard working and knows the world of marketing. But he is offering me a difficult solution. Do I want to speak to and write for interested audiences who will grow with me, who yearn for more simplicity, more spirituality? Do I want to leave the sometimes painfully difficult practice of psychiatry behind me? Do I want to take my twenty-five years of experience and let those years talk, hoping to prevent some of the atrocities that have filled my office so often? Of course I do. But at what price? Market, intensity, timetables, balance sheets, investors? I don't think so. I don't want a life consumed with worries about business ventures, worries that will crowd out my time for silence. I will take some of his ideas, but my path is too different. I cannot let a commercial venture, however attractive, sap my energies. I will carry on at my present pace, serving my patients and picking up a workshop here and there, getting my books into the hands of those like-minded wherever I can. Big business is a leviathan, waiting to devour the unwary; a digital Mephistopheles offering me a deal.

When does it happen?   Or is it even a proper question to wonder when? *The Light Within.* It starts as interesting concept, a comforting notion. Then the idea grows and is spoken of as if it were reality. In silence, you wait. You wait for God. You cannot make it happen. You cannot will it into existence. You cannot manipulate its appearance. You go on living as if it were real, you talk as if it were real.

Then one day, in silence, you sense its presence. The idea becomes a reality somewhere within you. The Light *is* there! The Light is there within. And it is everywhere else too. Personal and yet continuous with the Universe and beyond space. Light, alive, loving, personal, real. Light unbounded by time.

This morning, without fanfare, without pronouncements on my part; this morning I suddenly experienced the reality of the Light within me — illumination. Not something to be talked about. It is more like the first moment of conception, something important happening but no one else knows.

I run, light afoot, talking with the bare trees, the geese, and the few humans I meet running around my favorite route.

Oh, and I didn't mention that one patient overdosed yesterday and had a seizure in my office. I'm starting ECT on D* in the morning. And Gay is home from the hospital.

When I was talking about the marketing plan to increase my income from speaking and writing, Dan offered an analysis that summed up the conflict. He was offering you an outcome, not a

253

path. The path is more important than the outcome. The analog path lets me live richly in the present instead of pining away for some future whose shoulder I will look past once it arrives. The path, the process, the present, living in constant consciousness of the Light, yes. Not giving in to some Master Plan and then turning away from the very meaning and essence of my life.

And just as I begin to think of myself as being one of the spiritual elite, I meet my prideful self full force as anger intrudes on my simplicity and my silence. Anger, that most useless of emotions for settling human differences, that device underlying war, prejudice and abuse. Anger, my anger, stares me in the face and taunts me to let it have its way, if even only in fantasy. But no, I will go back to purgation, to letting go. Letting go of anger, letting go of that attachment which forcefully reminds me of my self-centeredness once again.

Anger? Yes, she called me timid. She called me competitive. And I feel angry, I want to tell her off, I want to shun her. But, no, I must let go. Not stuff it. Not stifle it. Not swallow it. No, let go of it. I must be effective in my dealings with her. Anger is only rarely effective. Like booze, its seeming benefits are at best temporary. Its long term consequences are totally disabling.

waning crescent₅

Our so-called energy-efficient house has a drawback in cold weather, it's chilly, very chilly. This morning we want to linger under our down comforter. I let go of my anticipated discomfort over the chill and get up to greet the rising sun. What a sight! A golden fleece blankets Warren Lake with downy softness several feet deep. The lawns are great expanses of crystals; shining, twinkling, reflecting, dancing. I go downstairs, light the candle, start the oatmeal and grind the coffee. I check the thermometer for its judgement: Nine degrees above. Isn't that seventy degrees colder than it was a week ago?

I am almost sad to see this moon draw to a close. Inside I feel like I need another quarter moon to get my contemplative work done. But not to worry, tomorrow the cycle starts again. And with it, new discoveries, new insights, new dances. I like marking time with moons rather than years, there are so many more of them. There are so many more beginnings and endings, so many more moods, so much more variety. Measuring years by numbers surely has hastened the demise of the poet in all of us.

I run, I pray, I read, I smile. I even feel joy. Then I clean up and head to work to do my part in lifting the depression of the world, if only in the lives of the few souls I will see today.

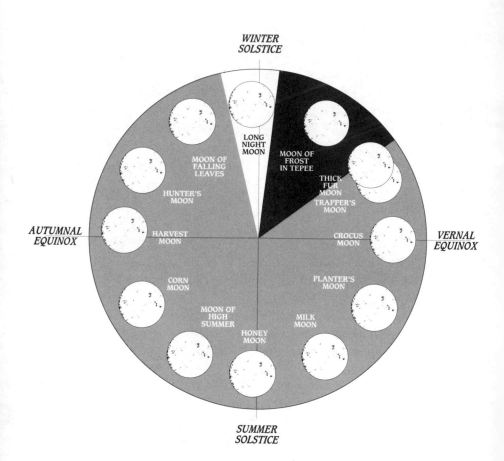

WINTER
SOLSTICE

LONG
NIGHT
MOON

MOON OF
FALLING
LEAVES

MOON OF
FROST
IN TEPEE

HUNTER'S
MOON

THICK
FUR
MOON

TRAPPER'S
MOON

AUTUMNAL
EQUINOX

HARVEST
MOON

CROCUS
MOON

VERNAL
EQUINOX

CORN
MOON

PLANTER'S
MOON

MOON OF
HIGH
SUMMER

MILK
MOON

HONEY
MOON

SUMMER
SOLSTICE

Chapter Eleven

LONG NIGHT MOON

THERE ARE SEVERAL NAMES for this moon: Christmas Moon, Yule Moon, Cold Moon, Moon of the Popping Trees, or The Long Night Moon. In medieval times pagans held festivals at the winter solstice. Recognizing the need to reclaim the promise of lengthening days and the return of spring, they burned bonfires, brought colorful plants inside, and prepared feasts to fortify themselves for winter's onslaught. Christians, not knowing the date of Jesus's birth, decided to crowd in on the festival, make it more "sacred." That lasted a while, but now Christmas has been crowded out by crass commercialization that would make any self-respecting pagan ill. Bright reds and greens still adorn the indoor atmospheres as do lights, the little electric bonfires on indoor trees.

As their names for this moon suggest, Native Americans lived through the cold of this time of year, more readily accepting the weather than longing for spring's warmth. My favorite name is _The Long Night Moon_. It is astronomically correct and also serves as a metaphor. Long, dark nights are inevitable for seekers who open themselves to the mystery of life. I will dance with these cold, long nights and learn to savor them just as lovingly as I savored the voluptuous spring breezes, lazy summer evenings, and fall's splashy show of color. It is winter. I embrace it. The days are short, the nights long, and all is right with the world.

waxing crescent₁

Tomorrow night I may be a fool, a saint, or a yawn. For seven years I have taught positive humor. My travelling medicine-humor show is well greased, smooth and comfortable. So long as I vary my audiences, the well-worn material sounds new to my listeners; fresh, funny, informative. Tomorrow night I am going a step further, I am going to talk about love; but no jokes, no sermonizing, no new-age pizazz. I will risk saying that love exists outside of us, just like radio waves exist outside of us. You need a receiver to pick them up, to make sense of them. You may not even know they exist. You are the receiver, you can choose to tune yourself in, clear the static, enhance the music or you can ignore it, leave your receiver off. Worse yet, you break it. But the radio waves exist nonetheless.

Love exists. We don't create it. We discover it. And with the right effort, we can amplify love and pass it on. Just as I have been teaching people how to increase humor in their lives, I now take the chance of teaching my companions how to increase love in their lives. I believe it can work, but am I woman enough for the job?

waxing crescent₂

Mark comes over to put the final touches on the show. I feel nervous. I never get nervous before a show. Then again, I have never been so audacious as to think I can tell other people how to discover and practice more love in their lives. We discuss the admission fee, food for the homeless shelter. We talk of my decision not to go ahead with the zealous marketing plan to make the big time. Mark's dry reply, "You know, the bottom line really isn't _the_ bottom line."

waxing crescent₃

It worked, or at least I think it did. There were tears in abundance, hugs all around, many kind words. I think it worked, but then there is really no way to know for sure. Popularity is no insurance of serving as a conduit for grace. (If anything, the contrary is the case: Rather than confirming grace, popularity almost assures the achievement of some narcissistic goal.) I give myself a B. Now I will let the ideas season for a while and wait for the next opportunity to talk about love. I guess I am waiting for some doors to open.

The day is radiant blue. There is still no lasting snow. The balmy temperatures melt the night-formed ice from the surface of Warren. During the morning hours geese choose to rest on the mirror-like plates of ice, tucking heads under wings, appearing to feel rested and safe. You can almost watch the sun set further south every night. This evening the crescent moon, delicate as lace, rises higher in the sky, accompanied at a respectful distance by the evening star.

waxing crescent₄

How simple is love? I believe, in its essence, it is probably divinely simple. But applying love with my imperfect will, trying to control it, modify it, question it; love seems more complicated. When do I as a therapist confront manipulation, co-dependence, deceit? When and how do I as a friend confront prejudice or hostility in those closest to me, those whose friendship I dare not lose? What do

259

I do when I look inward and see myself feigning love, seeking instead popularity or acceptance? I don't really know. For now I make some approximate answers to these questions and then live on, flubbing-up as I go along.

_____ *waxing crescent₅* _____

Things don't always work the way you want. Things break, plans go astray, people fail. Over a moon ago, my car's battery died. No big deal. But some clever technician coded my radio so if its electrical supply were ever interrupted, it wouldn't work again unless the right code was reinserted; a theft-discouraging device, a workable idea. But what if you don't know the code? I didn't know it, the garage didn't know it, and after three tries the radio is kaput — ninety-six dollars to take it out and reinstall it with a new code. For over a moon, I have been driving in silence and, as much as I like music and the news, I am beginning to like the silence more. I will probably get it fixed, but not just now.

D* is failing to achieve any positive results from ECT. She only has the negative side effects of memory loss and confusion and no reprieve from depression. I am running out of options. I honestly don't know what to do next. She is so very broken. I am supposed to be the fix-it technician of the human heart. And I am failing. I must be patient. I must wait. I must keep trying. I have nowhere else to turn.

_____ FIRST QUARTER _____
Dallas, Texas

Fancy, fancy, fancy: The Anatole Hotel is somewhere between Oz and the Taj Mahal. Huge, it spreads out for acres, sparkling with light-studded trees, fountains, sculptures and twelve story high tapestries. A home away from home for the very wealthy, "President

Bush stays here." I am here doing my thing, offering some educators my perspectives on positive humor. I weave in courtesy, respect, and love, and no one seems to mind.

One idea nags me. The teachers talk of how fifty-five per cent of their students are on free lunch programs. They lament the unstable mobility of their students' families (if the family exists as a unit at all), the high drop-out rates, the drugs, the violence and the too-frequent sexual abuse. Above all, they lament the absence of money for what they need to accomplish with their hungry children, demoralized families, and growing abyss of hopelessness. And here I am, in the arms of luxury, opulence. There is a radical discontinuity here. I admit total ignorance of economics, but that does not discourage me from critically wondering if there isn't a better way, if our government (or if we, the people, individually and collectively) couldn't help the underprivileged more. I realize that merely throwing money at the problem is not the solution, though money will be required. And I do know that just like the wolves, the poor must be approached with courtesy and respect or they will remain distant, distrusting and unwilling to sing together to the Origin of Life.

This is just a quick trip, I'll be back home tomorrow. The night doesn't seem so long in Dallas. Could it be that much further south? I don't know.

waxing gibbous₁

Home

I come home to what feels like a little cousin of a maelstrom. The days are overfilled, crowding out time for silence (though I still manage a little) and exercise (I haven't jogged a step). My days are patient-filled from seven to seven. When I get home, the mental marathon I've been running leaves little energy, so I content myself with music, mindless reading, or even television. As a depressed patient put it, the squirrel in her mind's cage can only run on the treadmill for so long before it collapses.

261

I see fourteen people in twelve hours. Why so many? I am trying to make up for the time I missed from my practice when I was on the road. More importantly, most of my patients are feeling particularly pressured. This is the long night moon and Christmas is coming. Lofty, light-studded and colorful expectations are surrendering to an impending, prolonged darkness; a darkness which doesn't hide, but paradoxically magnifies imperfections and magnifies the pain of admitting to them.

I talk to Gay; he is better, much better. He is more peaceful. This is a miracle of sorts, love operating in its own special way. And it is science too. Its results would be called miracles a hundred years ago. Today they are simply called facts.

<hr>

waxing gibbous₂

It's the weekend again. I have time — precious time to catch up on meditation, reading and exercise. And I have time for getting my priorities back in line. We buy a Christmas tree. Decorating it floods me with memories, some good, some bad. Many lofty expectations died in the darkness of my past. I remember how my father took such pleasure in looking at the tree. He would put on a white shirt, a tie, shine his shoes, and then sit for hours quietly looking at the tree. We didn't have music to distract from the silence. He was more peaceful during those hours than at any time in his life (except for the last two weeks before his death). I like sitting in front of the tree too. It is almost as if I partly become my father. I often feel that way. We look a lot alike, we act alike, we have the same sense of humor. Only I am educated and have succeeded in securing a joyful marriage. At times, when I feel particularly joyful, I hope he is feeling some of the joy as well. I know he wanted joy and laughter in life. But, for him, circumstances weren't too conducive to his achieving joy and laughter.

Carol and I go shopping. We both are wimps about shopping. We hate it. The malls are like Pacific rivers during the salmon spawn. We try to balance gifts for the kids, keeping needs and equivalent value in mind. We both notice how little we need or even want anymore. About the only things that attract me are books and music.

---

waning gibbous₁

Twenty-one years ago yesterday, I soloed a high-performance military aircraft for the first time. Twenty-one years ago today, I assisted in delivering my second son to life. Two days ago, while decorating the Christmas tree, I took the little ornamental plane, a replica of my first flight and threw it in the garbage. Last night I talked to Chris on the phone as he prepares for final exams. I have little doubt he will partake of some libations tomorrow, now that he is finally *legal*.

The day is cloudy and cold — very cold. I have communed with the moon very little and I miss it. Instead, I have been busy with my job, dealing with persons encountering their personal forms of darkness.

My mind is a jumble, a mixed up collection of seemingly-unrelated topics: Broken airplanes, nostalgic remembrances, encounters with ice and cold in real life and in the human heart. Most of all, I reflect on how suffering is an inescapable fact of life. Coming in diverse forms, its one certainty is its constant presence and transforming power in every life. I am here to help others out of their suffering, but can I? Really? Do I? Does anyone?

---

waning gibbous₂

A dream has recurred to me for who-knows-how-long. I discover spacious, though dusty, dark and foreboding rooms in a house I inhabit. Bit by bit, over these years I have stumbled into these rooms and felt slightly more comfortable. They appear cleaner, less foreboding, but still uninhabited. I wonder why I, or other people, don't make use of them. Then this morning I happened upon them again. How beautiful they've become; furnished tastefully, freshly painted, an elegant sculpture right outside the window. And I say this is so nice, I want to live here from now on. Somehow I know Carol was responsible for the repainting and tasteful decorations. Somehow I also feel this is a room for my contemplative work as well.

The rooms are parts of my own unconscious. How splendid that the love of another can bring such beauty to your innermost parts where once they were filled with foreboding darkness.

waning gibbous₃

Driving in the darkness of the winter morning, I need not quantify the cold temperature. My radio is broken and I'm not reading the paper in the mornings anymore. But I know it's cold; the car exhaust is cottony white and hangs in the air for several seconds. I am driving to the hospital for ECT.

One of my old patients, a woman stricken with manic depressive disease has a date with me. Eight years ago, when I met her, fresh from two years in the state hospital, she had returned home only to descend into psychosis, uttering growls instead of words, biting all who attempted to help her, and smearing feces on the walls of her bare room. Why had no person offered her ECT? I don't know. I did. Her husband signed. The court concurred. And *voila*, she cleared. After that, I prescribed a different regimen of drugs and she returned to work. A baker, she is eccentric, but loved by all. Twice in the last eight years she has "fallen off the deep end" and required brief courses of ECT. Each time, she failed to see it coming and succumbed to the terror of her disease. Now is different, she called four days ago, "Doc, it's coming. I need another treatment." Last night I talked to her and her husband. Both understand, both are ready. Both are grateful she senses the monster at the door of her hidden room.

When I arrive in the treatment room, she is ready with IV in place. I hold her hand as she falls asleep. The treatment is simple. Then ten minutes later, as she is awakening, I hover by her ear offering affirmations. I tell the nurse to do the same as my friend regains consciousness. Then I go to the dining room, eat a couple of bran muffins, drop in on a clinical conference (on PMS), and then go on to a team meeting on my in-patients. Then I have a dozen people to see in the office. Although it is a busy day, I finish it feeling fulfilled.

Carol has a simple meal prepared after which the evening slips away as I lie on the sofa, my head in Carol's lap. I watch the fire dance and the Christmas tree sparkle in the darkened room. I don't know when the evening ends. It just sort of slips away. Carol takes me by the hand in the darkness, we go upstairs. I brush my teeth and fall asleep, hoping to visit the beautiful room of my unconscious once again.

waning gibbous₄

Jung said, "Hurry isn't of the devil, it *is* the devil." Hurry is the greatest excuse for neglecting a spiritual path and the most common accompaniment for psychological violence. In our world digital is hurried. Analog is leisurely. This morning is once again a weekend. I linger long in prayer. I watch the snow falling. The scene is gray and white, no color. Tonight there will be colors everywhere and lights on trees. These colors don't celebrate the birth of Jesus as much as they symbolize our faith in the coming of spring with all its color. We need that now as we enter the darkness and the cold. So be it. I am prepared to linger with winter, with its darkness and its cold; linger just as I did with summer's warm breezes and the birds winging through the late evening twilight.

_waning gibbous_₅

First day, silent meeting. Christmas time. This morning I look out on the snow hoping to see rabbit tracks, but there are none. Bunny is safe and sound in Mr. Herbst's kennel.

At meeting, my mind is more active than usual, wanting to compose a novel I should one day write, rather than settling down to listening for The Origin whispering within. Finally, using words, I ask God to quiet my literary plans since I seem incapable of doing so.

Then, jolted, I remember. I remember V*, a Viet Nam vet, one of many. Medications didn't help. Therapy didn't help. He dropped out a month ago. Thirty-one weeks of therapy were no match for thirty-one months of combat. Bitter pain and witnessed atrocities became demons consuming his psyche. He remembered this time of year, in fact this specific date, as the worst of all. Some hill, somewhere in Southeast Asia, one they had _taken_ on two other occasions. A hill without a name, just numbers (how damned digital!). On that hill, twenty-one years ago this very morning, thirteen of his fifteen comrades were killed. Though wounded himself, all he remembers is their dismembered, chalk-white corpses, their screaming and his own helplessness and rage. As I recall our conversation, I become aware of the children in the next room singing Christmas carols, songs of hope and peace among all men, songs of God with us, God within us. And I remembered telling V* as we parted that I didn't know what else I could do, but I would be here, I would listen, I would not leave him alone with his pain. He asked if I prayed, I said yes. He asked for me to remember to pray specifically on this day, not just for him, but for the thirteen dead boys left on that hillside. I promised him I would. So in the silence, I remember my promise and I speak aloud to my silent Friends that they may pray also. As I pray, I let go . . . and I pray that V* learns to let go, too. Then, tempest past, I once again hear the children sing. My mind settles into silence and I listen for the murmurings of The Light within.

waning gibbous₆

It is too cold to run. I still do read thermometers at times. Though the bright morning sunlight looks warm and inviting, it says nothing of the cold. The thermometer warns that it is eight below, too cold to run. Digital or not, I accept the advice. Carol goes to swim, I immerse myself in my books. Reading on cold days is rather pleasant, but its success is a function of the warmth of one's long underwear when the house tends to be chilly.

In my warm underwear and robe, I think of those with no heat at all. Coldness, if sufficiently severe, will consume your consciousness just focusing on survival, let alone comfort. Too bad the opposite isn't the case. When warm and comfortable, too many people go on manufacturing problems to consume their spirits instead of giving thanks to the Origin of the fire.

And then I itch. Our dry air and our very soft water add up to this being the dry-skin-itches-too-much-moon. Somehow, as I get older, my skin gets drier. Curse it? No, I will be the jolly itcher. With each scratch I experience being alive and growing older. This is just one more gentle tease from this winter moon. I don't think I will shower today — just wash the essentials and apply plenty of lotion.

LAST QUARTER

Every year I look for her Christmas card and every year she delights me with one more variation on the theme. Christmas wasn't always good to her, though. When we met ten years ago, she came in depressed, hopeless, helpless and ready to die. But love for husband and love for her three grown children drove her to seek my help. Her story is familiar to those of us in the business. Only it's more gruesome than most, more heartless; you might say more evil. The summer before coming into therapy her defenses crumbled at her father's funeral when two older sisters took her aside and

267

confided she was not actually their *real* sister. She was born to an older sister, now deceased; their father was not her father. It was obvious. After all, she was the only red haired child in the family of nine kids.

That revelation broke the shaky defenses she erected thirty-two years before when, at knife point, she threatened her father that if he ever raped her again, she would kill him. She meant it and he believed her. So it was at thirteen she became free of his assaults which had been commonplace since the first sadistic rape when she was nine. Secluded on a farm in Iowa, she had nobody to turn to. Her *mother* was distant and cold. We now know why.

As our therapy developed, the pieces fit together. She was conceived by her oldest sister, now deceased, and her father. Her *mother* (really grandmother) kept the secret, raising her as if she were her own child. But she showed no love, only neglect and contempt — contempt which the rest of the family readily picked up on and practiced with sadistic perfection. Not until she was five years old was she ever in a family picture, and then only because she forced her way in.

In the second grade she worked on an art project, the manufacture of Christmas gift wrapping paper from the brown store variety. It was the Depression, and fancy gift paper was unheard of. She decorated her paper with the angelic hosts; several of the angels bearing lovely red hair. The family found her creation to be particularly ludicrous. Everyone around the supper table laughed at it and then her father ceremoniously tore it up and threw it in the kitchen stove. Anyone knows angels can't have red hair. There isn't such a thing.

She recalled this as we approached our first Christmas of therapy. I asked her to close her eyes, relax, and follow me as we imagined we were children together, a long time ago.

"We're best friends, you and me. Nine year-old shepherd's kids. But tonight we don't stay in Bethlehem with the women, we go out in the country because there is excitement in the air. Is it the census and the crowds? Or is it that very bright star? Where did it come from anyway? What does it mean?

"Too excited to sleep, we sit out on the hillside away from the fire where the men are watching the sheep, watching the sky, and talking about things we don't understand. And then it happens. A sound never heard before fills the sky. It's like wind and music all at once — a sound so deep you feel it more than hear it. Beyond words . . . . singing, unlike any we have ever heard. Spellbound, we can only listen in awed silence. We watch the sky, we look at each other, and then gradually we make out tall figures — incredibly tall. Comforting us, they make us feel so very safe. They are mostly human form, but oh, so big . . . . so protective. And their music, it's beyond words. . . .heavenly.

"Take my hand. Look. Can you see them? Look closely, they are very much like us. And look very closely now. See their hair? Isn't it beautiful? What color do you see?"

Eyes closed, tears streaming, big smile, she nodded, "Red. The angels have red hair."

Now, every Christmas, I get a different card from her — a card bearing an angel with red hair. Do you know how many angels have red hair? Infinitely many. That's how many. And merry Christmas to you, my friend.

_____*waning crescent₁*_____

Winter Solstice

Oh, the plans of mice and men . . . I planned to celebrate the solstice in the manner of the ancients; a few friends gathering at Carl's to build a big fire, one big enough to convince God to remember us and not take the sun entirely away. With days growing shorter all the time, something must be done to insure a turn-a-round, to assure lengthening days and finally the return of spring. I intended to bring prayer sticks to the fire, pieces of wood bearing old sins, guilts or angers we wanted to discard. We would throw them in

269

the fire and symbolically see ourselves freed of their domination as the fire consumed the wood.

The reality of the day is very different. First it turned out to be only Carl and I. Then he had to go and pick up his daughter from college. Then the temperature cascaded down to twenty-seven below, so cold that brushing the snow off the car left my hands on fire.

And how do I end up spending my evening? I spend it in the video studio for eight hours putting together a demonstration videotape; one required to further my plans as a professional speaker. I spend my time in a room filled with electronic boxes, video monitors, hundreds of cables and monotonous views of myself speaking. The video has to be in New York in four days. There is no more time to procrastinate.

waning crescent₂

This Christmas season is unlike any before in my life. Nostalgia and carols and hustle and bustle were the order of things for me in years past. This year, I have found time to get all the business of Christmas completed ahead of time. I have only attended two parties, my office and the Montessori school. I have eaten fewer Christmas cookies. The Christmas music in the shopping malls jangles hypocritically in my ears. Rudolf and Santa and elves and reindeer are out. I am spending less money and enjoying it more. I am taking more time for silence, more time for candles, more time for reading, and more time to dwell deep within myself: Seeking, hoping, reaching inward for the experience of Emmanuel, God within me — wanting very much for it to be real and not so many words. Christmas has moved inside of me this year.

I revel in the white *winter wonderland*. I accept the cold. This is the way Nature unfolds herself. It has really nothing to do with Christmas. Instead, I see Christmas as announcing a radical view of God dwelling within humankind. God is not at a distance. God is not a humanoid judge somewhere. God is not a law of thermodynamics. God, the Origin of the All, is present everywhere, including inside of me. The new physics shows how terribly logical that proposition can be. My task is to harmonize with that Presence and live congruently from that center. Jesus, a prime example (a unique embodiment?). We celebrate his coming to life now. And in the process, I, in my silence, seek to come to life in a similar way. And then, of course, such a birth will have consequences — consequences I can't imagine. I'm sure Jesus and the assembled folks at his birth couldn't imagine his future. They were pretty excited by the phenomena happening before their eyes — red haired angels and the like.

The arctic grip is letting up. Today I run again. Run off some of the Christmas cooking. I'm on call today, too. I am seeking to be aware of _that of God_ in each person today. Such a mind-set takes willingness and a good degree of concentration as well.

waning crescent₃

I'm making hospital rounds the Christmas weekend. I volunteered to cover for part of the holidays. An on-call colleague wanted to be out of town for the week. Hospitals are interesting places at Christmas: Typical decorations, the usual hustle and bustle and unbelievable amounts of homemade sugar-butter confections at every nurses' station. I have four patients to see, all non-paying, all needing not just my services, but my understanding, and justice from our society.

First, I see a young Vietnamese woman showing every evidence of schizophrenia; her English is poor and her culture so distant that my evaluation is less than definitive. Her alcoholic and battering husband is of little help and her uncertain tuberculosis status only complicates matters. She threatened to kill him with a knife a couple of nights ago and now cries to go back home to him. I search for signs of psychosis and discover a few. Medication is in order, but I

271

know it is merely a band-aid — a necessary band-aid, but a band aid just the same. Where is home for her? Anywhere?

A young woman originally from Latvia, here now eight years, is deeply depressed and suicidal. A supportive husband and sound family structure help. She spent the last two days in ICU recovering from a near lethal overdose of her anti-depressant. A pleasant young woman, she speaks almost flawless English. She needs anti-depressants, she needs therapy, and tomorrow she hopes to be allowed out of the hospital to attend Christmas Eve services with her family. I have real hope for her in the long run; she has a good support system and a treatable illness.

Next I see a sixteen year old girl, who last night drank a fifth of vodka. At her party, her friends became frightened when she passed out. They carried her unconscious body to the ER. Her blood alcohol was just under the lethal limit. Admittedly alcoholic since she was fourteen, she needs more than emergency treatment. There is no father in her family, no money, no insurance. We will have to see whether Medicaid will pay for an in-patient treatment program. I seriously doubt we will find funding for her. Her life is in steady decline already. She has dropped out of school and her mother feels she is out of control. We talk awhile and, for starters, I direct her to the AA meeting in the hospital in the morning.

Finally I see a young Hispanic woman. Twenty-three years old, she has three children the oldest of which is eight. She works forty hours a week at McDonald's which manages to pay her rent and utilities. Otherwise she lives on ADC and Medicaid. There were no presents at her house and in an impulsive expression of her desperation, she overdosed on aspirin. Seeing the risk that she might actually die, she came to the hospital by herself. The medical team did its job. Now I have one visit before her discharge to convince her Christmas is of the heart and not of materialism. (Easy for me to say.) I succeed in convincing her to go for therapy and give her a referral card to an agency that accepts Medicaid and focuses on families at risk. I think she will be OK in the short run. But in the long run? I'm afraid there will be more poverty, more single-parenting, more desperate frustration, more moments of despair.

These people are not simply mental patients, they are bearers of our society's shortcomings; its failure to adequately care for its underprivileged people, the ones who started out "a day late and a dollar short," the ones who really don't believe in their heart-of-hearts that capitalism is for everybody. They see it is only for those endowed with money or skills or social class or family of origin.

I remember to look for The Light Within each I meet. I look inside seeking the Christ child within. I do the same with the people I meet at the post office and the grocery store and the dry cleaners. This mind-set of Christmas should be an everyday perspective on life. Returning home, I don't feel defeated by what I have seen. Interestingly, I feel some hope.

waning crescent₄

The weather warms. Warren is a great white table top of snow and ice. Along the west shore some neighbors have shoveled a skating rink. Across the lake the white expanse is broken by the solitary figure of a single dead goose still lying on its breast, but its head has doubled over resting on the top of its beak. As I jog along, I hear shotguns in the far distance. For some, the sport of goose hunting is their way of spending Christmas eve morning.

I linger longer with my hospital visits. The Latvian woman is worse. She spent the night nearly chewing her thumbs off. I have to make a number of medication adjustments. I talk longer with her family and plan our next steps. This afternoon she is completely psychotic having switched her attention from her thumbs to her breasts which she says need to be cut off. I put her on a one-to-one suicide precautions and look for the Light within her wild, other-worldly eyes. It is there.

Our house is full. Our empty nest is overflowing with young adult life with young men too long for the new twin beds. Hot water is in short supply. The music on the stereo changes every time you turn around. And food is consumed at a rate that would frighten a football coach. We are at that stage of life with our young adult children. Each has a separate set of hopes and plans. Each expresses some unique individuality. We are years away from grandchildren (I think), so the gift exchange is casual, low-key, punctuated with laughter and fortunately, not very materialistic. Shirts and socks and ties and books and calendars are orders of the day. Above all, there is warmth and even a certain sense of pride that we, a blended family, have succeeded. We are not all love and perfection, but each of us is growing and seeming to respect the growth of the other.

I continue my visits to the hospital. Though I could turn the patients over to the next on-call psychiatrist, that would involve these people being seen by a different psychiatrist every two days this week. Psychosis is terrifying enough. We should not worsen the experience with new, unknown faces, offering new and different treatment strategies. The psychiatric unit on Christmas morning is a special place — a place where we can have an opportunity to show love, to be love, to nurture those deprived of their reason. The Latvian woman's mental status is still touch-and-go.

The nights are long. The weather is warmer than usual — a distinct relief from the severe cold of the last quarter. I am busy with family and a few patients. There is little room in the house to sit undisturbed in silence. I recall my early years as a parent; little time and scant space for silence. At this point in life, I can hardly do without it.

And Christmas? It is everyday. It is a state of mind. It is an orientation in life. Bethlehem is everywhere. And the Christ child comes in babies everywhere and of all colors and is being born everyday. And the Christ child within does not disappear as a person ages, it only becomes harder to see, covered by layers of frustration, layers of accumulated abuse or neglect, layers of mistakes in narcissistic gratification. The Light within, the Christ within, I don't care what it is called. And I seek no debate with those of other minds. I know this inner core is loving and capable of growing. Our original state of being is one of blessing, not of hate or sin. Those are layers on top of something very pure, something very good, something very simple, something very present . . . in all.

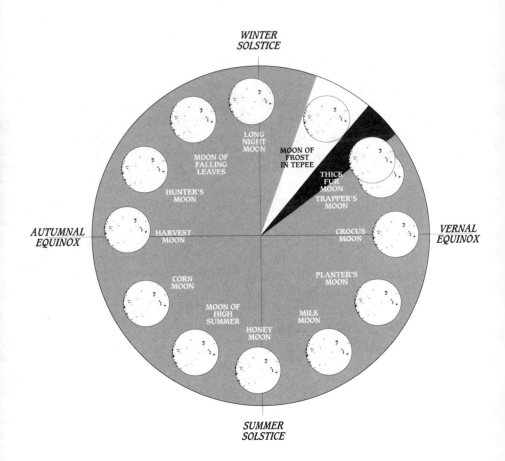

WINTER
SOLSTICE

LONG
NIGHT
MOON

MOON OF
FROST
IN TEPEE

MOON OF
FALLING
LEAVES

THICK
FUR
MOON

HUNTER'S
MOON

TRAPPER'S
MOON

AUTUMNAL
EQUINOX

HARVEST
MOON

CROCUS
MOON

VERNAL
EQUINOX

CORN
MOON

PLANTER'S
MOON

MOON OF
HIGH
SUMMER

MILK
MOON

HONEY
MOON

SUMMER
SOLSTICE

Chapter Twelve

MOON OF FROST IN TEPEE

THE COMMON NAME for this moon is the rather unimaginative Winter Moon. For reasons unknown to me, the Algonquin Indians preferred the term, Wolf Moon. Somewhere deep in eastern hardwood forests, the songs of the wolves must have been particularly haunting during this, the coldest of moons. But I am a prairie boy; the Lakota are closer to my home and heart. Their name for this first full moon of the new year is delightfully descriptive: The Moon of Frost in Tepee. Can you imagine how cold that is? You awaken in the morning and the buffalo robe you are sleeping under is frozen stiff, covered with the frost from your breath.

During the summer moons, I chatted with Carl about how nostalgia is a pleasant exercise, but far removed from real life. We spent wonderful hours in his tepee. But did we ever endure a blizzard out there? Change a baby's diaper out there? Nurse a sick child out there? Suffer through a bout of pneumonia out there? Go

277

hungry or even insane out there? No, we modern white eyes sit in a canvas lodge. We eat and we drink. We pass the pipe. We speak of lofty spiritual ideas.

I love the name of this moon, but on reflection, it speaks to the utter hardness of life. As a result of their physical hardships, the Lakota often died at an early age. And during their lives they weren't all that comfortable either. But did their adversity shape a sacred attitude toward life that we no longer share? The life of the Lakota is by and large lost to us now. We have a few documents, some romantic images, a few surviving descendants. (Most descendants have been destroyed by welfare, the loss of their land, and the loss of their spirituality; all drowned in bourbon and beer.) Now in our centrally heated, gasoline powered, polypropylene insulated lives, many (if not all) of us appropriate God as a part of our culture and use Him to justify our particular social or political aims.

The Lakota revered The Spirit. They must have wrestled with it, implored it, feared It, loved It. And they centered their lives around it and experienced the presence of God deep within their own being. But nowadays, upon what does the modern digital man center his life? Comfort. Wealth. The cult of Being In Touch With Your Feelings. The idol of self worship, hardbodies and the latest rock music.

waxing crescent₁

I have known her for seven years. She lives alone, her sole (soul?) companion, her cat. She works sixty-five hours a week for four-and-a-quarter an hour. We first met when she was nineteen; her brother brought her in, having pooled money from the family for her treatment. Something was wrong. She was, in the family's mind, quite crazy from time to time. They were not misjudging the situation. She was manic-depressive. When manic, she behaved in ways most people would call crazy. I called her behavior crazy:

Bizarre dress, double earrings in her nostrils, multicolored hair, numerous phone calls to the President, and constantly trying to buy a new Mercedes. The first few years were a tussle as she struggled against her diagnosis and against those who wanted to help. But about three years ago she hit bottom: She had too many rubber checks, big troubles with the law, and a roaring suicidal depression. She finally came to me of her own free will. With lithium and psychotherapy she improved, but the situation in her wake was a mess. My pleadings to the court and to her host of bill collectors succeeded. She reshaped a reasonable future for herself.

Slowly extricating herself from debt, she has been faithful with her treatment but still has mood swings. Manic-depressive disease is like a bad back, you manage it, but it doesn't completely go away. This past autumn she fell in love — the real thing. For once she had a man who would care for her, one she could have a future with, raise a family with. At least so she thought. Despite condoms and rhythm she became pregnant. When Mr. Right found out, he left. For a month she denied the reality of his leaving and her own fullness with child. But when she admitted the reality of her pregnancy to herself and then to me, I had to remind her that lithium harms fetuses. Her child could be born with congenital defects. We didn't discuss her poverty, her lack of a mate, her genetically transmissible disease, or her own relative immaturity. She wanted the baby. She didn't want an abortion. But then again . . . .

There are no simple answers to many of life's greatest problems. Surely abortion as a convenience, abortion on demand, is as lethal to the spirit of the mother as it is to the physical existence of the fetus. And perhaps such a policy, applied with no spiritual sensitivity, will be lethal to the society that sanctions its cavalier use. Yet what about my patient? The answer was not simple. It was not pleasant. She elected to have the abortion. But with no money and bad credit she went to Denver to a place that would accept no money down and easy monthly payments. Her experience was dreadful — unnamed doctors and unnamed nurses performed the abortion within her full sight and hearing. It was done so quickly the local anesthetic had little time to take effect — physical pain, psychological pain, spiritual pain.

Calling me today, she is ambivalent: She has no money and she says she doesn't want to bother me, she just wanted me to know. I say to myself, I am my sister's keeper. I say to her "come in, we'll talk." This will be on the house. She refuses my offer saying she wants no charity. I explain one day later in her life she will give to another. That will constitute sufficient payment. I don't need her money. I do know she needs to forgive herself. She needs to love herself once again. I want to do my part so she can live her life in such a way that the loss of this pregnancy is not without meaning.

waxing crescent₂

The digital mind counts years, decades, centuries and the like — a necessary activity, I guess. But the moon just goes round and round, and the geese, heads tucked under wings, sleep out on the ice. This is the time when digits marking years turn over. It is a time for merry-making, tooting horns, watching the ball in Time's Square, drinking too much, making resolutions you know you won't keep, and hugging people you hardly know.

Pledged to the analog life, I spend the day the way I want to spend it. In the early morning darkness we join five hundred souls at the city auditorium to meditate on peace for the world. Following that, we breakfast with two new friends. Then I take a mid-morning nap. What a luxury. The afternoon passes helping Carl and Karen cut and wrap the meat from Karen's first elk. Besides the good company, we get a share of the elk meat, a true delicacy. Then in the nighttime darkness, I run in a race with another five hundred souls just for the fun of it. Being a golden retriever, not a whippet, my motto when racing is "start slowly and then taper off." A fabulous crescent moon watches over our race in cold night air. As I run I think of the Lakota and I smile. I bet they smiled at this moon on such nights, too. Afterwards, we meet Fred and Nancy for a dip in their hot tub and shoot one another with Silly String. We cap the evening with toast and milk and then go to bed while the New Year is just being ushered in on the East Coast. It's been a good day, a very good day: Time with friends, time in silence, time for peace, time to dance by the light of the crescent moon.

waxing crescent₆

It was after Christmas and she was said to be manipulative, needing the shock of the state hospital to behave better. I didn't agree with them. I said her brain chemistry was distorted. The failure of medications didn't mean they should ship her to Pueblo for an indefinite stay, especially when she had a nine month old daughter at home. I argued for ECT. They said if I wanted her as a patient they would gladly transfer her to me; only be advised, she had no job, no insurance, no money.

I accepted and started ECT. She has had three treatments since Christmas. I discharged her after the first. She called this evening saying she was *actually happy*. She just wanted me to know she had spent the day skiing with her husband. And she wanted to confirm the time for her next treatment. I told her Friday and then suggested it might be the last one for now. Four ECT's versus an indefinite stay in the state hospital. A contrast? ECT is simply saving this woman's life. Only two weeks before she had attempted suicide. Today she skis, she laughs, she lives, she loves.

Miracles do happen in psychiatry — miracles of a sort. Only our stringent ethics prevent our parading success stories before the public. Instead, our positive clinical outcomes (confidentiality foremost in mind) are relegated to statistics in our sometimes-too-dry journals. It's too bad. While ECT has been a total failure for some, for this woman it is the treatment of choice.

In our country, ECT has become reserved for the middle and upper classes, the educated, and the white. All others do not receive ECT because well-intentioned liberals suggest that by using ECT on the poor, the black, the uneducated, we are expressing our contempt and bigotry against the underprivileged. If I could only let those people see her.

---
waxing gibbous₄

I need to be careful about making hasty generalizations, but I wonder what our world would become if every person took time every day for silence, if everyone sought to clear away the layers of false ego from their inner core and sought to unite with God.

The January thaw continues in a big way. Our days are almost as warm as summer. The snow is gone. Lakes are melting puddles on top of unsure ice. Ice groans like some huge aching cello, a sound audible only to those who take the time to listen.

---
waxing gibbous₆

Colorado Springs, Colorado

I spend the evening talking to medical colleagues about positive humor. In the manner of most physician audiences, they are restrained, wanting hard data, graphs and statistics. I tell them that altruism is one of the ways they might live longer and get more out of life. And as I talk, I realize how altruism has been absconded from the individual and deposited in the government. Charity has been delegated to the government, the very instrument which we look upon with suspicion, if not outright contempt.

FULL MOON

Home

It may not be global warming, but it sure is Colorado warming. There is no frost in the tepee this moon. We are breaking all-time records for warmth. The snow is gone from the countryside, leaving the slender green winter wheat shoots vulnerable to drying winds. The wintering bird population is singing as if it were spring. I see four magpies playing bridge on the greenbelt.

Some people are running in shorts and bicyclists are out spinning a few miles now that they are safe from ice patches. Die-hard golfers are out on the links. We all know this balmy reprieve is just temporary. More harsh winter will follow for sure.

Tonight Carol and I sit on the back porch admiring the gibbous moon. I feel sad, knowing the thirteenth moon is just around the corner, and with it, the completion of this project. Do I feel different from a year ago? Is a butterfly different from a caterpillar?

Comment:

Towards the end of your Portrait Journal you will begin to sum up the experience. You will feel the need for closure. It will come naturally. Be reminded that the real closure and final evaluation will come several months down the line when you pick up your Portrait Journal and re-read it in its entirety.

waning gibbous₂

Lara called me at home, wanting me to see a patient of hers who is seriously depressed and considering suicide. I agree to see her as an emergency before office hours. Assessing for suicide is a tricky process. Essentially, the decision comes down to whether to hospitalize or not. On first consideration, hospitalizing might seem the wisest decision in every case. Protection is paramount. But twice in my professional life, I have coerced hospitalization because of

283

acute suicidal risk and the patients so resented me and the whole therapy establishment, that once out, they broke away from all counselling and then committed suicide a few months later. On the other hand, is the case of the man who I believed I could trust to call me if things got worse. He made a *no-suicide contract*. Then he blew his brains out two days later. Most often I have chosen what must have been the best alternative because ninety-nine percent of the time I do the right thing. But when the other one per cent involve death or near-death, evaluating for suicide is always a very scary matter.

I meet the young woman. She is considering very lethal methods, gunshot or carbon monoxide. Then she says she has no gun and no garage. I go through all the clinical steps of evaluation and then I reach deep to find the dimmed Light within her. I speak to her with passion borne out of my own fear for her and out of my own reverence for life. We make contact. Our eye contact lingers and she promises to call if she feels any worse and agrees a few days in the hospital is better than dying. I prescribe some meds (in small amounts) and Lara and I set up alternate days of contact and plan to manage her as an outpatient.

waning gibbous₃

The mountain men named him, *"Sounds-like-Minnie"* because of his small, slightly nasal voice. He looks like Popeye, except his forearms aren't as large and he doesn't smoke a pipe. I knew him as Arlen, an acquaintance from grade school. We lost touch for the last thirty years until our high school reunion where we talked again. What struck me was how he gave up the digital life and retired to a cabin on the North Dakota-Canada border to practice the art of woodcarving. It takes a whole month to find one mallard in a single block of wood. He finds it feather by feather.

He drops in for a brief visit on his way to art shows in warmer parts. The arctic cold, 91 below wind-chill, doesn't bother him. "I just haul more wood and carve more decoys." A friendship, dormant for thirty years, springs back to life in minutes. He became tired of five jobs and no time. Life is too short for that. He discovered a skill which for years went unnoticed. As we talk, I discover the origin of his skill. Art is more a matter of seeing than of doing. As a little boy, his mother sternly admonished him never to go out of the yard. He followed her instruction and, after exploring the yard, became absorbed in examining the yard in six inch square patches; noticing every ant, blade of grass, every patch of dirt. He learned to see, really see. Now he sees ducks in blocks of wood. He studies each new duck he meets as if it were the first bird ever created.

His kids are grown and on their own. Does he make enough money? Enough? Enough for what? He owns his pick-up truck, his travel trailer and a small cabin on the lake. Enough for a pension? Doesn't care. Enough for food? Of course. And he has enough not to burden others if he gets sick, but no more.

We share some elk with him and he launches into a talk I myself give on how to care for the game so you don't waste it. His philosophy of life is simple: Never waste, always share. He gives Carol a pair of delicate feather earrings, carved from wood. He is on his way with a hug and a "good-bye, friend." I know I will see more of him in the next thirty years. He has much to share. After all, he is a happy man.

---

waning gibbous₄

The Wall Street Journal? And they want to talk to me? Could it be I have been discovered? Could it be that *A Laughing Place* is going to be reviewed? Could it be that the big time is right around the corner?

Her voice is professional, experienced, oozing confidence in her subject. She is calling to hear of my experiences from six years ago when I attended (and stood up alone to protest their message) a small church in a nearby community where Neo-Nazi hate is peddled under the guise of Christianity. I shake out my memories, clear away the cerebral cobwebs, and do my best to tell her what I remember. The church is a small group of people willing to believe that Jews are here to torment Christians; that the ten lost tribes are in fact the white people of America; and that all Blacks should be returned to Africa as soon as possible. Also they preach that the Baptist Church is too liberal to be called Christian any more. She says that while the Ku Klux Klan membership is declining, those that live by hate are finding sanctuary in right-wing churches who proclaim their beliefs under the banner of Christ's will.

I try to tell her that those people are really a minority of our community and that most people here are doing charitable, altruistic work. She acknowledges my rebuttal, but notes that news is in exposing this lunatic fringe. Maybe she is right, but when will quiet acts of peace be given equal exposure by national media? Does it not, by the stories it chooses to publish, also shape the perceptions and thus the expectations of our country? If we heard about fewer murders and drug busts, couldn't it be that (just perhaps) they might diminish by being deprived of the attention? In childhood the best way to extinguish unwanted behavior is to ignore it. But I am not a journalist. I'm probably naive to think that the choice of news reporting could move our violence-addicted country in the direction of peace.

She doesn't ask about *A Laughing Place*. I don't tell her I am an author who teaches positive humor, a psychiatrist who believes in loving his patients, and a contemplative who is discovering that God dwells deep within the heart of every person (including those Neo-Nazi hate mongers). I could tell her, but I doubt she wants to listen, not now when she is on the trail of Neo-Nazis right here in river city.

We laughingly call him Saint Thomas. He shyly smiles, shakes his head and changes the subject. After all, no one who is a saint would ever admit to it. To do so immediately exempts one from sainthood. But he has done it. He quit his pediatric practice with its focus on the middle and upper classes; kids covered by excellent insurance. He quit and opened a clinic for those children who are neglected, abused, too poor to get medical care without their parents going into debt. He saw the need and answered it. Taking a massive cut in pay, he has rallied many about him who also seek to help the poor. He didn't have to go to inner city ghettos or some third world country. He found poverty and disease going untreated here in our own back yard.

I told him he had a blank check: Whatever I could do, I would. Not being a child psychiatrist I doubted he would need me. He found a need, though. Come, he says, and talk to us. We need to be reminded of our purpose. We are like a family and we have our problems just like any other. So I come, I listen, and do what I can. He is right. They do need me. These very good people, seeking to serve the poor, are occasionally contentious with one another.

I start out by saying that they are the bearers of justice. Their acts are the start of bringing justice to the oppressed. Justice is the necessary precondition for peace and hence they are peacemakers, not just health care workers. Where does peace start? It starts within. Each person must start by _being peace_. Then peace extends to those they rub elbows with; then to those they serve; finally then, to the community. Just as the hate movements, hiding behind Jesus and the American flag, begin with hate in the individual heart, peacemaking must also start with peace in the individual human heart. I am honored to work with these people; honored that I can be an assistant to Saint Thomas. (Stop blushing, Tom, you're a good guy. I'm only kidding you. Only God really knows about saints. The rest of us? We just flap our gums on the subject. But She forgives us for our little fun.)

LAST QUARTER

I don't know why I thought of him today. It must be about twenty-four years since we met our one and only time. I was a senior medical student being allowed on the floors where the private (paying) patients stay, and he was a cheerful, barrel-chested man in his mid sixties. He was reading the paper when I came to do his work-up. He put his reading down and, with what felt like respect, seemed to enjoy all the time necessary for my examination. He was to have surgery the next day for an aortic aneurysm. We talked. He was cheerful and openly unafraid of death. Of course he wanted a good outcome. At the time of our talk, he felt fine, in the pink, but he knew how serious his problem was. We talked long after my examination was complete. He told me he hoped I would be a very good doctor, that I should always take time with people. As we parted, he smiled and said he would see me in the morning.

He did see me, just as he was going to sleep, he winked and gave me a thumbs up. The surgery was difficult, the aneurysm bigger and more dangerous than anticipated. In the middle of the procedure he hemorrhaged. It was too much to control and he died. The surgeon kept stitching and the anesthesiologist kept "bagging him" until he was closed up. Thus he died post-operatively and not "on the table." Investigations are too messy when people die during surgery, it looks bad on the records.

He died and I felt a loss of this man, my teacher, even though I couldn't remember his name. Why do I remember him now? Maybe because I am beginning to feel the same way about death and about life. I feel I am accepting my own death. I don't want it any time soon, but I have let go of clinging to life as if it were a result of my own labor. It is a gift, or maybe a loan, for me to enjoy.

waning crescent₁

Gentle, feathery, deep, silent snow. The beauty of winter at its finest. For two days, snow has fallen. Knee deep, it is a winter gift. A snowfall, not a blizzard. This morning, evergreen boughs are laden with snow, bending them like fruit trees in late summer. This snow is the purest manifestation of white. Shoveling the sparkling blanket in the warm sun is a gift. This is one of those ideal winter days, a day epitomizing the great beauty of this moon.

But all is not beauty in the minds of humankind. Not even here in our quiet community. Across town last night, competing gangs had a gun fight. No one was killed, but it stirred us from too much complacency, from a self-satisfaction that we might somehow live apart from the world and its violence. Fortunately, the wounds were minor, but the fight remains a grim reminder of the proximity of chaos.

This morning I read words of George Fox, "We utterly deny all outward wars and strife, and fightings with outward weapons, for any end, or under any pretense whatever." And with that reading my mind is jarred to recall a dream of the past night.

A couple of middle eastern men hold me prisoner and tell me they are going to execute me. I reply I am committed to non-violence and will not fight back. Though unjust, I accept their execution. I ask only that they give me paper and pen and time enough to write to Carol and my friends. My feeling was one of sadness at dying so early in my life, but I also felt a sense of rightness and inner peace. It was not a nightmare. The dream didn't awaken me. It waited till morning to re-emerge.

289

Ski Tip Ranch, Colorado

Take a heaping tablespoonful of winter. Drive high into the mountains; find a hidden out-of-the-way place; eat a wonderful meal with your best friend and then go for a walk at night. The wind chill is about twenty below. We encounter a dark moonless night and a deserted country road. We walk and marvel at the stars, so bright, so close. It is so cold we need to cover our faces except for our eyes and nose. The snow crunches underfoot as the sharp wind makes the trees tremble. We walk, wrapped in cold, and experience the essence of winter night. Carol wonders if we could survive this night with nothing more than the clothes on our backs. I doubt we could. As we walk along, we recall our childhoods in North Dakota and Montana; childhoods where long underwear was an essential fact of life, not an option. We walk more and we laugh. Finally we turn back, faces turning directly into the north wind. This is winter. This is night. And we dance. Not figuratively, we dance literally. We dance down the middle of a snow-packed road with the wind our music and the stars our approving audience. This is life and the fullness thereof.

Now as I write, I sit before a mammoth fireplace — fire, humankind's companion for winters untold. We gaze into the dancing flame and smile. I continue to feel very happy.

In the eyes of the IRS this is a business trip. I present my show at the nearby resort for doctors and nurses specializing in emergency medicine. My message is intended to help them survive and even thrive in the midst of daily death. They complain that their greatest stress comes from unfeeling administrations rather than the struggles of their patients. The world encroaches on their altruism, threatening to choke the life out of it. I not only talk about humor, I talk about wolves and dancing with life. What a wonderful job; I teach people how to find more love and laughter in life and get paid pretty well to boot.

We spend the afternoon on remote ski trails. The north wind, the snow and bare aspen trees are the gifts of the day. My nose runs too much. Carol laughs saying the sight of my face is easy to take, after all she does teach kindergarten. I use a gross of Kleenex, but still the nose is a problem. When we return to the lodge we have a treat the Lakota probably never enjoyed, a hot bath. Then we nap the rest of the afternoon, holding hands.

Evening brings another fine meal and another walk down the same empty country road. It is darker tonight. There are no stars, but it is still amazingly easy to see, the snow reflecting what little moonlight filters through the low-hanging clouds. When we return, Carol wants to go to sleep but makes the mistake of looking at her watch. It's only eight o'clock. And we both yearn for a life where watch and calendar disappear; where we live only by nature's rhythms, not mechanical-electrical devices. A dream? One day we may. One day we may.

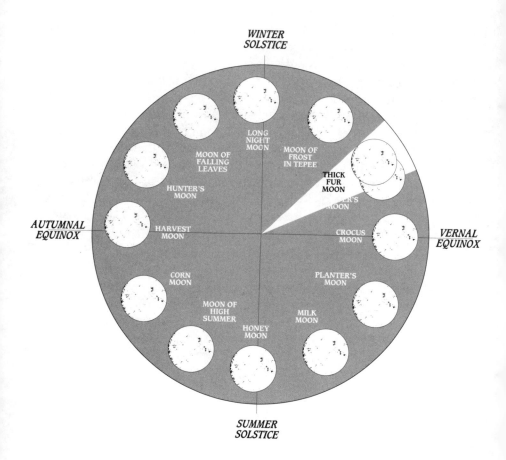

WINTER
SOLSTICE

LONG
NIGHT
MOON

MOON OF
FALLING
LEAVES

MOON OF
FROST
IN TEPEE

HUNTER'S
MOON

THICK
FUR
MOON

...ER'S
...OON

AUTUMNAL
EQUINOX

HARVEST
MOON

CROCUS
MOON

VERNAL
EQUINOX

CORN
MOON

PLANTER'S
MOON

MOON OF
HIGH
SUMMER

MILK
MOON

HONEY
MOON

SUMMER
SOLSTICE

Chapter Thirteen

THICK FUR MOON

WHEN I SAW the crescent moon on the horizon's rim last night, I felt sad. The thirteenth moon is here. The time allotted for this work is nearly finished. The year has been one of growth. I feel more peaceful and rightly-placed in life. When I look at myself, I know I have so very far to go. And my writing is still rough hewn. Like a piece of wood, it needs more care and polish.

Ah, dear crescent moon, the days of this little project are coming to an end. We have become friends. Never fear, I will dance with you forever. I have said I need to let go of everything, to purge myself of all my ego and become empty if I am to become filled. That means letting go my cherished dream of being a writer, of ever having anything to say to anyone. Maybe I need to be like you, my silver sliver friend. Maybe I ought to be myself and not try to be anything else. I don't need to let go of you, because I never possessed you. In fact does any of us ever really possess anything?

293

Why the name, *Thick Fur Moon*? There is no such name in any reference I could find. I made it up. This is the Trapper Moon again. Trappers trap during this moon because it is now that fur is the thickest. The winter exerts its maximal cold and the animals respond with their best fur. Animals' defense against winter's cold is so much more aesthetically appealing than our crude psychological defenses against the coldness of our lives. Not all animals get trapped. Most go on to shed their fur, mate and then dance with the summer moons.

_____ *waxing crescent₆* _____

You can't enter Mark's house by the front door. Instead, you come through the kitchen, but not for *old down home* reasons. The front door is blocked by his Steinway. The whole living room is dedicated to one purpose: To create the optimal environment for the creation and appreciation of music. From its hardwood floors to the simply decorated walls, it contrasts state-of-the-art digital and state-of-the-art analog. Twelve black boxes huddle around a computer while three keyboards form a stairway of sorts above the digital side. The analog portion is comprised of one solitary Steinway grand piano. Tonight we find out why the word, grand, is so appropriate.

Carol and I have come for the sole purpose of lying on the floor under the piano to experience the wood singing at a distance of two feet. Mark says it isn't a matter of how loud a piano can be played that counts, it is how soft. We lie down and are borne away on melodies. Some are familiar, some not. Transported to some distant planet where music is all that matters and time has no meaning other than the measurement meter. As we listen I reach up and touch the sounding board of the piano's tender underparts, feeling the vibrations flow like a warm electric current throughout my body. Earth time pauses. We simply exist. Holding hands, we smile. And as Mark closes with Bach's _Jesu, Joy of Man's Desiring_, I break into full belly laughter.

It's a school night and we should be home by ten — but not tonight. We are on Mark's time. A nocturnal creature, he creates best when the rest of humankind sleeps. At some late dark hour we dance back home.

FIRST QUARTER

You would think after watching the moon for thirteen cycles that I wouldn't be surprised by any new associations. But I have been looking as a lover, not a scientist. Much of my observation has been wrapped in awe and wonder, not devoted to calculations. Tonight I observe an all-too-clear relationship. The first quarter moon is at highest mid-heaven around the hour of sunset. That means, of course that the last quarter is at mid-heaven during sunrise. How symmetrical. With our days lengthening, the twilight provides a deep blue background for the pure white half illumined moon. I stop driving, pull off to the side of the street and just absorb the scene.

waxing gibbous₂

I chat with Kathy this morning. Her passion for writing has taken back seat to the demands of mothering her two small children and to her husband's Ph.D. Sharing a similar love of writing, we don't know if it is our inexperience, our lack of success, or that we are temperamentally different from the great writers. We aren't depressed. We aren't alcoholic. In fact, we are actually quite pleased with life. Writing isn't a great struggle, it's a wonderful pleasure. The only problem is finding the time to write when our other responsibilities demand so much of our attention. Is it possible for a happy person to write anything of value?

295

waxing gibbous₃

Every day I run the very real risk of being a very real hypocrite, especially in my silence; I run the risk of my silence degenerating into a process of going through the motions. I risk taking the process for granted, of not being present with God as an intimate companion. I run the same risk with my wife, my children, my friends, my patients — just go through the motions of living empty words, empty therapy, empty silence, empty piety, empty writing. When we start going through the motions of life, when we take life for granted, when we let our attention wander from the present pregnant moment, we are penalized. Time speeds up and life passes us by. We exist in a semi-narcotized state; a slumber of sorts, a stupor brought about by our own complacency, lack of attention, laziness. Conversely, time moves slowly when we live in intimate contact with each moment, nursing at Earth's breast.

waxing gibbous₄

I awake this morning and step out of bed. My left foot falls into a hole. I spend the next hour trying to walk upright. Today is one of those days when, for no particular reason, I am off balance all day. Actually, I feel like staying in bed, but such a luxury is not to be mine.

I stumble through my silence with a ping-pong mind; returning time after time to anger at a colleague. I don't know the man. He is a psychiatrist in Denver. I saw a patient of his yesterday. Depressed, recently having suffered the death of her mother and one child, the abandonment of her husband (he found another woman), and a diagnosis of rheumatoid arthritis, her previous therapists failed to help her out of the abyss so she sought out ECT. The psychiatrist performed the series on her, which helped. But what enraged her was his failure to return her phone calls, his failure to speak to her at the time of treatments, and his exorbitant charges which I discovered were double my fees. Despairing, she senses the need for more treatments, but cannot bear to be ignored and go bankrupt at the same time. How angry I get at colleagues who value money and prestige above love and compassion. Little wonder so much of the public distrusts and dislikes medical practitioners; so many of them have lost their altruism, their compassion, their capacity to love.

To straighten up my psyche I go to the swimming pool for a quick workout before office hours. I didn't plan it that way, but I run into Carol and her kindergarten class learning to swim. Little water spirits in constant motion, the children strike a sharp contrast to my methodical lap swimming. We finish our workout at the same time and head for the shower. The room provides a remarkable contrast: Five little boys squealing, a psychiatrist with one foot still in a hole, and a paraplegic young man using the handicapped shower in the corner. The children look, but do not stare. I look, but do not stare. The young man has large healing decubitus ulcers on his legs and works on the end of his penis to apply a condom of sorts with an attached catheter tube. He does it so naturally that no one stares, no children giggle with embarrassment. Feeling a mixture of gratitude and respect, the psychiatrist shakes his foot from its hole and walks evenly to the dressing room.

waxing gibbous₅

Make a joyful noise unto the Lord. Stuffy words. Certainly not the kind of thing any self respecting twentieth century person (let alone card carrying psychiatrist) would say out loud and mean it, not unless he were some sort of weirdo.

My day is busy, very busy; depressions running deep. Some are better, some not. Insurance companies demand, deny, threaten or remain mute. I keep up with the schedule, but I am not rushed. I recall my morning silence and look at my candle.

Carol fixes a most succulent fish, smothered in some hard-to-pronounce Japanese mushroom sauce. We take time and linger. Then we sit on the back porch, drinking the evening's moonlight, listening to music, and we laugh; deep, hearty, belly-wrenching laughter. And then I understand what the phrase means, *Make a joyful noise unto the Lord.* Laughter is the most joyful noise the Origin of Life can hear. Laughter, a product of love and gratitude.

FULL MOON
San Diego, California

Six hundred extroverts crowd one room. Handshakes, hugs, first names, smiling eye-contact, glad you're here. If I am ever to speak to a wider audience, I need what is here, how to learn the fine points of professional speaking. I'm not really switching careers, I'm only seeking an audience greater than one solitary patient sitting across from me in my consulting room. The time at this conference is linear, closely clipped, and unforgivingly digital. Since I'm neither Jewish or Southern, several of the pros doubt I have any business teaching humor. Can a Norwegian psychiatrist be funny? I explain it's more than humor, it's . . . it's . . ., well, analog, . . . a loving, wonder-filled, good-natured life I want to portray, a life of awe and inner peace. In fact, as time goes by, I want to teach love, taking time with Nature, learning to experience gratitude for being alive. Above all, I want to teach people to slow down. *Kiss of death*, they say. The topics that sell are sales, change adaptation, strategic planning, motivation, one-minute anything, and paths to greater profits. But no — no *touchy-feely* stuff; nothing smacking of spirituality. That won't sell. I don't tell them about howling wolf monks. Deep in my heart I know if I could bring them, one-on-one, to Mission Wolf, they would thrill to the experience. While I am here to learn, it is only too clear, I have no choice but to say what is growing in my heart. I just have to find a way to package it so those living the rat race of digital intensity will hear me out and not fear that my message will be the *kiss of death* for their enterprises or their productivity.

The walk to my hotel takes me past a small, tree-lined square. And, of course, the schizophrenics, the winos, and assorted other street people are there. Here are people who dearly need motivation, but are they capable of hearing? It is certain they can't pay. Again, I am struck with the contrast of the high paid motivators in fancy hotels next to the hopelessly addicted or mentally ill. I stop. Dominating the whole scene is the full moon in all her regal splendor. Looking up, I talk briefly to her.

"We meet again. Wherever I go, you are there. You are so wonderfully predictable. I think I love you." A schizophrenic black man stops his chanting next to an empty bus and walks over beside me. He looks at the moon, looks back at me. And then, shaking his head, he returns to some incomprehensible chant and ambles down the street dragging a large plastic bag behind him.

I wonder if the intense, digital minds aren't as lacking in spiritual depth as are these winos. The suit-clad digitals talk a good game about God, but is it spirituality or is it the bottom line? The winos don't talk, they drink from a brown paper sack and thumb through porno magazines, passing the time till the next bottle or their last breath.

Sister moon, you preside over so many contrasts, you see so much come and go. Still you keep your rounds, quietly observing the evolution of human societies and the human mind. I wonder what role I have in this process. Am I aiding the evolution towards unity with God? Or am I merely in a back wash, a side stream, talking schizophrenic to myself with no one to hear?

---

waning gibbous$_2$

Home

It's so cold the little hairs in your nose freeze. Snow, like icy goose down, blankets everything in sight. Winter returns, not with a vengeance, but with a clear affirmation of what winter is all about. All is cold and white. The sky, a light shade of gray, constantly adds more fine white feathers to the blanket. I light a fire and sit back reading Tolstoy and how he transformed in mid-life. The subjects of his writing went from the aristocracy to the peasantry. He stopped describing the debauchery of the time and focused on the simple spiritual struggles of the poor. He declined to entertain and opted (some say too heavy-handedly) to preach, to convert. Tolstoy's time differs from ours only in the speed and technology with which we are able to debauch ourselves. The choices are the same. We can live in the fast lane, satisfying our every whim, seeking out the new and the modern, the stimulating and the clever, all the while ignoring injustice. Or we can settle deep within the bottomless well we call our soul, let the superficial life run by, settle on the deep matters of the heart, and meld our souls with the Origin of the All. We can accept the gift of life, not in the form of gadgets, but in Nature. Take care of Nature, coddle her and help her regain her former vitality. Say "thank you" over and over again. And then look about and ask yourself what you can do so others may feel the heartfelt gratitude for the gift of life as well. It's that simple.

waning gibbous₅

Just as the moon has cycled through the year, the earth has completed its revolution around the sun. Nothing is finished. The process goes on and on. I go on and on. Ending is an illusion. Ending is arbitrary. Ending isn't ending at all.

My parts live within me, now non-violently participating with one another. My parts no longer interact by voting, vetoing or coercing, they operate by consensus. Therapy has helped in bringing out the shy parts and letting them speak in the forum of my mind — being heard rather than acting out behind the scenes. Consensus takes longer, but is the way of inner peace.

This morning the sun is bright; even now the snow is beginning to thaw. I shall go out and shovel our sidewalk. Maybe I will talk to neighbors as they do the same. There are rabbit tracks in the back yard, little ones of the resident cottontails. The redwings are singing in the cottonwood branches. Life is common, ordinary and an occasion for all my various parts to sing a *thank you* deep within. A *thank you* followed by *yes. Yes* to what? *Yes* to whatever is coming next. I don't know what it will be and I don't want to know. But we, every part of me, all say *yes* just the same.

I do not speak with one voice. Does anyone? I am not one uniform personality. Is anyone? I am comprised of many parts, some quite dissimilar. Just like everyone.

I am a man and I am woman too.

I am a psychiatrist and I am a patient too.

I am a husband, deeply loving and dependent on my wife,
    and I am a hermit too.

I love deeply and still struggle with bitterness too.

I seek God within and yet I often ignore God's presence.

I am industrious, hardworking and yet I often *vege-out*,
    watching sports on TV.

I am an extrovert, loving the stage and yet I am shy
    and reserved, frequently preferring the corner of a room.

I am a writer and yet my letters to my children are clipped
    and telegraphic.

I love animals and yet I kill some of them.

I love Nature and yet I squander Her resources.

I want to give of myself to all persons
    and still I charge a healthy fee for my services.

I am analog and I am digital too.

Above all, I am in process.

I am unfinished

The Mystery

The mystery does not get clearer by repeating the question.
Nor is it bought with going to amazing places.
Until you've kept your eyes and your wanting still for fifty years.
You don't begin to cross over from confusion.

Rumi
(Translated by Coleman Barks)

Endnote

NOW YOU HAVE *seen one*. Your next step is to decide whether you will *do one*. If you do, surely your journal will motivate you to *teach one*. And the process can go on and on and on.

Bear in mind your journal will be vastly different from mine. I offered *A Thirteen Moon Journal* to give you a sense of how to go about the process. The content of your journal is up to you.

When a Portrait Journal is completed, a most important part is re-reading it after having let it season for several months. I have elected not to share what conclusions I came to when I re-read my Portrait Journal. I will let you speculate about them.

Index